The Communist Movement in Iran

The COMMUNIST MOVEMENT in IRAN

by
SEPEHR ZABIH

UNIVERSITY OF CALIFORNIA PRESS

Berkeley and Los Angeles   1966

University of California Press
Berkeley and Los Angeles, California

Cambridge University Press
London, England

To Ramin and Leyla

Preface

This study has two interrelated objectives. One is to examine the contents and evolution of the Communist doctrine of social and national revolution in the East by a case study on Iran. The other is to treat the Iranian experience as an indigenous phenomenon and to inquire into the circumstances that influenced the Iranian Communist movement.

The first objective required an investigation of the functions of Communist doctrine as both theoretical concept and policy guide for native Communist parties, and also of the interaction between the traditional and revolutionary elements of Soviet diplomacy. The second objective required a determination of the nature and scope of the Communist appeal and of the social characteristics of those strata of Iranian society that have been most susceptible to communism; it required further an exploration of the interplay between traditional and modern forces, such as Islamic religion and nationalism, to identify their functions as impediments or catalysts of communism.

The first chapter discusses the initial formulation of the Communist revolutionary doctrine and the attempt to apply it to Iran. This attempt raised important issues. First, the original Marxian prophecy that the independence of colonial and semi-colonial people was contingent on the triumph of revolution in Europe came into conflict with the desire to spread the Communist revolution to the East. Second and third, a solution had to be found for the two major questions of the Communist attitude toward bourgeois nationalism and of the possibility of skipping the capitalist stage of development to pass directly from the precapitalist to the socialist mode of production. As for the second, Persia along with Turkey figured prominently in the first Lenin pronouncement on the temporary nature of the Communist cooperation with national revolutionary forces. As for the third, the early revolutionary experience in this part of the world prompted the Comintern to resolve that with the help of the proletariat of the more advanced countries, the backward people could proceed directly to a soviet regime.

The obstacles that Soviet Russia encountered in Iran in its initial attempt to extend the revolution to the East greatly influenced the later evolution of the Communist attitude toward the colonial and semicolonial lands. It was, for example, the failure of the Gilan separatist movement that led the Communist leaders to wonder if a full bourgeois development were not a prerequisite to revolution in the East. The episode of the Gilan soviet also provided evidence of the subordination of the indigenous Communists to Soviet diplomacy, a factor that was destined to play a significant role in the disillusionment of many Persian sympathizers with the Communist movement.

Chapter 2 discusses the period between the two World Wars. With the normalization of relations between Iran and the U.S.S.R. by the conclusion of the 1921 treaty, Soviet diplomacy abandoned its revolutionary tactic of using native Communists as a lever of pressure on the new regime of Reza Shah. Instead it relied on the new Iranian nationalism to complete the process of bourgeois development and create the objective conditions for revolution. When these conditions failed to materialize in Iran and elsewhere in the East, the Comintern, in its Sixth Congress in 1928, adopted more radical policies envisaging a return to the concept of agrarian revolution as the only means of Bolshevizing the Eastern people. The bourgeoisie was considered unable to carry out a radical change because of its vested interest in landlordism. In Iran, as in other countries with similar social and economic conditions, all Communist hope was pinned on an agrarian revolution, but no direct or serious attempt was made to revive the native Communist parties as a vehicle for the revolt of the peasantry.

Chapters 3 and 4 examine the wartime involvement of international communism in Iran (which provided another opportunity for the Sovietization of this area) and trace the change and continuity of Soviet diplomacy and the doctrine of revolution in the East.

This experience and its aftermath, extending to the period of the nationalist movement of 1951–1953, is further discussed in chapters 5 and 6 with emphasis on the post-Stalin revisions in such important concepts as the composition of the anti-imperialist patriotic fronts and the role of the native Communist parties in them. These chapters treat the Communist movement after the Second World War as an indigenous political force, mainly expressed in the Tudeh party and its various clandestine and cover affiliates. Since the Tudeh party was an integral part of the political developments in Iran at least up to 1953, my treatment of the postwar period necessarily covers the principal features of the country's political evolution as a whole. In the final pages, I take up the future prospects of communism in Iran.

Source materials used in this study fall into two main categories: those having a general bearing on the subject matter, including Western and non-Western literature on doctrines and practices of communism and Soviet diplomacy in the Middle East; and those dealing with the specific Iranian Communist experience. Persian works belonging to both categories have been used, but the bulk of primary Persian sources falls in the former category.

The vast collections of original works at the Melli and Majlis libraries of Teheran, the Persian collection of the Hoover Institution at Stanford University, the New York Public Library, the Department of Orientalia of the Library of Congress, and the British Museum have all been consulted. I have also made use of primary Soviet and Persian sources. Except when otherwise stated, the translations of the Persian sources are mine. Russian and Persian titles are given in transliteration, and a translation of the latter is also provided in the notes and the bibliography. In the absence of a standard method of transliteration of Persian names, a fairly simple method has been used to permit their reasonably accurate pronunciation by those unfamiliar with the language. The terms Persia and Iran are used interchangeably depending on the choice of the authors and the chronological order in which a cited work has appeared.

Many persons who have been either directly involved in the movement or have had intimate knowledge of its earlier phases have been interviewed. For obvious reasons, most of them must remain anonymous. Others whose accounts of the evolution of the movement is a matter of public record have been so cited.

I am indebted to Professor George Lenczowski, a pioneer in scholarly research on Soviet diplomacy and the Communist movement in Iran. He has read the whole manuscript and made many valuable suggestions. To Professors Ernst Haas, Eric Bell-quist, John Schaar, and Carl Leiden I owe much for unfailing encouragement and support during my graduate studies at the University of California. Geoffrey Wheeler of the Central Asian Research Center in London, Jean Vigneau of the Centre de documentation et de synthèse, and Pierre Rondot of the Centre des hautes études d'administration musulmane, both in Paris, generously put at my disposal valuable research materials. I am also grateful to Shirley Taylor for her competent editing of the manuscript. Finally to my wife Joan, on whose valuable advice and patient secretarial assistance I have confidently relied, goes a word of special appreciation. Needless to say the responsibility for the contents of this work remains exclusively mine.

This study was made possible by a grant from the Ford Foundation under its Foreign Area Training Fellowship program extending over a two-year period of field work abroad and writing in Berkeley. The Departments of Political Science of the University of California at Berkeley and St. Mary's College of California rendered assistance in research and in the final typing of the manuscript. The publishers of *Problems of Communism* have granted permission to use portions of an article of mine previously published in their journal.

Contents

1
PERSIA AND THE
BOLSHEVIK REVOLUTION

Of the countries on the Russian periphery, Persia, in 1917 and 1918, presented very favorable conditions for the extension of the Bolshevik revolution. The events in Persia since the constitutional crisis of 1905–1909 had made her vulnerable to external political pressures. Already in 1907 Russia and Great Britain had joined to partition her territory into their respective spheres of influence. When the First World War broke out, activities of the belligerent powers surrounding Persia on all sides nearly caused a political disintegration. Despite her declared neutrality, various foreign armies occupied her outlying regions at one time or another until late 1920.

With the triumph of the Bolshevik revolution, Persia, particularly its northern provinces, became directly exposed to a revolutionary movement which found a ready-made catalyst in that country's chaotic conditions. The Russian March Revolution of 1917 had spread the move for organizing soviets of the "Workers and Soldiers' Deputies" in Russia's sphere of influence. Simultaneously Bolshevik cells had sprung up in areas where Russian soldiers and workers were stationed. The October Revolution intensified this process and extended it to the considerable number of Persians who had migrated to Russia's neighboring regions in the preceding years.

What facilitated the spread of revolutionary agitation to Persia proper was the outbreak in the immediate postwar period of a number of local uprisings on the part of several of Persia's numerous minorities. Two uprisings had particularly far-reaching consequences, for they occurred in the politically sensitive Azarbayjan and Gilan regions. The Azarbayjan uprising was led by Sheikh Mohammad Khiyabani, a veteran of the constitutional revolution; the Gilan uprising was led by Mirza Kuchek Khan, who also had been involved in that revolution.[1] These two harbored strong anti-British and anti-Russian sentiments along with pan-Islamic aspirations (both of which had been actively cultivated by Germany and Turkey). After the conclusion of the Brest–Litovsk Peace, the Bolshevik regime took immediate action to align itself with Persia's anti-British nationalists by renouncing all imperialist aspirations and seeking to exploit revolutionary sentiments in the interest of world revolution.

Doctrinal Questions

In pursuance of this objective Russia's Bolshevik leaders were compelled to cope with a number of ideological and doctrinal issues. Although basic Marxist–Leninist doctrines on under-developed countries such as the national and peasant questions had been formulated before 1917, it was necessary for them to be modified somewhat in order to be effective in extending the revolution to the countries bordering Russia to the south and east.

Primarily, the problem was that of promoting revolution in one of the world's least industrialized regions where none of the necessary "objective conditions" for the rise of the proletariat was present. Furthermore, Marxist doctrines had predicted that "liberation" of the East could not be achieved before the tri-

---

[1] For a comprehensive treatment of this revolution, see Edward G. Browne, *The Persian Revolution of 1905–1909* (Cambridge, Eng., 1911).

umph of the Communist revolution in Europe, where both the economic development and the existence of a large industrial proletariat were favorable for its realization. When the Bolsheviks assumed power in Russia, they anticipated revolutionary expansion in the West. Partly because this failed to materialize, but largely because Russia included so much Asian territory, the East became the focus of Bolshevik attention.

On a doctrinal level two questions concerning the East had to be answered. The first was the question of nationalism. Most of this region was either directly under Western European rule or under its strong, and at times exclusive, influence. Nearly everywhere, there existed nationalist movements, of varying strength, which sought to end Western domination. The first question for the Bolsheviks was therefore what attitude to take toward these movements. The second question stemmed from the social and economic conditions of the Eastern countries, where the capitalist stage of development had either not begun or was not completed. Could the East skip this stage and proceed directly from a precapitalist to a socialist mode of production?

In an attempt to answer both questions Bolshevik leaders recruited prominent Marxists of Asia, such as M. N. Roy of India and A. Sultan Zadeh of Persia. Concerning nationalism, Lenin and his Eastern colleagues had divergent views. Roy found no common ground between communism and bourgeois nationalism and opposed any compromise with the latter. Lenin, on the other hand, favored a temporary alliance with the national movements, which he termed "national revolutionary" rather than "bourgeois democratic." Lenin hoped a situation would be created where the alliance could be terminated at some future date in favor of Communist leadership.[2]

Inspired by Lenin but bearing in mind the particular case of his own country, Sultan Zadeh, a prominent Persian Communist writer, suggested that the attitude toward bourgeois nationalist movements should be flexible and adapted to local requirements.

---

[2] See Walter Z. Laqueur, *The Soviet Union and the Middle East* (New York, 1959), p. 18.

These movements should be supported only where they were still in an embryonic stage; in countries where they had existed for ten years or more, new movements, purely Communist in nature, should be created to oppose bourgeois nationalism and to shift the revolutionary struggle from a national level to a social and class level.[3] Persia was clearly in this category, for the constitutional revolution dating back to 1905 had contained all the elements of a bourgeois nationalist movement; only during the First World War had it acquired an Anglophobic character. Sultan Zadeh's compromise formula was accepted, and Persian Communists received the ideological sanction to campaign for the extension of communism to Persia.

The second doctrinal question, whether or not the capitalist stage could be bypassed, also necessitated modification. Before the October Revolution Lenin had on a number of occasions rejected such a possibility as an illusion of those who sought to broaden the scope of revolution without due regard for conditions of capitalist development in countries where industrialization had not yet been achieved. But the Russian revolution itself had weakened this argument, for capitalist development had hardly been completed when the revolution occurred and succeeded. Hence, a new theoretical modification had to be effected to abet revolution in the East, which socially and economically was much like a large part of Russia.

At the Second Congress of the Communist International in 1920, Lenin sponsored a resolution declaring that, with the help of the "class-conscious proletariat of the advanced capitalist countries," the masses in the backward countries would indeed proceed directly to the establishment of Soviet republics.[4] This line of thinking was ardently supported by both Russian and non-Russian Asian Communists, for whom it reflected a change in Bolshevik emphasis from the West to the East. Thus, for ex-

[3] A. Sultan-sade, in *Protokoll des Zweiten Weltkongresses der Kommunistischen Internationale* (Hamburg, 1921), p. 169.
[4] Laqueur, *op. cit.*, p. 21. A supplementary document to the resolution, drafted by M. N. Roy, makes this point clearly.

ample, Sultan Galiev, the Moslem commissar in the Commissariat for Nationalities, went so far as to develop a thesis for forming a colonial rather than a Communist international, believing that the hegemony of the colonial people was more real than that of the international proletariat.[5] Classic Marxists, he thought, made a mistake in concentrating on the industrially developed West; the backward people of the East were genuinely propertyless and in that sense more progressive than the Western working class, which, despite Marxist prophecies, had not as yet been pauperized to any large degree. Furthermore, Galiev argued, there was no reason to apply the doctrine of class conflict to the East, where, in contrast to Europe, all classes— even the upper class — were subject to colonial control. A colonial revolution clearly called for an alliance of all classes, relegating the class struggle to some future date.

Ingenious as they were, few of Galiev's recommendations were accepted by the Communist International; indeed, it was not until the post-Stalin era that they received any attention by the leadership of international communism.[6]

Having laid the doctrinal grounds for revolution in the East, the Bolshevik leaders assigned the task of formulating policies and action programs for Eastern Communists to Stalin, who little more than a year after the October Revolution had addressed himself to this question. In 1918, in a speech to the First Congress of Moslem Communists meeting in Moscow, he suggested that no one could erect a bridge between the West and the East as easily and as quickly as the Moslem Communists, who held the key to Persia, India, Afghanistan, and China. The liberation of these countries from the yoke of the imperialists, Stalin assured his listeners, would guarantee and consolidate the freedom of their own countries and, at the same time, under-

---

[5] Alexandre Bennigsen, "Sultan Galiev: The U.S.S.R. and the Colonial Revolution," in Walter Z. Laqueur, ed., *The Middle East in Transition* (New York, 1958), pp. 398–405.

[6] Galiev's views were first expressed in a series of articles published in *Zhizn Nationalnostei*, the organ of *Narkomindel* or Commissariat of Foreign Affairs in 1918–1919 (hereafter cited as *ZN*).

mine the foundations of imperialism. To this end, he said, social-ist education in the East must be the first task of the congress.[7]

On Stalin's recommendation, a resolution was passed estab-lishing a Department of International Propaganda for the East-ern Peoples, attached to the Bureau of the Moslem Communist organization of the Russian Communist party. Its task was to organize agitation in the East, to explain the Russian revolu-tion and the coming world revolution to the peoples of the East, and gradually to bring the revolutionary masses to an under-standing of world communism.[8] The department was divided into twelve subdivisions, including sections in Persia and Azar-bayjan, under the direction of natives of these countries.

At the Second Congress of the Moslem Communists, held in Moscow in November, 1919, Lenin proclaimed that because the masses in the East were peasants, the revolutionary struggle there would be against the remnants of feudalism and not against capitalism directly. He stressed the importance of directing ap-peals to the masses in each country in language they could understand.

We must clearly understand that the vanguard alone cannot achieve communism. The task is to awaken revolutionary activity and the sense of independence of the toiling masses and to organize them irrespective of their cultural level. The Moslem Communists had to interpret for their people the true Communist teachings, which had been actually drawn from the Communists of the more advanced countries, in the language of each people, applying to life the practical tasks which are to be accomplished immediately and uniting with the proletariat of all countries in a common struggle.[9]

The resolution passed by the congress of the Moslem Commu-nists embodied most of Lenin's recommendations. Emphasizing

[7] Joseph V. Stalin, in *ZN*, XIII (November, 1918), 2, as quoted in Xenia J. Eudin and Robert C. North, *Soviet Russia and the East, 1920–1927* (Stan-ford, 1957), pp. 77–78.

[8] For the full original text, see *ZN*, XV (February, 1919), 4; quoted in *ibid.*

[9] V. I. Lenin, *Sochineniia*, XXIV, 550–551; quoted in *ibid.*, pp. 78–79.

the indispensability of the East to the proposed international socialist revolution, it identified two directions for revolutionary activity in that part of the world. The first was toward a gradual formation of local Communist parties as branches of the Comintern and as dictated by the class struggle of the world revolutionary movement. The second was toward intensification of the struggle against Western imperialism by supporting this region's rampant nationalist movements. Support for national liberation struggles should, however, the resolution cautioned, in no way compromise the class revolutionary aspirations of the international proletariat. Instead, intensive organizational and propaganda work should be undertaken to accelerate the overthrow of West European domination. To assure the Bolshevik party's control of these activities, the congress recommended that the central organ of the Communist Organization of the People of the East create separate territorial sections and functional departments which would operate under the direct control of the Bolshevik party's Central Committee.[10]

At the suggestion of the Turkistan delegation it was resolved that to coordinate the action of the oppressed Eastern nationalities with that of the revolutionary proletariat of the West, the Third International must declare that the national liberation movements in the East and the socialist revolution in the West pursue the same general aim: the overthrow of capitalist imperialism.[11] This was clearly in line with the Communist solution of the attitude toward bourgeois nationalism already adopted by the Bolshevik leadership.

Of the countries of the East, Persia was definitely considered to be most ripe for application of these policies. Writing on "Revolution and the East" in 1918, K. M. Troianowsky claimed that the ground for revolution in Persia had long been prepared by the imperialists of Great Britain and tsarist Russia. Only a jolt from the outside and the initiative and determination of the Comintern were necessary to unleash revolution. Troianow-

---

[10] *ZN*, XLVII (December, 1919), 2; quoted in *ibid.*
[11] *Ibid.*

sky believed that, because of the geographical position of Persia, a revolt there could become the key to general revolution in the entire East, and therefore she must be the first to be conquered politically. He concluded very frankly: "This precarious key to revolution in the East must be in our hands; Persia must be ours at all costs; she must belong to the revolution." [12]

It is worthwhile at this point to examine the Communist evaluation of the situation in Persia in 1919, about a year before the Comintern embarked on its first attempt to export communism to the East — specifically Persia by means of the existing rebellious Jangali movement in Gilan. In 1919 the exact nature and social content of this uprising were not yet crystallized. It was still little more than a guerrilla revolt against the nearly impotent central government of the Qajar dynasty, which was looked on by the nationalists and liberal reformists as an instrument of British and, until 1917, of Russian imperialism.

The Communists' appraisal of this situation had undergone numerous changes and occasional reversals, but there is sufficient evidence to reveal the lines of thinking that immediately preceded the decision to transform the Jangali movement into a bridgehead for Communist expansion. A document entitled "The Nature of Propaganda to Be Carried Out in Persia," which appeared in the Russian journal *Zhizn Nationalnostei* in the spring of 1919,[13] argued that the importance of the Jangali leaders lay not in their armed strength or their opposition to the British but rather in the possibility of using them for revolutionary propaganda in the entire country. Kuchek Khan was recognized as an important socialist agitator, not so much because he was the leader of an armed uprising, but because he had advanced socialist slogans even before British forces entered Gilan. His work was closely connected with communism, and though it was interpreted by Persians in a different sense, it represented a seed that with careful and skillful cultivation was

---

12 Eudin and North, *op. cit.*, p. 92.
13 Original text in *ZN*, XIX (May, 1919), 2, and XX (June, 1919), 1; quoted in *ibid.*, pp. 177–178.

likely to produce a good harvest of revolutionary spirit among the Persian masses.

The document cautioned that, as long as the country was in the grip of the British, revolutionary work had to conform clearly to Persian life and psychology — that is to say, agitation must first of all concentrate on the general hatred of the British. Only later could the revolutionary materials be effectively used.

As for disseminating socialist ideas in general, and communism in particular, party agitators were instructed to rely principally upon local cells and organs of the Persian Socialists. Before the European war, Socialist activity had been largely confined to Azarbayjan, but following the October Revolution, and the establishment of Russian revolutionary war committees in northern Persia, the influence of revolutionary and socialist ideas had increased. Furthermore, thanks to the hard-working agents of the Persian Socialist Democratic party's central committee in Baku and Astrakhan, these cells had increased in number and had become more coordinated in activity. They were therefore the logical place to begin revolutionary undertakings in Persia, even though they were in many instances weak and had nothing that resembled a cadre of dependable and class-conscious socialists. The primary task of the Communist activists was to be that of creating a sense of class consciousness within a welter of existing political elements, always with the aim of preparing the people for the forthcoming revolutionary venture.[14]

In the spring of 1919 Communist sources gave further evidence of being preoccupied with ways of utilizing the Jangali movement in Gilan. Another article in the same Russian journal acknowledged that Kuchek Khan was attracted to communism and suggested exploiting his rebellion to spread communism to Persia and, indeed, throughout the East.[15]

The Anglo–Persian Treaty of August 9, 1919, in effect legalizing Britain's hold on Persia, provoked much anti-British senti-

---

[14] *Ibid.*, p. 178.
[15] *Ibid.*, p. 97.

ment which the Communists were able to exploit. In a lengthy message to the "Workers and Peasants of Persia," Georgii Chicherin, Soviet commissar for foreign affairs, appealed directly to this sentiment over the heads of government authorities.[16] Reviewing the differences between his government and the British government in the two years since the October Revolution, he described the treaty as a scrap of paper whose legal validity could not be recognized; Soviet Russia backed Persia in opposing it. Persians were assured:

The time for your liberation is near, the hour of death will soon strike for English capitalism against which a broad revolutionary movement is spreading evermore threateningly among the toiling masses of Britain itself. The working people of Russia stretch out to you, the suppressed masses of Persia, their fraternal hand. The hour is near when we shall be able, indeed, to carry out our task of a common struggle with you against the robbers and oppressors great and small who are the source of countless sufferings.[17]

Both diplomatic preparation and doctrinal formulation had thus been completed for a Communist offensive in Persia barely three years after the October Revolution. But the move itself could not have been successfully launched before the Communist hold was consolidated in Russian Azarbayjan. On April 28, 1920, after a good deal of upheaval and uncertainty, a soviet republic was at last established there: Moscow was now in a direct line of control of the Communist offensive south of its Asian borders. In a thinly veiled statement of purpose, Sultan Galiev openly declared that this was indeed the aspiration of Moscow: "Now Soviet Azarbayjan with its old and experienced revolutionary proletariat and its sufficiently consolidated Communist party will become a revolutionary beacon for Persia, Arabia, and Turkey . . . From there it is possible to disturb the British in Persia and stretch friendly hands to Arabia and to lead the

---

[16] G. V. Chicherin as quoted in Edward H. Carr, *The Bolshevik Revolution: 1917–1923* (New York, 1953), III, 241–242.
[17] *Ibid.*, p. 242.

revolutionary movement in Turkey until it assumes the form of a class struggle."[18]

The Communist offensive in Gilan used three elements which varied in importance and effectiveness throughout its more than two-year course: the physical presence of the Red Army on Persian territory; the Jangali rebellion; and the small Persian Communist party, which owed its existence to the support of Asian, notably Caucasian, Bolsheviks. The Red Army, the traditional tool of Russian diplomacy, was only a temporary expedient, but the other two elements were more directly employed and deserve some examination.

All the existing historical accounts of the origin of the Communist movement in Persia refer to the activity of a group called Adalat (Justice) among the Persian and Azarbayjani workers and the inhabitants of Baku as the first attempt to form a political party along Communist lines. At the outbreak of the Russian revolution this group had over 6,000 members recruited in the Caucasus and Turkistan.[19] One account identifies several Adalat committee leaders involved in an attempt to take over the Persian consulate in Baku — Mirza Assadollah, Ghaffar Zadeh, and the four Aghayev brothers.[20] Adalat committee leaders had promised the Bolsheviks to mobilize up to 10,000 Persian workers for the Red Army in return for the latter's support of the committee's revolutionary adventure in Persia. At that time there were about 20,000 workers of all nationalities throughout the oil installations in and around Baku.

The attempt to storm the Persian consulate in Baku, made in April, 1918, was the first recorded revolutionary incident in which the committee participated. The majority of the Persian colony succeeded in thwarting this attempt, but a second attempt a month later was successful; the consulate was seized and the consul general, Mohammad Saed, forced to flee. Within days the committee sent a delegation headed by its leader, Ghaffar

[18] *ZN,* XIII (May, 1920), 7; quoted in Eudin and North, *op. cit.,* p. 96.
[19] A. Palmieri, *La Politica Asiatica dei Bolscevichi* (Bologna, 1924), I, 238.
[20] Mohmommud Ali Manshur, *Siyasate Dowlate Shoravi dar Iran* [The Soviet Policy in Iran] (Teheran, 1948), pp. 41–42.

Zadeh, to establish contact with Mirza Kuchek Khan, the Jangali leader. Ghaffar Zadeh arrived in the Iranian Astara and was on his way to Enzeli to meet Kuchek Khan when he was assassinated by a personal opponent who had followed him from Baku.

Despite the loss of its leader, the committee continued to function, and during the Bolshevik regime of Stepan Shaumian in 1918 it readied the impressive strength of 4,000. Much of this success was due to the party organ, *Bayraghe Adalat* (Banner of Justice), a paper directed at workers and freedom fighters of the early phase of the constitutional revolution. The Ottoman occupation of 1918 reduced party strength to less than 40, but with the end of the war and the departure of the Turks, the committee resumed its activity, starting a new biweekly paper called *Horiyat* (Freedom), printed in Persian and Turkish. This journal advocated unity of the workers, aid to the poor, and unity with the workers of the world; it opposed the monarchy, the clergy, and the privileged aristocracy.[21]

Ghaffar Zadeh's successor as committee secretary was Mirjaafar, later to be known as Javad Zadeh and, still later, as Pishevari. Javad Zadeh was a native of Khalkhal, Persian Azarbayjan, and was fluent in both Persian and Russian, as well as in his native Azari. He held the post of secretary until the Red Army landed in Enzeli, after which the committee moved to Persia. Javad Zadeh and the four Aghayev brothers, together with other leaders of the worker committee of Adalat, became the native forerunners of the Communist offensive.

Official Soviet views on the origin of the Communist movement in Persia more or less confirm the non-Communist accounts. One writer describes the Adalat Committee as a Social-Democratic party founded in 1916 by Persian workers.[22] In an account of the Jangali revolt in Gilan, Emile Lesueur, a former professor in the Faculty of Law in Teheran, records that of the

---

21 *Ibid.*, p. 43.

22 M. N. Ivanova, "The National Liberation Movement in Gilan Province of Persia in 1920–21," first printed in *Sovetskoye Vostokovedeniye*, No. 3 (1955). English summary in *Central Asian Review*, Vol. IV, No. 3 (1956), 308 (hereafter cited as *CAR*).

5,000 regular soldiers which at the height of the movement constituted its miliary force, more than 600 were Persian Bolsheviks from Baku who belonged to the revolutionary party of
Adalat.[23] These figures are confirmed by other Western sources
on the relations of Bolshevik Russia with her southern neighbor.
It is commonly conceded, however, that the real work of the
Persian Communists started with the arrival in Gilan of the Red
Army, which installed the Adalat Committee in the province
as the first step in the offensive against Persia.[24]

The Gilan Republic

The significance of the Jangali movement lies in the fact that
this was the first instance since the Russian revolution of direct
Soviet military intervention in Persia's affairs and, more importantly, the first creation of a soviet republic within the territory of an independent country in the Middle East. It constituted
the first real chance of the Communists to implement the doctrine of revolution in the Eastern colonial and semicolonial
countries.

There is, however, considerable disagreement on what exactly
happened, and on how to interpret what happened. The Soviet
habit of fitting historical data into changing ideological interpretations has clouded not only the facts themselves but also the
background of the event. As recently as 1955, in the post-Stalin
era, during which there was systematic rehabilitation of old victims and a reinterpretation of historical events, new accounts of
the happenings in Gilan appeared in print, adding to the already
considerable confusion by presenting new data and by drasti-
cally reappraising the roles of the major actors. None of the
surviving leaders of the movement, who sought asylum in Soviet
Russia, has supplied an objective account of the event. Persian
literature also lacks objectivity and often is colored by national
istic sentiments depicting the Jangali leader either as a hero

---

[23] Emile Lesueur, *Les Anglais en Perse* (Paris, 1922), p. 53.
[24] Eudin and North, *op cit.*, pp. 99–100.

exploiting the Russian revolution to advance his own cause or as a naïve and innocent nationalist betrayed by Communist infiltrators.[25]

Confused though it may be, the Jangali movement is so important to our inquiry into the evolution of the Communist movement in Iran that we must make some attempt to separate fact from fiction and to review the events in proper perspective. Certainly a few facts are clear.

The movement arose in the province of Gilan primarily as an anti-British phenomenon. The British then occupied the entire northwestern region of Persia and had organized a military mission under Major-General L. C. Dunsterville to pass through Gilan to Baku and thence to Tiflis. After some resistance by the Jangalis to this mission, an agreement was reached with Kuchek Khan on August 12, 1918, terminating hostilities between the two antagonists.[26] At about that time a Soviet committee was formed in Enzeli, a town on the Caspian Sea (renamed Bandar Pahlavi in 1925), which was eventually to serve as a beachhead for the landing of the Red Army.

Soviet authors writing on the Jangali movement during the decade after the October Revolution not only acknowledged this committee but often overemphasized its significance; later Soviet versions have tended to minimize its role. Thus, in 1927, Irandust described this committee and its connection with the Jangali movement in some detail. According to him, in 1918 — on the initiative of Russian revolutionary soldiers — local soviets, including Russian soldiers as well as Persians, were formed in Resht and Enzeli, and gave new impetus to the partisan movement of the Jangalis.[27] Since the death of Stalin, Soviet writers and historians have stressed the indigenous and nationalistic character of the movement, only briefly referring to the exist-

---

25 Typical of this kind of treatment are Hasan Tehrani-Afshari, *Mirza Kuchek Khan* (Teheran, 1941), and Ahmed Tamimi-Taleghani, *Jangale Iran Che Budeh?* [What Was the Jangal of Persia?] (Teheran, 1945).

26 Ivanova, *op. cit.*, pp. 305–306.

27 Irandust, "Aspects of the Gilan Revolution," *Istorik-Marksist*, No. 5 (1927), as cited in *CAR*, Vol. IV, No. 3 (1956).

ence of these soviets.[28] It is beyond doubt, however, that these soviets were largely composed of Russian soldiers left in Persia after the collapse of the tsarist regime and of Communist elements from Turkistan and the Caucasus, as well as of members of the Adalat Committee, which a year later took over control. Enzeli was then part of the concession to tsarist Russia, and since there were as yet no diplomatic relations between Persia and Bolshevik Russia, no action could be taken against the Russian garrison of that city. [29]

Before the Communist offensive in early 1920, the social composition of the Jangali movement had undergone several transformations. At the core was a fighting force of peasants, laborers, and urban and village petty bourgeoisie, but the leadership was in the hands of the Ettehad-e-Islam (Unity of Islam) Committee, which had bourgeois nationalist and pan-Islamic characteristics.

The political and social background of Kuchek Khan reflects the initial orientation of the movement. As a turbaned theological student, he joined the constitutionalists in Gilan in the course of the 1905–1909 revolution and came to Teheran with them when they won their battle for parliament and formed the Etedalion (Moderate) party. In 1912, two leaders of the Turkish pan-Islamic movement, Bahabey and Roshanibey, had arrived in Persia to join some members of the opposition Democratic party and to form the Ettehad-e-Islam Committee. Kuchek Khan was one of the founders of the committee, which used pan-Islamic slogans. When the First World War broke out, the Democratic members of the opposition deserted the committee and resumed their former political activity. Kuchek Khan returned to Gilan. During the war he received arms and technical aid from the Turkish and German armies and gradually managed to gain control of Gilan. Up to this point, he had been extremely religious, with no clear goals for his revolution; his political

---

[28] M. S. Ivanov, *Ocherk istorii Irana* (Moscow, 1952), as quoted in *ibid.*

[29] Manshur, *op cit.*, pp. 41–42. Se also Major-General L. C. Dunsterville, "Military Mission to North-West Persia 1918," *Journal of Royal Central Asian Society*, Vol. VIII, No. 2 (1921), 83.

program was to be defined only after he joined with the Persian and Baku Communists to declare the establishment of the republic of Gilan in June, 1920.[30]

Early in 1918 two major groups emerged among participants in the movement. One, which had a great influence on Kuchek Khan, represented the upper middle bourgeoisie, landlords, and clergy; although it advocated reforming the state by limiting the Shah's power and feudalist domination, it did not conceive of any drastic overhaul of the social and political order. The other group consisted of petty bourgeoisie and the miserably paid seasonal agricultural workers, who were to become the focus of attention of the Communists dedicated to drastic changes in existing agrarian conditions.[31]

But not all authors agree with even this much of the early orientation and composition of the movement. Some early Communist sources find the movement of interest primarily because in the course of its evolution it attempted to solve the agrarian problem.[32] Even before the formation of the Gilan Soviet republic, leaders of the movement had confiscated the holdings of the feudal landowners who had escaped to the capital. Kuchek Khan, however, was not particularly in favor of land confiscation; his agrarian policy was tinged with strong religious undertones and in general advocated a return to what was vaguely described as "the old democratic order of Islam." This was taken to mean a system of property taxation and religious charity for the care of the poor and similar measures based on Koranic injunctions.

The program of the autonomous government of the revolutionary movement was nationalistic and pan-Islamic. Primarily, it stood for the overthrow of the monarchy and the establishment of a republic in Persia, for the defense of individual rights and property rights, for the liquidation of all "unjust agreements"

---

30 Mohammad Taghi Bahar, *Tarikhe Mokhtassare Ahzabe Sisyasiye Iran: Engheraze Qajariyeh* [A Short History of Iranian Political Parties: The Fall of the Qajars] (Teheran, 1944), I, 166–167.

31 Ivanova, *op. cit.*, p. 304.

32 Irandust, as quoted in *CAR*, Vol. IV, No. 3, 305.

concluded between the Persian government and foreign powers, for the equality of all nations, and for the defense of Islam.[33]

The summer of 1919 marked a turning point for the movement, which, following its defeat by forces of the central government, became more vulnerable to Communist infiltration and subsequent transformation of its character and orientation. The leaders of the movement, particularly Ehsanollah Khan, who was destined to play an important role in its evolution, believed that revival of the movement depended on Soviet Russia, and acting on this theory sought to make contact with the Soviets. According to one account, Kuchek Khan himself went to Lankoran, a province of Russian Azarbayjan, where he learned that Kolomiytsev, the official Soviet representative in Persia, was trying on his own to establish contact with the Jangalis.[34]

In the early spring of 1920 the Jangalis received a letter from the Bolshevik commander in the Caucasus informing them of the imminent seizure of Baku. They rightly interpreted this as a prelude to intervention on their behalf in Gilan. On the eve of the Soviet landing in Enzeli, the Communists of the Adalat Committee who favored such intervention issued a manifesto, signed by Haydar Khan and Javad Zadeh, calling upon all Iranian Communists and radicals to rise up on the day of the Russian invasion of Iran, to seize all government offices and military establishments and to arrest all members of the government, aristocrats, merchants, landlords, and any others who had collaborated with British authorities in Iran. It was, in short, a call for insurrection on the day the Red Army set foot on Persian soil, an event eagerly awaited by the Adalat Committee since the Bolshevik consolidation in Russian Azarbayjan.[35]

On May 18, 1920, Soviet military and naval detachments, under the command of Fedor Fedorovich Raskolnikov, landed in Enzeli with the professed intention of "returning the ships

---

[33] Ivanova, *op. cit.*, p. 305.
[34] George Lenczowski, *Russia and the West in Iran, 1918–1948* (Ithaca, N.Y., 1949), p. 59. This work is based on the memoirs of Ehsanollah Khan.
[35] *Setarehe-Iran* (Teheran), Feb. 23, 1923.

that had been taken away by the interventionists and liquidating the threat from the British and White Guard forces stationed in Gilan."[36] Although this was the official excuse for the intervention, the Soviets have readily acknowledged the connection between this step and the Jangali movement. In a historical account of this episode, they boast that a powerful impetus was given to the mass struggle of the Persian people and thus the national movement developed with new strength in Gilan.[37]

In a secret cable to Raskolnikov, L. M. Karakhan, the Soviet deputy commissar of foreign affairs, revealed the political purpose of this operation. The cable read in part:

> The reaction of Kuchek Khan to the establishment of the Soviet system in Iran must be carefully ascertained. . . . The toilers and the bourgeois democrats should be made united in the name of Persia's liberty and be instigated to rise up against the British and expel them from the country. . . . It is necessary to unite the Kuchek Khan forces and the Persian Communist and Democratic groups against the British. I will not oppose the establishing of . . . the Soviets . . . but I believe the principles should be changed, for I fear any haste in establishing Soviet principles there could result in class antagonism and weaken the struggle in Persia.[38]

In an account of this operation and its political significance, the commander of the Red Army and fleet in the Caspian admits that, as soon as a foothold was established on Persian territory, his emissaries encouraged the Kuchek Khan forces to continue chasing British and central government forces out of the area.[39] At any rate, with Red Army units secure in Enzeli, the Jangali movement was launched on a new course. In terms of Communist involvement, the new era of the movement falls logically into three phases.

---

[36] *Noveyshaya istoriya stran zarubezhnogo vostoka* (Moscow, 1954), I, 251, as quoted in *CAR*, Vol. IV, No. 3, 307.

[37] *Ibid.*

[38] Text in *Majelehe Forough* (Resht), May, 1928; quoted by Manshur, *Siyasate Dowlate Shoravi dar Iran*, p. 71.

[39] Eudin and North, *op. cit.*, pp. 179–180.

First Phase: The United Front Alliance

This phase covers the time from the landing on May 18 to the end of July, 1920, a period that could be characterized as a time of common struggle against remnants of British influence in the northwest region of Persia. For the Communists, this phase was one in which "a national united front was engaged in a struggle against British imperialism and its supporters — the ruling clique of the feudal aristocracy and the entire bourgeoisie." [40] This description was based on the composition of the revolutionary government and deduced from the numerous declarations of intention and policy.

The Gilan republic, proclaimed upon the arrival of detachments of Jangali forces and Red Army units in Resht on June 4, 1920, was styled after the Bolshevik model with eight commissars. [41] The messages sent to Lenin and other Bolshevik leaders, however, reveal the haziness of the regime's ideological principles. In a message to Lenin, Kuchek Khan said, in part:

We consider it to be our duty to draw your attention to the fact that there are a number of criminals in Persian territory — Persian oppressors, English traders, and diplomats supported by English troops — and as long as these enemies of the Persian people are in our country there will be an obstacle to the introduction of our just system all over Persia. In the name of humanity and the equality of all nations, the Persian Soviet Socialist Republic asks you and all the Socialists belonging to the Third International for help in liberating us and all the weak and oppressed nations from the yoke of Persian and English oppressors. . . . We have firm faith that all the world will be governed by the ideal system of the Third International. [42]

---

[40] Ivanova, *op. cit.*, p. 308.

[41] Manshur, *op. cit.*, p. 78, lists the following commissars: (1) interior, Mir-Shamsseddin; (2) external affairs, Seyd Jaafar; (3) finance, Mirza Mohammad Ali Pirbazari; (4) justice, Mahmud Agha; (5) post–telegraph–telephone, Nassrollah; (6) education, Haji Mohammed Jaafar; (7) public welfare, Mirza Mohmud Ali Khomami; (8) commerce, Hirza Abolghasem Fakhrai.

[42] Text in *Novyi Vostok*, No. 29 (1930), pp. 106–107; English summary in Eudin and North, *op. cit.*, p. 97.

The new republic and Leon Trotsky, the Bolshevik commissar of war, exchanged messages linking the Gilan revolt with the world revolutionary struggle. The Gilan message, after claiming victory over the counterrevolution allegedly engineered by international capitalism, announced the formation of Soviet power and a Persian Red Army for the purpose of "destroying the enslavers of our people." [43] This message carried the signature of Kuchek, chairman of the War Council, which included Ehsanollah, commander of the army, and Muzaffar Zadeh. The council had been set up by the Council of People's Commissars soon after the proclamation of the republic. In his reply Trotsky spoke of the struggle of the toilers of Persia for their freedom in the preceding decade and a half and expressed a firm conviction that under the guidance of the revolutionary War Council Persia would conquer for itself the right to freedom, independence, and fraternal toil. [44]

To show his appreciation for the valuable aid of Russian Azarbayjan in the success of the revolution, Ehsanollah sent a similar message to Narimanov, president of the Council of Commissars of the Soviet Republic of Azarbayjan in Baku. This message optimistically pictured the situation in the northern region, which was next in line for the Communist offensive. The revolutionary army, Ehsanollah declared, held the key to Mazanderan and the strategic line of Shahsavar and Lahijan to Gilan along the Caspian coast; revolutionary committees were already functioning in these parts, and the peasants were rallying in large numbers. More than a thousand peasants, he claimed, had enlisted in the new army, and the masses of workers of Mazanderan had appealed to the Soviet republic for liberation. These people awaited the help of the Third International and hoped they would not be abandoned in political or diplomatic deals. [45]

---

[43] Text in *Izvestia*, June 16, 1920, p. 7; quoted in Eudin and North, *op. cit.*, p. 181.

[44] Eudin and North, *op. cit.*

[45] *Izvestia*, July 13, 1920; quoted in Georges Ducroq, "La Politique du gouvernement des Soviets en Perse," *Revue du Monde Musulman*, Vol. LII (December, 1922), 146.

Clearly, Ehsanollah was one of the spokesmen of the new regime. Authority was ostensibly vested in a nine-man executive committee, with a presidium including Kuchek, Ehsanollah, Abrahamoff, and Javad Zadeh, but the real power was in the hands of the last three. Kuchek was merely the figurehead, for as long, at least, as the appearance of the alliance was maintained. Ehsanollah himself was convinced that the more violent the peasant movement was, the more complete would be the collapse of the feudal system, which would not only facilitate the present reforms but would also ensure future economic reconstruction.[46] Under one of the first decrees all estates were confiscated and distributed among the supporters of the regime. As head of the army, Ehsanollah was able to enforce the decree; and he firmly believed that the army, the police, and the people's courts were instruments of the people for the oppression of enemy classes and hence should be made use of to eliminate the feudal system within their domain.

There were problems facing the new government — religion, in particular. The Communist leadership at once embarked on a policy of antireligious propaganda, and in so doing precipitated its own downfall, as a consequence of the split with moderate elements and the disillusionment of the predominantly religious peasantry. In the first few weeks of its rule the regime reportedly closed nineteen mosques, prohibited religious instruction, and decreed forceable unveiling of women. The Moslem clergy, who vigorously opposed these measures, were ridiculed publicly and even used as hostages for the good behavior of the masses.[47]

Soviet authorities condemned most of these measures in the postmortem analysis of the revolution, but it was only after the failure of the movement that they were able to appreciate such factors as the religious devotion of the peasantry. Thus, in an article on the "Five Years of Iranian-Soviet Relations," Iransky says:

---

[46] *Jangal* (Resht), Sept. 20, 1920.
[47] Based on the report of the Governor General of Gilan to the central government cited in the newspaper *Setarehe-Iran*, June 26, 1924.

In view of the backwardness, ignorance, and apathy of the Persian peasantry the revolutionary movement in Gilan never found staunch supporters. The peasants were delighted to grab the land, but they never understood the content of the revolution. Having played its historical role it lost its dynamism and its historical sense of mission and began to disintegrate internally. Lack of understanding of the Communist ideology, personal jealousies of the leaders, religious fanaticism, and mistakes of the new government jointly were responsible for its failure.[48]

Long before any of these measures were allowed to be completed the uneasiness of the alliance between Communist and non-Communist elements, partly stemming from personal conviction and political background, became apparent. The principal figures around whom evolved the controversy over the aims and tactics of the revolution and the future of the Soviet republic in Gilan were Kuchek, Ehsanollah, and Sultan Zadeh. The latter two have written about this phase, and although their accounts do not always correspond to historical fact, they reflect their ideological orientation at the time they led the movement's left wing.

Ehsanollah relates that even before the proclamation of the republic Kuchek harbored misgivings about Bolshevik aims, despite the fact that he had formed a revolutionary alliance with their agents. Kuchek, says Ehsanollah, wanted to enter into treaty relations with the Bolsheviks before extending his revolution to Teheran.[49] Ehsanollah was opposed to negotiation with the Bolsheviks, lest it create misunderstandings between the Jangalis and the Russians. At the insistence of Kuchek, however, negotiations were undertaken in Enzeli on May 20, and Kuchek wrested from the Bolsheviks a promise of noninterference in Jangali's domestic affairs.[50] Even after this pledge Kuchek did

---

[48] Iransky, "Russko-Persitskiye otnoshenia za piat let," *Novyi Vostok*, Vol. IV, Nos. 3–4 (1923), 218; cited in Lenczowski, *Russia and the West in Iran*, p. 58.

[49] Based on the memoirs of Ehsanollah Khan in *Novyi Vostok*, Vol. XXIX (1932), 88–107, as cited in Manshur, *op. cit.*, p. 72.

[50] Carr, *op. cit.*, pp. 243–244.

not yield to Ehsanollah, who advocated an immediate march to the capital where a revolutionary government would be established and treaty relations immediately taken up with the Bolshevik government in Moscow. Instead, the Jangali forces marched into Resht and set up their republic.[51]

Apart from differences about the nature of the soviet republic's actions, there was a fundamental divergence of opinion concerning the popular basis of the regime. Kuchek apparently believed the object of the new government was to achieve consensus among various interests, expressed through elected representatives dependent for reelection on the satisfaction of the majority of their constituents. The Communists held themselves responsible solely to the executive committee of the Third International and rejected any form of parliamentary government. They stated frankly that all members of the soviet government in Gilan should faithfully accept the authority of the Third International, and if they participated in parliamentary government, they should always be ready to destroy it if so instructed by the party.[52]

Soviet authorities showed misgivings about Kuchek's lack of enthusiasm for their goals, a lack they considered responsible for the eventual failure of the Gilan republic. In the first phase of the movement Kuchek was accused of half-hearted decisions and endless compromises with the central government.[53] The major complaint against him, however, was that his government sought to limit the revolution to the Gilan province rather than to turn it into a liberation movement on a pan-Iranian scale. Clearly, Soviet diplomacy hoped for rapid expansion of the revolutionary movement in accordance with the strategy Ehsanollah had so candidly revealed. Had the strategy succeeded, the Soviets would have been supplied with a much stronger lever of pressure in their relations with Persia

---

[51] Manshur, *op. cit.*, pp. 72–73.
[52] *Golshan* (Resht), June 28, 1922.
[53] Ivanova, *op. cit.*, p. 308.

and Great Britain than was the case with the isolated Gilan
experience.

From a doctrinal viewpoint, the Bolshevik dilemma at this
point was that short of a united struggle rallying the forces of
the Jangalis with those of the Persian Communists, there was
no way of expanding the revolution. The Bolsheviks were quite
aware that the Communists of the Adalat Committee were
neither numerically nor ideologically capable of achieving this
alone. The Bolsheviks, therefore, were equally critical of the
extreme leftist provocation of the Communist wing of the Jangali
leadership which urged immediate action irrespective of Kuchek's opposition.

This view has become increasingly popular in Soviet interpretations in the post-Stalin era. Thus charging the Communist
leadership with counterrevolutionary policy, a recent Soviet
source complained that Sultan Zadeh's faction, which had made
its way to the leadership of the Communist party, was guilty
of extreme leftism. This group is criticized for demanding far-
reaching radical measures such as confiscation of all lands, even
those of small holders, and requisitions among the peasants,
petty traders, and artisans. Furthermore, the extremists are
criticized for having demanded an end to cooperation with the
petty and middle bourgeoisie, and above all for having engaged
in antireligious propaganda which "bore a provocative character, considering the social composition of the movement."[54]

That such a policy indeed deviated from the approved
line of action was only gradually admitted by the Soviet government and its native Communist supporters. Official evaluation of the Gilan soviet shortly after its formation was indicated
in an essay by A. Vozhesensky, head of the Eastern Department
of People's Commissariat of Foreign Affairs, in which he conceded that the composition of the Gilan government was far
from Communist.[55] The government was regarded rather as a
united front which had brought together many elements of

---

[54] *Ibid.*
[55] *Izvestia,* as quoted in Eudin and North, *op. cit.,* p. 98.

varied social backgrounds under the banner of an anti-British struggle. A look at the composition of the cabinet is sufficient to substantiate this conclusion, for it contained mostly representatives of the democratic petty bourgeoisie of northern Persia.

Despite this evaluation, considerable trust was put in Kuchek Kahn by the Soviet officials directly in charge of operations in Persia. For example, Raskolnikov expressed hope that Kuchek's cooperation with the wealthy class was merely a tactical necessity which would soon be replaced by more drastic measures to attract the peasantry through land distribution.[56] The course of events showed the fallacy of these assumptions. It eventually became evident that the united front, which formed the backbone of the republic, would not work. On July 19, Kuchek resigned from the government and moved with his followers from Resht into the forest, bringing to an end the republic's initial phase. To save face, the Central Committee of the Persian Communist party issued a decree removing Kuchek from all positions in the Gilan soviet hierarchy.

Although the Communists generally were optimistic about the movement's achievements in this phase, not all Bolsheviks were enthusiastic. Within a week of the proclamation of the republic on June 4, the prominent Turkistan Bolshevik Sultan Galiev cast doubt on the firmness of the regime, which he said was not entirely Communist, notwithstanding Kuchek's expressions of sympathy for communism. Only in retrospect, however, were the weaknesses of the regime really allowed their full weight. Soviet writers, after the event, blamed the united front for lack of progressive policies. Its strategy was sound, but its very extremism was responsible for the collapse of the strategy. The Soviet Encyclopedia says that Kuchek, on the right wing of the bloc, was forced to resign as a result of his disagreement with the tactics of certain "Trotskyist" elements who were guilty of breaking the united anti-imperialist front.[57]

The Soviets now recognize that the chief underlying difficulty

---

[56] *Ibid.*, p. 180.
[57] *CAR*, IV, No. 3, 309.

in maintaining this alliance was the forces of nationalism. Even before the republic had failed, Chicherin, the architect of Soviet diplomacy, was warning of the dangers of nationalism. In December, 1920, in an address to the Eighth Congress of the Soviets, he characterized all the movements then taking place in the East as primarily nationalistic in content and xenophobic in form.[58] As Communists, he said, the Bolsheviks favored these anti-imperialist movements, but there existed serious differences between movements seeking national liberation and communism advocating international class struggle. In dealing with the East, therefore, the Bolsheviks were confronted with the task of finding a common language with these movements and advancing jointly against world imperialism. But Chicherin assured the congress that Soviet policy, recognizing the necessity and validity of struggle for independence against Western imperialism, was based on compromise with the Eastern liberation movements.

Numerous pronouncements and documents attributed to official Soviet sources clearly indicate that the Eastern united front alliance was to be temporary.[59] It is obvious, however, that the premature collapse of the united front phase of the Gilan republic surprised the Soviets and left them with only the leftist faction of the leadership and the members of the PCP to work with.

First Congress of the PCP, 1920

Toward the end of the first phase of the movement the PCP held its first congress under the chairmanship of Agha-Zadeh, a veteran of the Adalat Committee. Although the congress was held in Enzeli on June 23, preparations had been completed

---

[58] Eudin and North, *op. cit.*, p. 91.

[59] Ducroq quotes from *Internationale Communiste*, No. 12: "We utilize their revolutionary activity for the struggle against the world capital, for the triumph of social revolution in the whole world; but if later the interest of revolution demands, we can turn our weapons against our yesterday's allies." "La Politique du gouvernement des Soviets en Perse," p. 143.

previously in Tashkent in Russian Turkistan, and the idea of
holding this congress had itself been initiated by the Turkistan
Kray Committee of Adalat, which was second in importance to
that of Baku.[60] At the time of the congress Enzeli was still occupied by the Red Army, despite mounting pressure from the
central government and repeated promises of Bolshevik leaders
to withdraw the troops.

The congress approved the credentials of 48 delegates, purporting to represent 2,000 members and sympathizers[61] (this
despite the fact that, according to the best available information,
the numerical strength of the party, before the arrival of Soviet
troops, was 37, organized in two underground groups in Resht).[62]
Several resolutions were quickly passed stating that it was
the party's duty to join Soviet Russia in fighting world capitalism
and to support in Persia all forces opposed to the British and to
the Shah's government.[63] It was resolved that dictatorship of
the proletariat could be established in Azarbayjan and Gilan
only by slow degrees and with the support of Soviet Russia. According to a leading congress member, this "savior position" of
the Soviet Union also imposed definite obligations upon the
Communists in Iran, whose duty it was to defend the Soviet
Union against attacks of the capitalist nations.[64]

In an attempt to attract the masses to a common struggle
under the leadership of the Communist party throughout Persia,
the following policies were agreed upon: overthrow of imperialist domination; confiscation of all foreign enterprises; recognition of the right of self-determination for all nationalities within
the framework of the unity of the country; confiscation of all
lands of the big landowners and distribution of these lands

---

[60] Sultan Zadeh, *Sovremennaya Persiya* (Moscow, 1922), pp. 59–60; cited
in *CAR*, Vol. IV, No. 3, 403.

[61] Sultan-sade, "Der erste Kongress der persischen Kommunisten der
Partei Adalat," *Die Kommunistische Internationale*, No. 14 (Hamburg,
1923), pp. 225–230.

[62] Jane Degras, *The Communist International* (London, 1950), Vol. I,
110.

[63] *Ibid.*, p. 106.

[64] Javad Zadeh in *Jangal*, June 2, 1920.

among the peasants and soldiers of the revolutionary army; and alliance with Soviet Russia and the world proletarian movement.[65]

Sultan Zadeh, who was later accused of being partly responsible for the failure of the united front government, reported that this congress was apprehensive about Kuchek Khan's intentions to carry out the bourgeois-democratic revolution by drawing to its side various khans, large-scale landowners, and feudal lords on the grounds that in fighting the Shah and the British, the nation had to be united.[66] It was stated in the congress that the Communist party obviously could not approve of such tactics, for it was convinced that any revolution in a backward agrarian country that did not remove feudal oppression and liberate millions of peasants was destined to fail. Liberation of the peasants with the help of the feudal lords was considered an illusion which the party was obliged to oppose.

The Persian Communists, in effect, gave a far narrower interpretation to the concept of temporary alliance with the bourgeoisie than was accepted at the beginning of this phase, when the soviet republic was proclaimed. This was a return to Sultan Zadeh's hope of an independent formation of purely communistic parties in countries like Persia on the grounds that a bourgeois nationalist movement had long existed there. Ironically, this interpretation served to discredit its author later when the Gilan offensive collapsed and rationalizations had to be advanced for its failure.

Among the other items of business at the congress, the party formally changed its name from Adalat to Hezbe Komoniste Iran (Communist Party of Persia). It sent greetings to the Red Army and fleet and to the central committees of the Russian Communist party, and it elected Lenin and Narimanov as honorary chairmen in absentia.[67] In the final session, Sultan Zadeh was instructed to seek Lenin's assistance in adopting a correct

---

[65] *Ibid.*, June 6, 1920.
[66] Eudin and North, *op. cit.*, p. 99.
[67] *Ibid.*

policy and action program for the party. After a meeting with Lenin in July, Sultan Zadeh reported that Lenin listened attentively to the discussion in the commission but remarked that in backward countries like Persia, where the greater part of the land was concentrated in the hands of the landlords, advocacy of agrarian revolution would have a practical significance for the peasant millions. Bukharin and Zinoviev backed Lenin, and Sultan Zadeh and Pavlovich were asked to outline a thesis applicable to Persian conditions. This was immediately communicated to PCP's Central Committee, but by then it was already faced with new crises in the Gilan republic, which had moved too fast for this recommendation to be of use. For by July the schism between the nationalists and the Communists had come into the open and a new phase in the Gilan episode had begun.

Second Phase: Independent Communist Rule

The second phase, which lasted from the end of July to mid-October, 1920, is characterized by the disintegration of the united front of the Communist and non-Communist Jangali elements and by the independent attempt of the Communists to continue and expand the revolution on their own.

On July 31 a new government led by Ehsanollah took over in Resht. It was officially called the National Committee for the Liberation of Persia, and its membership consisted solely of followers of Ehsanollah and of Sultan Zadeh. The new government was in control of a force of about 200 Russian, Armenian, and Georgian soldiers and about 1,200 Persian workers from the Baku oil industry, and in one of its first steps it created a Communist youth league to intensify propaganda and agitation and to organize armed groups for operation against Kuchek's followers, now the main adversaries.[68] To replace the former commissars of the Gilan soviet, seven new commissars were appointed from among the PCP members and a small faction of Jangalis

---

[68] Manshur, *op. cit.*, pp. 87–88.

led by Khalu Ghorban, who had deserted Kuchek and gone over to Ehsanollah.

The regime also had at its disposal two journals, *Komonist* and *Enghelabe Sorkh* (Red Revolution), which printed certain information about the organization and action of the new government. According to *Enghelabe Sorkh,* two committees wielded the real power under the mandate from the larger revolutionary committee. One, called the Committee of Revolution, was to chart the regime's ideological course. The other, called Special Branch, was to see to it that the prescribed line of action was pursued by the commissars and subordinate organs, such as the Communist Youth League and the armed detachments which were being mobilized to defend the regime.[69] In other words, the new government adopted a program of action later criticized by the Soviets for being based on a "dogmatic philosophy of Socialist revolution in Persia at a time when there was no firm social base for putting it into practice, in view of the small size and weakness of the proletariat."[70]

That Ehsanollah always favored radical and violent action is partly confirmed by his political background before accepting communism, and especially so by his membership in a terrorist organization which was active in Persia before the Russian revolution. The organization, known as Komiteye Mojazat (Punishment Committee), was responsible for several political assassinations in 1918–1919 in Teheran. In 1919, when the government took measures against the committee, Ehsanollah was one of the few who managed to escape to Russian Azarbayjan.[71]

Ehsanollah strove hard in the early years of the revolution to follow the methods of the Russian Soviet government. To him, the situation in his native country was akin to that of Russia

---

[69] *Ibid.,* p. 92.

[70] Mme Ivanova blames Ehsanollah in this fashion, yet at the end of her article acknowledges as one of the failures of the Gilan republic the "local character of the revolutionary events." In his memoirs published in *Novyi Vostok,* Ehsanollah says he believed that "we ought not to limit ourselves to one province but ought to develop our movement throughout the whole country." See *Novyi Vostok,* No. 29 (1930), 102; *CAR,* Vol. IV, No. 3, 328.

[71] Bahar, *Tarikhe Mokhtassare Ahzabe Siyasiye Iran,* pp. 32–33.

in 1917, and he therefore attempted to emulate the Russian experience, first of all by applying the method of war communism by militantly focusing on the forcible elimination of all opponents of communism and rejecting any cooperation with other social classes. When this method proved unsuccessful, he recognized the necessity of winning over the peasantry and petty bourgeoisie by economic concessions — an attitude akin to the "New Economic Policy" which resulted from a similar failure in Russia.

Typical of the early measures taken by his regime were those concerning property and taxation. Once established in Resht and in the surrounding regions, his government decreed that all rent moneys were to be paid to the revolutionary government's treasury instead of to the landowners; that the owner's share of crops was to be handed over to the government's treasury; and that country houses of rich landlords were to be confiscated and all houses large enough for more than one family were to be requisitioned for government officials.[72]

The climax of this period was an unsuccessful mid-August march on Teheran, a march for which Ehsanollah had clamored from the early days of the Red Army's landing in Enzeli in May, 1920. It was an utter fiasco, for the revolutionary army was defeated by the central government forces before it could even set out on the main road to Teheran.

The Baku Congress, September, 1920

Meanwhile, preparations were under way in Moscow and Baku for a congress of the People of the East, to be held in Baku in early September. Planning this congress was by far the most elaborate attempt by the Comintern's Executive Committee to reach the Asian masses. As early as July the committee had appealed to the "enslaved peoples of Persia, Armenia and Turkey" to attend the proposed congress.[73] The committee cited the capitalist "oppression" of the proletariat of the West and the

---

[72] Summary in *Iran*, June 28, 1920.

masses of the East as a common cause for cooperation of all anticapitalist forces. Lenin's resolution to the Comintern Congress
earlier in the year had sanctioned the bypassing of the capitalist
stage of development in the backward East with the help of the
proletariat of the industrialized West. The Baku Congress in
effect sought to establish an organic link between the two.

The Baku Congress was attended by 1,891 delegates, the majority of whom, according to Zinoviev, the congress chairman,
were not Communists. Nevertheless, the bulk of the delegates
were sympathetic to the Party's anti-Western and indeed nationalist goals because they represented the part of the world which
for a long time had been under some form of Western colonial
control.

The Persian delegation of 192, the second largest after
Turkey's, which numbered 235, primarily represented the northern provinces. It included liberal anti-British veterans of the
1905 constitutional revolution, most of whom were more *against*
Great Britain than they were *for* the Communist formula for a
social revolution.[74]

In his opening address Zinoviev appealed for a holy war
against British imperialism and for establishment of the soviet
system throughout the East. He urged fighting on two fronts:
against the foreign imperialists, and for the education of the
masses in hostility toward the rich. Real revolution, he promised, would come only when the 800,000,000 people in Asia
were united with Russia, when the African continent was also
united, and when hundreds of millions of people were at last
on the move.[75]

Of the three Persian delegates who addressed the congress,
Haydar Kahn deserves most attention, for his speech re-

---

[73] Text in *Izvestia*, July 3, 1920; cited in Eudin and North, *op. cit.*, p. 99.

[74] The leading Persian delegates were Haydar Khan, Alioff, Sultan
Zadeh, Javad Zadeh, Lahuti, Zarreh, and Ehsanollah Khan. Most of these
men became involved in the final phase of the Jangali rebellion on their
return to Persia. See Nassrollah S. Fatemi, *Diplomatic History of Iran* (New
York, 1951), p. 168.

[75] A Persian translation of Zinoviev's speech appeared in *Haqiqat*,
Oct. 6, 1921.

flected the political attitude of a basically nationalist leader who was about to embrace communism as a matter of expediency rather than as a sincere conviction. He appealed for Russia's military support to organize an international Communist army. His views on the class nature of society and the unavoidable struggle between the oppressed and oppressors had more or less a Communist content. He spoke of a classless society which would rely on the Soviet army to resist Western hostility.

His views on bourgeois democracy showed a complete reversal from his earlier support of a constitutional brand of democracy during the 1905–1909 revolution. Now he thought only the dictatorship of the proletariat was able to liberate mankind from the "hypocrisy" of bourgeois democracy, which, according to Lenin, was only for the rich, unlike the proletarian dictatorship, which was the democracy for the poor.[76] This speech and similar statements of a primarily nationalistic character compelled Comintern spokesmen to warn against narrow-minded nationalism. Zinoviev cautioned that the character of the struggle was determined not by national boundaries but by the class against which it was waged. But since the East was not ripe for communism, Zinoviev conceded, the Comintern was willing to cooperate with the nationalist democratic and revolutionary elements, while continuing to support the still weak Communist movements.[77]

Specifically, the Baku Congress passed two manifestos and several resolutions. One resolution invited the "oppressed masses of the peasantry" to rely on the support of the revolutionary workers of the West, the Comintern, and the soviet states of the present and future, and to wage a determined struggle to set up soviet power in the East.[78] Another recommended the establishment of the "Soviet Government in the East" as the conclusive objective of the revolution against foreign and domestic oppressors.[79] The solution of the agrarian question was

---

[76] *Komonist*, Sept. 29, 1920, and *Jangal*, Oct. 2, 1920.
[77] Carr, *op. cit.*, pp. 264–265.
[78] *Ibid.*, pp. 247–248.
[79] Eudin and North, *op. cit.*, pp. 170–172.

also linked with the creation of such a government, which alone could attain the liberation of the peasantry. Only after the complete destruction of world capitalism, the congress declared, and with the help of the working class of the world's most advanced countries, could the peasants of the East proceed to the Communist regime. To implement this declaration, the formation of a Council for Propaganda and Action of the People of the East was announced at the close of the congress. This council was to have a presidium of seven members, two of whom were to be appointed by the Comintern's Executive Committee with the right to veto the council's decisions.

Despite an appearance of solidarity in the resolutions of the congress, strongly reflecting the Communist line, the assembled delegates were less than harmonious in political composition. Two groups were recognizable — the Communists and the much larger group of nonparty delegates. Because of this imbalance, the congress failed in its immediate task of spreading Communist propaganda in the East, as indicated by the proceedings of Comintern's Third Congress a year later in Moscow.[80] In Moscow, Javed Zadeh of the PCP admitted the disunity of the Communists in the East, where three parties existed in Turkey and two in Persia. But he blamed the disunity on the success of the ruling class in exploiting the Communist idea for its own ends by encouraging factionalism and dividing the party's leadership. Zinoviev's answer was that the Comintern could support only genuine Communist activity and should repudiate anything in the nature of pure nationalism, however it might be disguised. Some of the Moslem delegates maintained that it was typical of all Near East revolutionary activity to be nationalistic in its early stage.[81]

If anything, then, the Baku Congress and its aftermath merely emphasized once again the Bolsheviks' dilemma in the handling of nationalism. The best they could hope for was the transformation of the revolutionary movements after their initial,

---

[80] Hans Kohn, *Geschichte der nationalen Bewegung im Orient* (Berlin, 1928), p. 176.

[81] *Ibid.*, p. 148.

strongly nationalistic stage. In the 1920's, at any rate, these stages had not been completed. The large number of Middle Eastern leaders expressing extreme nationalistic sentiments proved this beyond doubt. As we have seen, these sentiments were not anticipated by the Russian Communists, who at the Third International charged the guest delegates with preaching nationalism, not communism, and warned that the first duty of the delegates was promotion of world propaganda against nationalism.

Third Phase: The Collapse of the Rebellion

The return of the Persian delegation from Baku coincided with the end of the second phase of the development of the Gilan republic. Toward the end of October, 1920, the PCP elected a new Central Committee, which set about trying to reconstruct the former united front. The party had already recruited Haydar Khan, the old revolutionist, and it now elected him secretary of the Central Committee, hoping thereby to increase the prestige of the committee. Some Soviet sources even went so far as to credit Haydar Khan with being a pioneer organizer of the Persian Communist party and workers' movement long before the formation of the Gilan republic.[82] There seems no doubt, however, that, although he lived in Baku after the close of the First World War, he joined the party only toward the end of the Gilan movement, primarily as a result of the Baku Congress.

With the election of Haydar Khan, the Central Committee also adopted a new thesis on the social and economic conditions of Persia and an action program. The new thesis analyzed the country's social and class composition during the various stages of the revolutionary movement before it achieved its goal. Acknowledging the impossibility of immediate introduction of such measures as outright property expropriation, and revealing the opposition that the earlier antireligious measures had evoked, the party drew a pessimistic picture of the prospects of

---

[82] Ivanova, *op. cit.*, p. 310.

destroying land ownership. It was clear to the Central Committee that the feudal system of property, in force in Persia for many centuries, could not be eliminated overnight.

Even Soviet propaganda was not successful in penetrating Persian society on the scale the party had expected, the new thesis stated, because industry and therefore an industrial proletariat were lacking. But the failure was also a result of the differences between Kuchek Khan and the Bolsheviks concerning such religious problems as the emancipation of women, respect for Koranic injunctions, and the over-all relation between Islam and political and state organs.

Izvestia, the organ of the Soviet government, construed the new thesis as the PCP's acknowledgment that revolution in Persia should be started by the bourgeois class because the Gilan experience had proved the futility of trying to set up a Bolshevik regime in that country.[83] In terms of doctrinal content, the thesis did indeed represent a drastic departure from the previously accepted dogma concerning the prospects of communism in Persia: there was to be no attempt at outright communization; Persia could not skip the bourgeois stage in its revolutionary progress; the best hope lay in a renewed attempt to reorganize a broad national front alliance in which Communists and other elements could cooperate to accelerate this process.

At this time it seemed that traditional Soviet diplomacy corresponded to the Comintern doctrinal injunctions. No less a Bolshevik than Chicherin interpreted the thesis of the PCP's Central Committee as relegating the revolution in Persia to that country's completion of bourgeois development. The new thesis, in other words, constituted the end of any policy to introduce a Communist regime in Persia. Thus an effort that had started with the local soviet government in Gilan had now to be abandoned in favor of more conventional diplomacy on behalf of Bolshevik Russia.[84]

After accepting the new thesis, Haydar Khan and other mem-

---

[83] *Izvestia*, Nov. 6, 1921; cited in Manshur, *op. cit.*, p. 143.
[84] *Ibid.*

bers of the Central Committee set out to establish a united
national front such as had existed in the first phase of the development of the Gilan republic. Contacts were established with
the Jangali leader, and finally on May 8, 1921, an agreement
among the Central Committee of the PCP, the Ehsanollah revolutionary committee in Resht, and Kuchek's faction of the Jangali movement was concluded for combined action against Great
Britain and the central government.

That the formation of this alliance in no way meant the loss
of the Communist party's separate identity was evidenced by a
number of Communist resolutions adopted after the formation
of the new Central Committee. One resolution put out by the
Central Committee in March, 1921, over the signature of Haydar Khan, contained detailed instructions for party committees
throughout the country. Emphasizing the importance of grass-
roots work, the resolution urged the immediate formation of
local Communist cells to increase the scope of party activity.[85]
Local cells were to pursue the long-range goals of overthrowing
the present government and preparing an armed uprising.

The immediate goals were designated as the creation of a
Central Committee composed of members of local cells in each
district, the preparation of new sections of party members, the
awakening of the revolutionary forces and their organization
under the Central Committee, and the preparation of local
groups to strengthen the revolutionary struggle. These goals
were to be pursued by means of propaganda in newspapers and
local discussion groups against English imperialism and the government, propaganda for the reorganization of professional cooperatives created in 1908 and 1909 by the workers of various
professions, and the organization of youth clubs and of a regular
service of intelligence with other organs of the party.

Interestingly, for the first time the party attempted to reach
beyond the Gilan province. Armed with the considerable popu-
larity of Haydar Khan, copies of this resolution were sent to

---

[85] Ducroq, "La Politique du gouvernement des Soviets en Perse," pp.
144–145.

Tabriz and other towns of Persian Azarbayjan. In Tabriz a Bolshevik committee was set up, including Tartars from Baku,
Armenians from Erivan, and Russians who ostensibly had escaped as a result of the October Revolution or its aftermath but
who in reality were Soviet agents. A Communist pamphlet distributed in Tabriz at this time carried the seal of the local Bolshevik commissar of Persia and contained assurances that bolshe-
vism would soon be introduced in Persian Azarbayjan now that
it had a foothold in the Gilan province.[86] There is no evidence,
however, of any very large number of Communist cells in Azarbayjan, or, for that matter, anywhere else as a result of the instruction issued by the new Central Committee.[87]

By and large, the Soviets were satisfied with this phase of the
Jangali development. The PCP was credited with having given
serious attention to propaganda among the agricultural workers
and the poorest peasants, as a result of which the party's authority
had allegedly increased and an attempt was made to mobilize
the peasantry as an auxiliary to the party.[88] At the end of July,
1921, a Peasants' Council of Jangal was organized, with Haydar
Khan as its president. The Revolutionary Committee, the official
governing body of the new alliance, also took measures to unify
various armed detachments and to form trade unions. Finally
on August 4, 1921, Gilan was once again proclaimed a soviet
republic.

Within a very short time it became obvious that the new alliance was not going to be any more lasting than the previous
one. The alliance's leadership was in sore disagreement as to
the conduct and scope of the revolutionary movement. According to recent Soviet sources, some revolutionary committeemen
secretly struggled for leadership. Ehsanollah was again blamed
for envisioning a triumphant march on Teheran. Other Soviet

---

[86] A photostatic copy of this document in Persian is contained in *ibid.*,
pp. 146–147.

[87] Ivanova cites proclamations of the PCP's provincial committee in
Mashad but fails to prove that there actually were such committees anywhere except in Tabriz and Gilan; *op. cit.*, p. 171.

[88] *Ibid.*, p. 311.

sources have attributed the dissension to Haydar Khan, who less than a year earlier had been hailed as the new blood of the revolutionary life. He was charged now with attempting to gain full control of Kuchek's Jangali domain.[89]

While these rifts continued, the central government increased its pressure for the military recovery of the province. Toward midsummer, 1921, preparations were made for a march on Resht and Enzeli. Accounts on how the adventure came to an end are so varied as to render its exact reconstruction impossible. What is certain is that as the pressure by the central government's army mounted, the leadership became more divided. Communist sources charged that the internal dissension was caused by Kuchek's fear of the expansion of the influence and power of the Communist party, and even went so far as to suggest that Kuchek was secretly dealing with agents of the central government and Great Britain.

There seems to be some truth to the charge that Kuchek had become apprehensive about the future of his cooperation with the Communists. Persian sources confirm that some contacts were established with a new cabinet in Teheran, which sent an emissary to Gilan in an attempt to break the alliance between Kuchek and the Communists. These came to naught in the face of Kuchek's insistence on Gilan's autonomy, but they more or less succeeded in their purpose of causing a break between Kuchek and the Communists.

The Communists decided to trap Kuchek by sending a mission of peace and reconciliation led by Haydar Khan and including Ehsanollah, Khalu Ghorban, Zarrah, and Hesabi. According to Persian accounts, Kuchek was tipped off about the plot and ordered his partisans to attack and set fire to the house in Pesikhan where the peace emissaries had assembled to await the Jangali leader. Haydar Khan was killed, but the others escaped unharmed. The break was now out in the open, and Kuchek ordered his followers to assassinate Communist leaders throughout

---

[89] Irandust, "Aspects of the Gilan Revolution," as quoted in *CAR*, Vol. IV, No. 3, 311.

the region.[90] Communist sources, in a somewhat different version
of the incident, accuse Kuchek Khan of open betrayal and claim
that it was as a result of a counterrevolutionary conspiracy that
Haydar was killed on September 29, 1921. Kuchek's partisans,
they say, then marched into Resht and destroyed the organizations and headquarters of the Communist party, both there and
in Enzeli, but since they were incapable of holding the town
for long withdrew into the forest, permitting the Communists to
return after four days.

Then, according to Persian sources — a column of the central
government's army, commanded by Reza Khan, launched a final
assault on Gilan toward the end of August. By the end of October the Communist forces of Ehsanollah were completely destroyed, forcing him to leave Enzeli on October 22 on a boat
for Russia, accompanied by about eighty followers. Before leaving, he promised that he would return "to raise once again the
banner of the Red Revolution, which this time would be extended throughout the country." This promise was never fulfilled; he disappeared from the scene completely by the late
1920's and apparently died in Turkistan in 1939.[91] As for Kuchek
Khan, soon after the assault against the Communist centers in
Resht he withdrew into the forest to await further developments.

The treaty of friendship between the Soviet government and
the central government, signed February 26, 1921, had opened
a new diplomatic phase in Persia's relations with the Bolsheviks.[92] The most important feature of this treaty was the provision of withdrawal from Persian soil of the Red Army by September 21, 1921. This withdrawal marked a reversal in Bolshevik policy toward Persia and had ramifications not only for the
revolutionary movement in the north but for the entire Communist prospects in the country.

After the arrival of government forces in Resht and Enzeli,

---

90 Manshur, *op. cit.*, p. 95.
91 *Ibid.*
92 Carr, *op. cit.*, p. 292.

Andrew Rothstein, the Soviet ambassador in Teheran, was persuaded to intercede between the central government and Kuchek
Khan. An examination of the messages exchanged illuminates
the Soviet atitude. In his original letter to Kuchek Khan, the
Soviet ambassador urged surrender, hinting that this could be
a temporary measure in anticipation of a more opportune time.
He criticized the attitude of the Ehsanollah faction and asserted
that his government considered any revolutionary action at that
time not merely useless but harmful and had for that reason
altered its policy toward Persia. Kuchek's reply, handed to M.
Kalantarov, the emissary of the Soviet ambassador, recalled that
he had welcomed the arrival of the Soviet army and that native
Communists, who enjoyed Red Army support, had corrupted
the goals and social content of the revolution.[93]

Numerous other documents confirm this change of direction
in Soviet diplomacy. It was now the opinion that experiments
in using Persian Communists and separatist movements had
been hastily undertaken, with insufficient regard for local conditions and possibilities.[94] The experiments were to be abandoned in favor of consolidating relations with the Persian government, culminating in the treaty of February 26, 1921. Two
years later Karl Radek wrote:

For the Soviet government it is completely unnecessary to create
in Persia artificial Soviet republics. Its real interests in Persia consist
in the fact that Persia should not become a base for an attack in Baku.
If the Persian government adopts a course of action in conformity
with the 1921 treaty, then the form of government in Persia, the
solutions in Persia of the agrarian question (the labor problem
barely exists there) will be exclusively the business of the Persian
people, of the spiritual influence of the Persian Communists, the
majority of whose responsible leaders understand very well that the
revolutionary movement in Persia will for a long time be possible
only in the form of peasant movement and that at this time com-

---

[93] The gist of these exchanges appeared in the newspaper *Parvaresh*
(Resht), Nos. 6 and 7, 1922; cited in Manshur, *op. cit.*, pp. 146–152.

[94] *Novyi Vostok*, Vol. II (1922), p. 261; cited in Carr, *op. cit.*, p. 294.

munism may go for a short distance on this road along with the
democratic intelligentsia.[95]

There is even some evidence suggesting that Soviet diplomatic
representatives in Teheran had become impatient with the delay
in the total destruction of the Jangali rebellion and had urged
Lenin to take action.[96]

After the Gilan rebellion, many attempts were made to analyze
its nature and discover the causes for its failure. The Soviet interpretation found both objective and subjective reasons for the
failure. Thus *Novyi Vostok* thought that the inertia of the peasantry was so profound that the revolutionary movement could
not find much support there, and that the bourgeoisie and the
traders were for the most part too dependent upon foreign trade
between the central government and Persia's neighbors to seek
their own demise by taking arms against the central government,
no matter how oppressive they might feel its feudalism to be.[97]
Another Soviet source attributed the failure of the movement
in part to the local character of the revolution and to Gilan's
isolation from the broad national liberation movement developing elsewhere in the country; these reasons were quite as important as the weakness of the newly formed Persian working
class, which proved unable to preserve the united front alliance
and received little support from the trade bourgeoisie and landowners, who deserted the movement when they understood its
revolutionary content.[98]

Despite this sort of postmortem analysis, Soviet sources credited the movement with being mainly responsible for the cancellation of the 1919 Anglo–Persian treaty and the subsequent fall

---

[95] Karl Radek, *Vneshniaia politika Sovetskoi Rossii* (Moscow, 1923),
p. 74; cited in Ivor Spector, *The Soviet Union and the Moslem World,
1917–1958* (Seattle, 1959), pp. 95–96.

[96] Louis Fischer in *The Soviets in World Affairs* (2d ed.; Princeton, N.J.,
1951), Vol. I, 288, reports that the "Soviet envoy in Iran, Rothstein, complained to Chicherin who in turn sent a personal protest to Lenin."

[97] *Novyi Vostok*, Vol. IV (1923) pp. 217–218, as quoted in Carr, *op. cit.*,
pp. 470–471.

[98] Ivanova, *op. cit.*, p. 312.

of the Qajar dynasty. They also regarded the Gilan experience as proof that nationalist sentiments could be exploited to rally the people of Persia into an alliance with Soviet Russia, "which the broad masses of the people welcomed, for they saw in such an alliance a guarantee for their freedom and independence." [99]

In sum, the movement showed the following characteristics: (1) a national liberation front directed against foreign powers, notably Great Britain; (2) a bourgeois democratic orientation aimed at overthrowing feudalism and changing the agricultural basis of the Persian economy and the system of land tenure; (3) a proletarian-Communist orientation which sought to give the movement an antibourgeois direction.[100] Soviet sources have for the most part tended to evaluate the movement in terms of the proletarian-Communist orientation. There are significant differences, however, between the evaluation of the early 1920's and that of the post-Stalin era. One disagreement concerns the role of the PCP. Post-Stalinist sources find it in no way to blame. Mme M. N. Ivanova, for example, maintains that throughout the revolutionary movement the party was always right; any wrong policies it may have adopted were due to "traitors and deviationists, the party itself being always correct and unanimous and hence deserving credit for whatever achievements gained in the course of the movement." [101] This is in great contrast to Soviet sources of the 1920's; they played down the PCP's significance, regarding it as but one factor in the Gilan revolution, which was throughout divided and confused. Its leadership was blamed for ideological and personal frictions, detrimental to effective party activity.[102]

One striking aspect of the Soviet treatments of the Gilan episode is their denial of any connection between the presence of the Red Army in Gilan and the evolution of the movement. The

---

[99] *Ibid.*

[100] Irandust has analyzed the rise and fall of the movement in a similar fashion in "Aspects of the Gilan Revolution," as cited in *CAR*, Vol. IV, No. 3, 312.

[101] Ivanova, *op. cit.*, p. 313.

[102] *Ibid.*

nearest hint at the direct implication of the Soviet army in any
Soviet writing comes from a commentary on the resolution of
the PCP's Central Committee adopted on September 30, 1920.
Paragraphs 9 and 10 of this resolution refer to the entrance of
the Red Army into Gilan in the context of international proletarian solidarity.[103] An appeal to this alleged solidarity for
seizure of power by local Communists was voiced by PCP delegates attending the Third International Congress held in Moscow June 22 to July 12, 1921. Agha-Zadeh, head of a five-man
delegation of the PCP, justified this appeal by acknowledging
the Communists' inability to capture power by themselves. In
the absence of close cooperation of the world proletariat, the
party, according to Agha-Zadeh, had adopted a minimum program corresponding to the needs of Persia's backward state.[104]

With all their points of disagreement, Soviet accounts of the
Communist failure in Gilan contain some elements of truth,
and, to one degree or another, place the responsibility on the
three major elements in this offensive — the presence of the Red
Army, the Jangali rebellion, and the PCP. It would appear that
the withdrawal of the Red Army was of most importance in the
failure, for if the military occupation of Gilan had continued,
the Communist offensive could have lasted much longer against
the weak central government. The central government's successful counteroffensive was in fact launched only after the evacuation of the last units of the Red Army, and, as we have seen,
with the support and active encouragement of the Soviet diplomatic mission in Teheran.

In short, after it was decided to turn to conventional diplomacy, doctrinal considerations and controversies became academic questions. This is not to deny the significance of the other
elements in this, the first Communist offensive in Persia. Undoubtedly, the Jangali rebellion was instrumental in the Soviet

---

103 *Ibid.*

104 *Protokol des III Kongresses der Kommunistischen Internationale*
(Hamburg, 1921), p. 1070. A brief English translation may be found in *The
3rd Congress of the Communist International* (London, 1921), pp. 159–160.

decision to select Gilan for an offensive. It supplied the Bolshevik leadership with the objective condition which could be successfully utilized by the subjective factor — the will to revolutionary action on the part of its leadership and that of the Communist cadres. That this failed to materialize conclusively was in part due to the social content of the movement and to the weakness of the Communist party.

The social content of the movement prevented the full implementation of Communist doctrines of socialist revolution and contributed to the transformation of the revolution into a militantly anti-British struggle. At the same time, the weakness of the PCP prevented it from seizing complete control of the rebellion and placing itself in the vanguard of the revolutionary forces. In their zeal for rapid communization of Persia, prominent party leaders like Sultan Zadeh and Ehsanollah Khan ignored these obvious factors. Indeed, the fallacy of Sultan Zadeh's thesis concerning the launching of a purely Communist party in Persia because of her experience with a bourgeois nationalist movement was conclusively demonstrated in this venture. The Gilan episode, quite apart from such theoretical justifications, emphasized the error of rigidly applying the concept of Communist revolution to a backward country like Persia. Whether the Communists profited from this experience will be the question taken up in chapters that follow. It is certain that the subordination of the revolutionary aspirations of the indigenous Persian radicals to the requirements of Soviet diplomacy served to disillusion the majority of participants in the Gilan adventure. This alone was a severe setback for an immediate revival of the Communist movement in the country. Instead, the center of Communist activity was shifted elsewhere and its control passed to various Comintern organizations. With few exceptions, this situation persisted throughout the reign of Reza Shah until 1941.

2

THE INTERWAR PERIOD,
1921-1941

Doctrinal Adjustments

Between 1921 and 1941 the Communist movement went through several phases in its working out of a doctrine for the East. The first phase, lasting until 1928, when the Sixth Congress of the Comintern adopted more radical policies, was a period of inaction in the offensive to communize the underdeveloped East. In the beginning of this period, as we have seen, the accepted doctrine of revolution was Lenin's formula as presented to the Second Congress of the Communist International in 1920.[1] Two elements of this formula were recognition of the need to assist bourgeois democratic movements of liberation in colonial and backward countries, and a declaration of simultaneous assistance to the peasantry against the big landlords and all other remnants of feudalism.

Lenin's doctrine did not, however, receive unanimous support from Asian Communist leaders. The reservation of Persia's Sultan Zadeh, cited previously, were moderate compared with the radical opposition of M. N. Roy of India, who sought to

---

[1] *Protokoll des Zweiten Weltkongresses der Kommunistischen Internationale* (Hamburg, 1920), pp. 101–103.

distinguish between the bourgeois national movements and the struggle of the peasantry in backward countries. While the former endeavored to achieve their political aims within the existing social order, the latter were seeking to eradicate every form of exploitation, and it was a mistake to sacrifice these high goals to even a temporary alliance with the bourgeoisie.[2]

Nonetheless, Lenin's doctrine remained the operational guide for the Communist parties of the East until 1927, when the Chinese experience cast serious doubt on its future implementation. Throughout this phase the Comintern leadership underrated the potential value of the intelligentsia in the national movements, and instead of taking advantage of the great propagandistic appeal of nationalist slogans, Communist organs continued to view them suspiciously. Thus, for example, at the Fourth Comintern Congress, Safarev complained about the strength of national movements and the predominance of the intelligentsia in their leadership, expressing hope that after this initial stage, the Communist parties would be able to make progress.[3] Stalin, on the other hand, thought the time was ripe for Communist parties in the Eastern countries to pass from a united national front to a revolutionary bloc of workers and petty bourgeoisie. In 1926 Bukharin cautioned against trying to predict the exact nature of revolution in the East; it would be entirely original, he said, and could not be a repetition of what had occurred in the Soviet Union.[4]

That Comintern leaders were not at all clear about the Eastern policy is evident from the inconsistencies in their numerous pronouncements on the subject. Their uncertainty was increased by the growing nationalistic trend in political developments throughout the East, including Turkey, Persia, and China; and finally, in 1928, at the Comintern's Sixth Congress, a radical shift in policy toward nationalist movements was undertaken. In its

---

[2] *Ibid.*
[3] Walter Z. Laqueur, *The Soviet Union and the Middle East* (New York, 1959), p. 79.
[4] *Ibid.*

new policy, the Comintern rejected any kind of alliance between the Communist parties and the reformist opposition, opting instead for complete political independence of Communist parties and a relentless struggle against bourgeois national movements. Although limited and temporary agreements for the coordination of isolated political activities in connection with definite anti-imperialist demonstrations were still permissible, the new policy demanded that the Communists be politically and organizationally independent of all petty bourgeois parties. In other words, the Communist parties were to preserve their identity at all costs and to refuse absorption into broader national liberation movements.[5]

National reformists and bourgeois national movements, it was charged, vacillated between imperialism and revolution and were only too ready to join the imperialists after independence had been achieved. Agrarian revolution, therefore, was the only way of achieving a real social revolution. The bourgeoisie, with its vested interest in the land-tenure system, could not be counted on to achieve such a revolution, and they only secured influence over the petty bourgeoisie by relying on empty nationalistic slogans.

Agrarian revolution was the policy for the East until the Comintern's Seventh Congress, held in 1935.[6] At the Seventh Congress, alarmed by the emerging Nazi danger, the Comintern opened the popular front era. In the East, where the absence of liberal or socialist parties made a popular front alliance impossible, the alliance had to take the form of a national anti-imperialist front. The main task of the Communists in the East was to create an anti-imperialist front by collaboration, and even active participation, with the national reformist elements on the basis of a concrete anti-imperialist platform.[7]

This policy represented a complete reversal of the policy held

[5] Text in *International Press Correspondence*, Vol. VIII (December, 1928), 1659–1676; hereafter cited as *Inprecor*.

[6] Laqueur, *The Soviet Union and the Middle East*.

[7] Walter Z. Laqueur, *Communism and Nationalism in the Middle East* (New York, 1956), p. 294.

for the previous seven years. Now, the Communist parties were told not merely to relinquish demands for leadership in any alliance with bourgeois parties, but even to abandon most of their revolutionary demands, including agrarian reform, for which they had clamored so long. In the words of a Persian delegate to the Comintern Congress, the new attitude was one of friendly persuasion instead of steamroller tactics. Rather than destroy the national reformists, the Communists would now rally them under the banner of the common struggle against imperialism.[8]

The Decline of the PCP

For the Middle East, these theoretical modifications amounted to little more than academic speculations, since the period 1921–1941 had given them no opportunity to test their validity. With the collapse of the Jangali movement, Persia had for all practical purposes been given up as potential ground for Communist expansion. After the death of Haydar Khan, the PCP had assumed a conspiratorial character. What remained of its Central Committee established itself in Baku at the end of September, 1921, and Sultan Zadeh, representing the extreme left wing, became head of the Near Eastern Section of the Commissariat of Foreign Affairs in Moscow. In this post he was able to exert considerable influence on the future course of Soviet diplomacy in Persia.

By the fall of 1921 the Soviet government had, as we have seen, reversed its policy of directly supporting the native revolutionary movement and the indigenous Communist undertaking, and it appeared ready to preserve a correct attitude toward the central government of Persia, with which it had established formal diplomatic relations. This did not, however, mean a total abandonment of the revolutionary content of its diplomacy; for it continued to shelter the native Communist parties under the Comintern cover.

The PCP now focused on the more progressive elements of the

---

[8] A. Naderi, *Inprecor*, Vol. XV (1935), 103.

working class and peasantry, working by means of political education and the creation of trade union organizations in the cities and peasant associations in the countryside. This shift of emphasis on education and propaganda rather than on an extensive recruiting campaign indicated the party's conviction that objective conditions did not favor massive response to its appeal.

Reviewing the party's progress, Sultan Zadeh claimed that by the fall of 1921 the party had four district committees and scores of local ones, with a total membership of 4,500 — a figure lower than that of the previous year, when the party was allied with the Jangali revolutionaries. The split in leadership, which occurred in the third phase of the Gilan revolution, was recognized as the reason for this decline. Sultan Zadeh himself, admitting this, stated that even the publication of the journal of the Central Committee, *Komonist*, was discontinued in Resht. Despite a membership decline and a change in strategy, the party now claimed that its trade union campaign had attracted more than 4,000 workers and tradesmen.[9] By this campaign, the party hoped to build up "an army of discontent organized in professional and trade unions, ready to strike at the behest of the Communist general staff when the opportunity presented itself." Soviet authorities did not conceal their belief that this was indeed the long-range policy for Persia. *Izvestia*, expressing satisfaction at the organizational work in Iran, predicted that Persian workers, solidly organized in professional unions, were ready to march on the same path as the Russian working class.[10]

Properly speaking, Persian professional unions at that time were not workers' unions, but rather resembled cooperative organizations of a guild nature. They existed mostly in the north, where the number of workers and artisans was considerable and where there was greater awareness of the Russian labor movement than in other parts of Persia. Apart from the Persian provinces — notably Gilan, with its two centers in Enzeli and

9 *Pravda*, July 16, 1921, as quoted in Georges Ducroq, "La Politique du gouvernement des Soviets en Perse," *Revue du Monde Musulman*, Vol. LII (December, 1922), 148.

10 *Ibid.*, p. 149.

Resht — the only other center of trade union activity was Teheran. In 1921, according to several estimates, there were ten
unions or guilds in the country, representing various trades including bakers, printers, telegraphers, tailors, street cleaners,
government employees, and others, with a total membership of
about 10,000.[11]

At the height of the power struggle between Reza Shah and
the Persian parliament, the Majlis, in February, 1922, the trade
unions were politically active in support of the Shah. The newspaper which more or less reflected their policies, *Haqiqat*
(Truth), was directed by an editorial board containing a number
of known Communists, among them Javad Zadeh, the veteran
of the Gilan soviet republic. The political stand of *Haqiqat* was
typical of democratic and liberal groups; it included demands
for the lifting of martial law, for amnesty for all political prisoners, for confiscation and distribution of lands of those who had
abused the peasants' rights, and for distribution of state lands
among the peasants.[12]

As Reza Shah's power became more consolidated, Communist
activities in Persia gradually declined. The Persian Communist party still participated in the internation congresses of the
world Communist movement, but, even there, its waning for-
tunes had to be acknowledged. Thus, at the Fourth Congress in
November and December, 1922, a report of the Mandate Commission read by Eberlein of Germany put the PCP's strength at
1,000, of whom only half were dues-paying members. Two delegates were invited to the congress but since three had arrived the
commission accepted two with a decisive vote and one with a
consultative vote. This report also revealed that early in 1922 the
Comintern had abolished the Foreign Bureau of the PCP, and
therefore admission was refused two delegates who sought to
represent the Bureau in the Fourth Congress.[13]

---

[11] V. Ossietroff, originally in *Novyi Vostok*, Vol. I (1922), quoted in
ibid. under the title, "Les Partis politiques de la Perse."

[12] *Pravda*, Sept. 17, 1922; cited in E. Palmieri, *La Politica Asiatica dei
Bolscevichi* (Bologna, 1924), Vol. I, 240.

[13] *Protokoll des Vierten Kongresses der Kommunistischen Internationale
Petrograd — Moskau, 5 Nov. bis 5 Dec. 1922* (Hamburg, 1923), pp. 366–368.

For all practical purposes, in the years following the collapse of the Gilan republic, these international forums were the only platforms for the Persian Communists. They could scarcely hide the party's decline, but they pretended to be optimistic. At the 1922 congress an accredited Persian delegate, Nik-Bin, confirmed the drop in membership from 4,500 to 1,000, but he spoke confidently of infiltrating the trade union movement and the press. He estimated that there were about 15,000 workers and traders in these unions, 12,000 in Teheran alone, and, though the party considered it unrealistic to attempt the organization of a mass political party, it was achieving good results among the unions. The party's main task, he said, was to strive for a common anti-imperialist front by establishing a democratic bloc to which all national and democratic groups might belong, but in which the leading role would be played by the PCP. He expressed hope that with the growth of an industrial proletariat the party's prospects would improve.[14]

The PCP continued to decline, however. A year and a half later, at the Comintern's Fifth Congress held in Moscow between June 17 and July 8, 1924, even the fate of the party in the congress itself was in jeopardy, when Russian delegate, Piatnitsky, reporting for the mandate commission about the strength of parties belonging to the Third International, reported that the Persian party, which at the Fourth Congress was credited with 1,000 members, now had only 600. Therefore, in the distribution of mandates the commission gave it only two decisive votes as compared with the ten it had enjoyed in the Third Congress.[15]

The Second Congress of the PCP, 1927

For three years more the PCP was on the wane, but in December, 1927, responding to policy changes by the Kremlin soon to

14 *Ibid.*, pp. 626–627.
15 Communist Party of Great Britain, *The Fifth Congress of the Communist International* (London, 1924), pp. 269–270.

be announced at the Sixth International Congress, the PCP held a Second Congress in Urumiyeh (renamed Rezaiyeh in 1930), primarily for the purpose of deciding what its attitude toward Reza Shah should be. Since the Shah was now securely established in power following his accession to the throne in 1925, both the Comintern and its Persian affiliate were obliged to examine this development in anticipation of the forthcoming radical policies for the Eastern countries.

A detailed report, published shortly before the Sixth Congress, reviewed the situation in Persia since the Fifth Congress; it also attempted to justify the forthcoming change in policies in the East and recommended a "correct" attitude toward the new Shah. The report alleged that Iran, despite all appearances of an independent state, was in reality a semicolonial country practically owned by the British. The Anglo–Iranian Oil Company ruled the south, exerting control over Reza Shah first by helping him crush the Gilan revolutionary movement and now by using the threat of tribal unrest. The new landlords, described as "a peculiar mixture of former feudal lords and the trading bourgeoisie," were said to be the principal social force supporting the Shah.[16] Unlike the economy of the former feudal owners, the economy of the new landowning class was tied to the world supply of raw materials, but it was no different from the old class in its exploitation of the peasantry. In return for its support of the regime, this class allegedly enjoyed the protection of the army, the main pillar of the regime's power.

The report maintained that the illegal Persian Communist party was the only organized political group, since the once powerful Democratic party had decayed and recent attempts to organize parties for the election had failed. Trade union movements, it said, no longer existed as a political force, and it condemned Reza Shah for accepting the support of the trade unions in his struggle against the Qajar dynasty only to suppress them after he had ascended the throne.

---

[16] Communist Party of Great Britain, *The Communist International Between the Fifth and Sixth World Congresses* (London, 1928), pp. 406–410.

For its part, the PCP in its Second Congress criticized the "opportunistic" views of some party leaders who believe that Reza Shah's regime constituted progress and that the party was incapable of securing his overthrow, not only because it was weak but also because it might indirectly assist reactionary forces if it engaged in such an overthrow. Only by organizing workers, peasants, and the petty bourgeoisie for a struggle against Reza Shah could it secure a people's republic "as the government of a revolutionary democratic dictatorship of the proletariat and the peasantry."[17]

In a review of the accomplishment of this congress, Sultan Zadeh claimed that the party had survived several governmental attempts to suspend it during the seven-year interval between the First and Second congresses. The first PCP congress, he recalled, had focused on the struggle against British imperialism and the Qajar dynasty, and the same sort of struggle was still urgent in 1927, even though the Qajar dynasty had been replaced by the dynasty of Reza Shah. Concerning the party's attitude toward the new shah, Sultan Zadeh referred to some of the delegates in the First Congress who had expressed the opinion that the end of the British occupation would secure Persia's complete liberation.[18] Now it was realized, he said, that this was wishful thinking because Reza Shah's regime represented landlordism and feudalism, which were just as detrimental to Persia's liberation; the departure of British troops in no way signified capitulation but only a change of tactics; Reza Shah had waged no basic struggle against British imperialism and feudal landlordism. "In the above manner," he continued, "the party congress in a firm and authoritative fashion put an end to the futile squabble about the national liberating role of Reza Shah and

---

[17] For a detailed analysis of the work of this Congress, see *Donya* [Universe], Vol. II, No. 4 (East Germany, March, 1959), 108–120. *Donya* was the theoretical journal of the Tudeh party after it established its claim as successor to the PCP.

[18] A. Sultan-sade, *Die Kommunistische Internationale*, No. 51 (Berlin, 1927), 2517–2523.

about the bourgeois nature of his coup d'état. It also showed that, far from contributing anything to the national liberation of the country, he has become in a short time a big landowner, strengthening his ties with the feudal aristocracy in various areas." [19]

The record of the Second Congress, particularly the two theses on Persia's international situation and on the new party program, becomes more illuminating when it is realized that Reza Shah's rise to power was at first regarded as helpful to the national liberation movement. Not only the Soviet government, which in accordance with the treaty of 1921 embarked on a policy of accommodation with the new shah, but even the local Communists who had been fully involved in the episode of the Gilan revolution, shared this optimism about Reza Shah.

A close examination of the PCP's two theses shows both the radical departure from this line of thinking and the way in which this reversal of policy was justified.

The PCP's New Theses

The first thesis, "Studies on the International Situation of Persia," reviews the general condition of the country in a rigidly Marxist–Leninist framework. Persia's "apparent" independence until 1917 is attributed to the Anglo–Russian rivalry that had prevented her complete colonization. When the British did attempt to colonize more completely in 1919 through the defunct Anglo–Persian treaty, the thesis contends, Soviet Russia and Persia's national revolutionary movement joined to thwart the plan.[20]

The thesis further sets out to prove that the change in the dynasty was really a British machination:

---

[19] *Ibid.*, p. 2519.

[20] *Donya*, Vol. II, No. 4. This interpretation has been echoed by some recent Soviet accounts of this phase of Persian history. See A. K. Bashkirov, *Ekspansiya Angliiskikh i Amerikanskikh Imperialistov v Irane 1941–1953* (Moscow, 1954); cited in Ivor Spector, *The Soviet Union and the Moslem World, 1917–1958* (Seattle, 1959), 15–17.

Having failed in its attempt at direct colonization, Britain tried to establish a government of its stooges, as she had done in Egypt and Palestine. She had lost hope and confidence in the Qajar dynasty and chose to engineer the change of regime. Thus preparations were made for the new Shah to take over. In his struggle to seize power, the latter tried to rely on the national bourgeoisie, but his endeavor never exceeded the framework of the feudal and landlord class. In fact, he deceived the national bourgeoisie and used it for the consolidation of his own power, safeguarding the feudal and landlord interest with the support of the upper level of the bourgeoisie. His *coup d'état* was the result of a struggle within the feudal class and the rift between the landlord ruling class and the bourgeoisie which sought to participate in government, and finally the clash of the feudal and upper level of the bourgeoisie against the incipient revolutionary movement.[21]

What facilitated the Shah's success, according to this interpretation, were the country's social condition, its class structure, and the power basis of the ruling class, including the Shah himself, who had become a major landlord and thereby acquired a vested interest in supporting the landowning class. In this, he joined the smaller of the two chief classes, which were, according to the rigid Marxist–Leninist line, the ruling landlords and their upper bourgeois associates and the much larger class of workers, peasants, and craftsmen (petty and middle bourgeoisie).

Persia's social and economic conditions, the thesis said, were far from improved under the new Shah. The plight of the peasantry had deteriorated, as evidenced by a number of peasant revolutionary outbursts across the country. Nor were the regime's other measures, such as the construction of railways and harbors, thought to have improved Persia's economic condition. Nothing could improve it, the congress said, as long as the British maintained their control over such major economic institutions as the oil industry. As for the party's earlier favorable appraisal of Reza Shah, the theses contended that the relative ignorance about the Shah's reliance on the British until 1925 had not allowed for a

---

[21] *Ibid.*, p. 110.

correct attitude; only after the Shah had intensified his suppression of revolutionary movements and in particular that of the
Communist party had his close ties with British imperialism
become evident.

Based on the above analysis and mindful of the futility of
such isolated action as that in Gilan, the PCP recommended a
broadly based united front to wage a coordinated offensive
against Reza Shah and Great Britain and to work for the creation of "the toilers' government." More concretely, some "hard-
won lessons" of the past struggle were singled out as guidelines
for future action: (1) It was not enough for the peasants to capture political power in the countryside; the cooperation of the
urban revolutionaries was necessary for this purpose. (2) The
revolutionary movement in cities needed the support of the
masses. (3) Workers and craftsmen often provide leadership.
(4) The peasant revolution needed the support of the army.[22]

This thesis reveals several aspects of the PCP's thinking in
this period. First, the party recognized the significance of an
alliance of the peasantry and the democratic elements of the
urban population for broadening the scope of the revolutionary
struggle. But this did not affect the prominent role that the ad-
mittedly weak proletarian class would play. Indeed, because of
its close ties with the "semiproletarian" craftsmen and small
traders, and in view of the absence of any competing political
party, the working class would succeed in assuming the leadership of revolutionary forces.

Second, an agrarian revolution was regarded as the immediate
object for which the party had to agitate systematically but without deviation from Leninist principles concerning the vanguard
position of Communist parties in this type of endeavor. Mindful of the numerical weakness of Persia's working class and the
party's relative youth, the PCP expected that its ties with the
Comintern and the support of the "semiproletariat" would com-
pensate for this liability — hence its choice of the trade unions
as the channel of mobilization and propaganda work.

---

[22] *Ibid.*, p. 112.

Third, the alliance of all revolutionary forces, once firmly established, was to be organizationally expressed by a new party known as Iran's National Revolution party in which the vanguard role and independent identity of the PCP would be assured. But in order to avoid such a rift as that which beset the Chinese Communist party and the Kuomintang, the formation of the new organization was seen as an eventual objective rather than an immediate undertaking.

Fourth, the PCP's solidarity with Soviet Russia was reaffirmed, indicating that the earlier Soviet abandonment of the movement had not disheartened the party. The defense of a pro-Soviet attitude was now couched in a language designed to appeal to anti-British sentiments: "The Capitalists, with Britain at their head, are preparing for a war with Soviet Russia in which they will use this country as a base. It is an obvious duty of the PCP and all other patriots to fight this policy and to endeavor to prove to the toiling masses that as long as the despotic monarchy continues, British imperialism and the plundering of the country will also persist." [23]

The specific actions which the PCP was to take were outlined in a second thesis prepared by the congress. The party was to pursue these aims: the elimination of the monarchy and the rejection of the parliamentary republic; the building of a republic based on the free alliance of all nationalities; the securing of internal autonomy and the right of secession for all nationalities; and the creation of a new army of workers and peasants.[24] Specifically, it demanded the confiscation of all installations of the Anglo–Iranian Oil Company; the abolition of foreign concessions; the establishment of agricultural lending banks; assistance to craftsmen and manual workers through the extension of loans and credit; the surrender of all public works, religious endowments, and big estates to the peasants; the confiscation of the property of the Shah, the aristocracy, and the tribal chief-

---

[23] *Ibid.*, p. 114.
[24] *Ibid.*, pp. 117–120.

tains; and the abolition of all debts owed by peasants to the government, to speculators, and to moneylenders.

The second thesis also made certain political demands: full freedom for political organizations, unions, cooperatives, and other associations of the workers; recognition by government and factory owners of trade unions as the official organs of working class organizations; freedom of assembly, strike, speech, and press for the workers. It also called for collective bargaining and contract rights for the unions, the establishment of a minimum wage, and housing for workers in the oil and fishing industries.

The PCP at the Comintern's Sixth Congress

Some seven months later, in July, 1928, a delegation of the PCP attended the Sixth Congress of the Communist International. For the first time in years, they showed spirit. When the Comintern leaders began their deliberations on the "Thesis on Colonial Revolution," A. Shareghi was quick to point out the nature of political conditions in Iran. The Comintern, he urged, should be more concerned with the problems of the peasantry in the Near East.[25] He thought Bukharin's report on the Near East and his proposed thesis for revolution in the colonial and semicolonial countries did not contain adequate guidance for the Communist parties of these countries. The PCP, he declared, was left without any doctrinal guidance on such critical issues as its relations with other political parties and its attitude toward parliamentary elections.[26]

Sultan Zadeh, who was also a PCP delegate, engaged in a heated debate with Hilferding, over the issue of finance capital. Hilferding had spoken of the domination of bank capital over industrial capital, whereas now he spoke of the unification of

---

[25] "Report of the 9th Session of the VI Congress of the Comintern," *Inprecor*, Vol. VIII, No. 48 (August, 1928), 834.

[26] This is a reference to the Iranian Socialist Party active in the mid-1920's and to the elections to the Majlis, in which the PCP had acted independently. *Ibid.*

the three (merchant, bank, and industrial), and not of the two forms of capital. Bukharin, quoting from Lenin's *Imperialism* and his own work, *World Economy and Imperialism*, argued that Hildferding's theory of merging capital was correct and that in reality the criticism of the Persian delegate was directed against what Lenin had said.[27]

On the question of revolutionary movements in the colonies, Sultan Zadeh protested that the pressing issue was not whether a particular country belonged to any of the four categories that Kuusinen's report to the congress envisaged. Rather, the issue was whether a country like Persia could bypass the stage of capitalist development. Was it possible to establish a soviet regime immediately, or must the party work instead for the creation of a democratic dictatorship of the proletariat and the peasantry on the day after a successful revolution? In other words, could the party hope to wage an agrarian revolution in Persia or should this be relegated to the future? It was incorrect, he suggested, to lump Syria, India, and China into a single category because in many of these countries the highest form of social living coexisted with the most backward form. He complained that the "Thesis on Colonial Revolution" disregarded the strategical importance of these countries, implying that Persia's geopolitical situation merited special treatment.

Sultan Zadeh was particularly skeptical about the Comintern thesis on the role of the bourgeoisie in the agrarian revolution. It was his opinion that the bourgeoisie would oppose the alliance of the proletariat and the peasantry and would seek to align itself with the landlords and foreign imperialists. Nor would the petty bourgeoisie serve any better as a pillar for an agrarian revolution. Thus the proletariat and the peasantry, organized by the PCP, were left as the only social forces capable of revolutionary action.

Another PCP delegate informed the Comintern Congress that the Communist parties in the colonies and semicolonies were not genuine proletarian parties. For example, half the members

---

[27] *Ibid.*, Vol. VIII, No. 59 (September, 1928), 1034.

of the Persian Communist party in 1922 were petty bourgeois elements. As he saw it, party organizers were confronted with three tasks: assumption of the leadership of the class struggle, mobilization of the peasants for an agrarian revolution, and struggle against imperialism.[28] In pursuance of the first task the PCP had to work independently and maintain its separate identity. The second and third tasks required the party's cooperation with the peasants, the traders, and the intelligentsia. Disagreeing with the Comintern thesis which had recommended the formation of proletarian parties everywhere in the East, the PCP delegate proposed that this be tried only where the peasant movement had developed rapidly. In Persia an attempt to form a labor peasant party in 1924 had failed precisely because of the absence of a well-developed peasant movement.

In sum, the PCP stood by policies adopted in its Second Congress. Since Persia was the only Eastern country where previous Comintern doctrines had been tested, the PCP's reservations about the thesis of the Sixth Congress sounded all the more plausible. However, these reservations were not reflected in the final draft of the Comintern thesis nor did the PCP find another opportunity to put its own version of them into practice. By the late 1920's the situation in Persia was rapidly moving toward consolidation of the authoritarian regime of Reza Shah accompanied by increasing apprehension about any kind of political opposition, to say nothing of a radical faction like the PCP.

The party managed to retain some influence with the professional and trade unions, however, and was continuously involved in labor unrest. In the spring of 1929, for example, the leaders of a strike waged by oil industry workers in Khuzistan were revealed to be party members with long records of agitation among workers.[29] A new tactic employed by the party was the use of cover organizations to conceal its identity. In 1931 several of these were discovered disguised as culture and sport clubs, in-

---

[28] *Ibid.*, Vol. VIII, No. 78 (November, 1928), 1469.

[29] Mostafa Fateh, *Panjah Sal Nafte Iran* [Fifty Years of Persian Oil] (Teheran, 1956), p. 487.

cluding an important one in Resht composed of a number of veteran Gilan Communists.

In June, 1931, in an attempt to cope with these Communist tactics, the Reza Shah government introduced a bill to the Majlis to outlaw all genuine or disguised political organizations engaged in Communist activity and propaganda.[30] This bill, which easily passed into law, was a clear demonstration of the anti-Communist orientation of the regime, and as such it might have been expected to clarify the Communist attitude toward Reza Shah. The Shah's strong nationalistic stand was sufficient to confuse the Communists, however, as they proved in their reaction to the D'Arcy oil concession affair which arose late in 1932. The D'Arcy concession was in Khuzistan, where the Communists had been carrying on anti-British agitation. Nationalist elements of various sorts rallied behind the Shah, and on November 27, 1932, the government annulled the concession as unjust and contrary to the sovereign rights of Persia.[31] The Communists wecomed this measure as another opportunity to agitate against the British, but by the same token, and at least by implication, they were compelled to support the regime in this particular case.

The oil dispute confronted the PCP, and indeed other opposition forces, with the problem of how it could join the government-sponsored struggle against British imperialism without allowing itself to be too closely identified with the Shah's policies.[32] Mindful of its earlier optimistic appraisal of Reza Shah

---

[30] The text reads in part: "Any person in Iran who under whatever name or pretext forms and directs a group, an association, or a faction thereof, whose aim and conduct is opposition to the Iranian constitutional monarchy, or contains communistic ideology . . . Any person who becomes a member of a group, association, or a faction thereof formed to pursue either of the aforementioned two goals . . . Any Iranian who is a member of a group or association which aims to oppose the Iranian constitutional monarchy or advocates Communist ideology or conduct, even though that group or association may be formed abroad . . . will be punished by imprisonment from 3 to 10 years." Morteza Ravandi, *Tafsir Qanune Assassiye Iran* [Interpretation of Iran's Constitution] (Teheran, 1944), p. 56.

[31] Fateh, *op. cit.*, p. 487.

[32] L. Mazyar, "Struggle for Persian Oil and the Task of the Communist Party of Iran," *Inprecor*, Vol. XV, No. 1 (1932); cited in *ibid.*, p. 488.

and the subsequent change of attitude necessitated by the Shah's anti-Communist measures, the party sought to chart a pragmatic and opportunistic course. It rejected the extreme stand that he was another imperialist agent, but it also rejected the idea that his policies, especially toward foreign powers, contained progressive and reformative elements. Instead, the party contended that the campaign had only the limited objective of securing better terms from the oil company. The PCP advocated expropriation as the only means of recovering Persia's natural resources from the British. Under these circumstances, party leaders sought to mobilize workers, particularly in the oil industry, and to broaden the struggle until it embraced the most radical objectives of the PCP.[33]

With the settlement of the oil dispute in 1933, anti-British agitation subsided and the Communists no longer had the opportunity to infiltrate labor and the lower bourgeoisie. By the mid-1930's the focus of their propaganda and recruitment campaign had shifted toward the intelligentsia, in line with an objective evaluation of conditions in Iran as well as the Comintern's doctrinal injunctions. At the Sixth Congress in 1928 the Comintern had noted the tendency of intellectuals to respond to Communist indoctrination, and indeed to predominate in the party composition. One resolution had stated: "An important, if not a predominant, sector of the party ranks is recruited in the first stage of the movement from the petty bourgeoisie and in particular from the revolutionary-inclined intelligentsia, very frequently students."[34] As a result of increasing Westernization brought about by Reza Shah, a core of Western-educated intellectuals had been created by the mid-1930s. Heretofore, the intellectual class had been largely limited to members of the aristocracy, who could afford the heavy costs of foreign education; under Reza Shah, public education had at last been offered to the middle classes. In early 1930 a scholarship program had been launched to send qualified high school graduates to Europe,

---

[33] *Ibid.*, p. 489.
[34] Laqueur, *Communism and Nationalism in the Middle East*, p. 273.

mainly to France and Germany, for university education, thus opening a hitherto exclusive privilege to the bourgeoisie and even the lower middle class. This new core of Western-educated middle class Persians was a potential source for recruiting and training Communist cadres, a process initiated even before the students returned home from their foreign studies. Small though it was, this was the nearest thing to a revival of the Iranian Communist party since its demise following the ban of 1931.

Dr. Erani's Marxist Circle

The new Communist activity in Iran was distinguished in a number of ways from the earlier experiences. For one thing, it was an attempt by a group of Western-educated Iranians to indoctrinate the intelligentsia in Marxist–Leninist ideology rather than to train party activists for immediate political action. For another, its participants were native Persians whose social and sectional backgrounds sharply contrasted with those of the majority of the Adalat committee and PCP, who had been recruited either from among residents of Russian Caucasia, Turkistan, and Armenia or who were Persian expatriates long living abroad. In addition, these Persian Marxists had been introduced to Marxism and scientific socialism in Western Europe rather than in Russia. These distinctions bore heavily on the evolution of the Communist movement up to 1941 and after, when the majority of Erani's circle, just freed from prison, set out to form the Tudeh party, the largest and most important organizational expression of the Communist movement in Iran.

The introduction of Marxist ideas into Iran preceded the organization of a party in the Western sense, dedicated to Marxist ideology in the wake of the October Revolution in Russia. The process of indoctrination and dissemination of Marxist ideas had begun early in the twentieth century, when Western ideas first began to penetrate Persia, and it had gone through two stages. The first period, as we have seen, lasted from the beginning of the twentieth century to June, 1920, when the PCP was formed from the Adalat Committee; it could be termed the period of the activity of social democracy in Persia. In the earlier part of this period such activity was usually centered on the publication of a newspaper, several examples of which may be cited from 1910 to 1914. One paper, *Etefaghe Kargaran* (Workers' Unity), was connected with workers' committees in Teheran. Later, the center of social democratic activity shifted to Russian Azarbayjan, notably Baku, and led to the formation of the Adalat Committee in 1916. The second period of dissemination and propagation of Marxist ideology, began with the formation of the PCP and was to continue throughout the reign of Reza Shah until 1941. The activity of Erani's group from 1933 to 1937, starting first in Europe and reaching Iran in 1935, can be considered as the highest stage of this period. The third period, about which this book is most concerned, began with the formation of the Tudeh party in October, 1941, and continues to the present.

An analysis of the characteristics of the second period of Marxist activity can best be undertaken by examining the content of the circle's theoretical journal, *Donya* (Universe), of which the first volume was published under the editorship of Dr. Taghi Erani, the Berlin-educated physicist from Azarbayjan. In the mid-1930's, when open Communist party activity was forbidden, this journal was the only channel through which Marxist ideas could be circulated in Iran. Certain expatriate Communists in Europe, where remnants of the PCP's leadership had sought refuge, attempted to carry on propagandistic work, including the publishing of a newspaper, *Paykar* (Combat), in Berlin; but in 1932 Persian diplomatic pressure resulted in court action against the staff, and a year later, with the ascendancy of the Nazis, it ceased publication.[35]

In Iran, party activity was successfully curtailed by the government's anti-Communist law of June, 1931, under which many Communists had been sent to prison — and which would in 1937

---

[35] E. Bassir, "Barkhi Moshakhassate Sabke Erani dar Tarvije Afkare Marxisti dar Iran" [Some of the Characteristics of Erani's Style of Dissemination of Marxist Thoughts in Iran], *Donya*, Vol. II, No. 4 (1958), 94–100.

be used against Erani himself.[36] Despite many risks, Erani's group set out to indoctrinate the intellectuals, whose number grew as the European-educated students returned to Iran. *Donya* was designed to carry on their education in Marxist doctrine, begun in Europe, and to extend it to other Iranians, in their native language, and on a sophisticated level.

The journal followed a strong anti-idealistic and antimetaphysical philosophy and an unswerving Marxist interpretation of history and political philosophy. Its views of the state and class interest and contradictions were typical of this orientation. The state, wrote Erani, in an essay on the materialistic view of man, was an apparatus organized by the most powerful class to ensure its domination over the weaker classes. Both the legislative and the judiciary systems, as well as the institution of education and art, were under the control of the state, he said, and therefore in a class society every aspect of social and political life was class-based and organized in the interest of the dominant class. Thus it was folly to think that such an organization could ever bring happiness and prosperity to all.[37]

The dominant characteristic of Dr. Erani's writing and teaching was its scientific method, which attempted to explain the main principles of Marxism–Leninism in relatively simple lan-language.[38] Erani was the first writer to introduce Marxist theories into different branches of the exact sciences in the form of a series of books on the "Exact Sciences." To this extent he was

---

[36] A Comintern publication put the number of Communist prisoners in Iran in 1931 at 150 (*Inprecor*, Vol. II, No. 25, 454). Police records indicated, however, that in 1937 there were only 30 or so active party members still in prison. Some of these were retroactively tried under the 1931 Anti-Communist Act, together with Erani and 52 others.

[37] Taghi Erani, *Bashar az nazare Maddi* [Man from a Materialistic Viewpoint] (4th ed.; Teheran, 1945), p. 38.

[38] Some of Erani's works did not see print until after the fall of Reza Shah: *Erfan va Osule Maddi* [Mysticism and the Principle of Materialism], *Bashar az nazare Maddi* [Man from a Materialist Viewpoint], *Materialisme Diyalectic* [Dialectic Materialism], and *Theorihaye Elm* [Theories of Science].

recognized as basically a scientist and not a propagandist, a claim justified by his training and teaching career. At the same time, his followers did not see him merely as an intellectual dedicated to modern scientific social and political undertakings. Rather, he was seen as a true Marxist humanist striving to relate the principles of Marx and Lenin to existing internal and international social problems and to "the struggle of the toiling masses for the vindication of their just rights." [39]

Erani's followers, who met often in groups to discuss his ideas, were recruited from among teachers, students, lawyers, judges, and trade union leaders, some of whom had a record of political activity in the mid-1920's. More than 65 percent of the circle belonged to the middle class, 15 percent to the upper middle class, and 20 percent to the lower bourgeoisie. Professionally, the group contained 35 percent teachers, 15 percent students, 25 percent lawyers and government employees including judges, 15 percent workers, and 10 percent others. [40] On April, 1937, Dr. Erani and fifty-two of the most prominent members of this group were arrested and charged with conspiring to violate the Anti-Communist Act of 1931. In early January, 1938, formal indictments were issued by the prosecutor general of Teheran, and a public trial was held from November 2 to November 13 of that year. [41]

During the trial articles from *Donya* were cited to prove the group's engagement in Communist propaganda in violation of the act. However, none of the fifty-three had mentioned communism as such in his cross-examination and defense, and each claimed he had merely learned about dialectic materialism and modern social theories by studying the journal and reading other relevant literature. In a long speech, Dr. Erani spoke vigorously in his own defense, contending that the law of 1931 vio-

[39] Bassir, *op. cit.*, p. 99.

[40] Based on bibliographical information contained in the records of the trial published in *Ettelaat* (Teheran, November, 1938).

[41] For a Communist version of this, see Bozorg Alavi, *Panjaho-se Nafar* [The Fifty-three] (Teheran, n.d.).

lated every principle of justice and was clearly unconstitutional; that he had merely advocated dialectic materialism; that the court was incompetent to try them, for it was an instrument of the State and in conspiracy with the police; and that it was illegal to make the law ex post facto to cover the alleged Communist prisoners from Resht who were already in prison when the law was promulgated.[42]

His attack on the constitutionality of the 1931 Act was based on its general prohibition against all freedom of expression, not merely that of a Communist nature. Throughout his defense he stressed the scientific character of the Marxist doctrine. How, he asked the court, could any state suppress opinions whose scientific basis dated back to the very beginning of human society and which viewed all aspects of individual and social life in terms of totally scientific and logical tenets? On no other social or religious doctrine had there been so much written as on socialism; obviously, a law could not ban these thoughts without a thorough study of its vast literature.[43]

The trial ended with the conviction of the fifty-three defendants. Ten of the leaders received the maximum penalty of ten years' imprisonment; the others received terms ranging from three to seven years. Erani himself died in the prison hospital on February 4, 1940, allegedly because of the deliberate negligence of hospital authorities, thus providing his followers with a martyr image which was exploited in the years that followed.

The imprisonment of the Erani group marked the conclusion of this phase of open Communist activity in Iran. It also proved of considerable value to the Communist movement as a whole, for in prison indoctrination continued relentlessly. If anything, the hard core became more than ever dedicated to communism, and many younger members, in their student years when arrested, turned the prison cells into classes for Communist education. When the group was released from prison in September,

---

[42] Taghi Erani, *Matne Defa* [Defense Statement] (Teheran, 1945).
[43] Ravandi, *Tafsir Qanune Assassiye Iran*, pp. 57–58.

1941, they formed the nucleus of the Tudeh party. It gave to the party leadership an intellectual cast which, among other things, disproved the Comintern's prophecy concerning the temporary nature of the predominance of the intelligentsia's leadership.[44]

Contrary to the expectations voiced in one thesis of the Sixth Comintern Congress, leadership in the later stages of the Communist movement did not pass from the intelligentsia to other classes. Once again the Communist party had to adjust its machinery for the consumption of the intelligentsia. It was a process that gave the party a dualistic nature of elitist and populist characteristics which has persisted to the present day.

The activities of the Erani circle coincided with a new phase in Communist doctrine, climaxing in the Comintern's Seventh Congress which, meeting in Moscow in 1935, formally inaugurated the popular front era. In the East, where fascism did not constitute an immediate danger to international communism, and where liberal and democratic parties were nonexistent, the proposed front was to assume the form of a united anti-imperialist alliance of all progressive forces.[45]

During the discussion of a report entitled, "The Preparation for an Imperialist War and the Task of the Comintern," Naderi, purporting to represent the PCP, pledged his party's support for the new line. In order to form the broadest anti-imperialist front, Naderi told the congress, the party would mobilize the workers, peasants, and the petty bourgeoisie, temporarily postponing its class struggle.[46]

Although this was the approved line of action for the Communist parties in the East, there is no indication that the Erani circle attempted to apply it. Indeed, the doctrinal framework of the Erani circle was much closer to the more radical injunctions of the Sixth Congress than to those of the Seventh, inas-

---

[44] Laqueur, *Communism and Nationalism*, p. 273.
[45] *Ibid.*
[46] *Inprecor*, Vol. XV, No. 39 (August, 1935), 718.

much as its emphasis lay in a pure Marxist conception of class
conflict. Furthermore, there is no evidence to suggest that this
group was in direct communication with its expatriate com-
rades in Europe. By and large it was an isolated group that endeavored not so much to revive the Communist party per se as
to continue and intensify Marxist indoctrination at a level in-
conceivable in the earlier phase of the movement.

3

WARTIME REVIVAL
OF THE MOVEMENT:
THE TUDEH PARTY

In September, 1941, with the overthrow of Reza Shah's regime following joint Anglo–Soviet military intervention in Persia, the Persian Communist movement revived. The presence of the Red Army in the north in effect reintroduced to Iran the traditional and revolutionary elements of Soviet diplomacy, both of which had been absent since the late 1920's.

In view of the increasingly authoritarian nature of Reza Shah's rule, its overthrow marked an almost automatic return to a large measure of political freedom. As a matter of principle, as well as for tactical reasons, the Allied powers were eager to facilitate the democratization of Iran. The anti-Nazi war and the championing of democracy had justified intervention in Iran and the overthrow of a pro-German regime. The desire to win over the people at a time when Iran's strategic importance was increasing constituted a second factor for the revival of the movement, which readily embraced the Allies' anti-Fascist orientation and wholeheartedly joined the campaign to discredit the deposed Shah and his pro-German policies.

Unquestionably pro-German though the regime was,[1] a case

---

[1] Germany occupied the first place in foreign trade, as well as in technical

could be made to support the contention that the pro-German
bias was in line with Persia's traditional desire to balance the
Anglo–Russian influence by relying on a third major foreign
power. Furthermore, Germany had participated actively in the
modernization and industrialization of Iran during the late
Shah's reign, so there were many in the government and in the
politically conscious elite who were understandably sympathetic
to the Germans. When Nazi Germany declared war on Great
Britain and Soviet Russia, both of which in the eyes of Persians
had long held territorial designs on the country, these pro-
German sentiments were intensified.

Curiously, the many changes in the material condition of the
country under Reza Shah made it easier for the Communists to
revive their movement. In that relatively stable period between
1921 and 1941, considerable social change had occurred as a
result of reforms designed to modernize the country's social and
economic life.[2] The creation of a middle class, well represented
in trade, government service, the army, and institutions directly
involved in the modernization process, was one aspect of the
social change. Another was the emergence of a labor force as a
result of the introduction of industries, one of the paramount
goals of Reza Shah's regime.[3] A third factor was the significant
growth of the intelligentsia, which became the primary target
of the movement's revived offensive soon after restoration of
political freedom. The various factors were of differing degrees
of relevance during the turbulent course of the movement in
this new period.

In this chapter we shall be concerned with the first two phases
of this period, covering the years 1941 to 1946. Our inquiry will
pursue two major themes — one tracing the movement as the

---

assistance for the industrialization of the country. George Lenczowski, *Russia and the West in Iran, 1918–1948.* (Ithaca, N.Y., 1949), pp. 154–161.

[2] For a historical account of these see Amin Banani, *The Modernization
of Iran, 1921–1941* (Stanford, 1961).

[3] The labor force doubled in size between 1929 and the end of Reza
Shah's rule, when it numbered 600,000. See Iraj Eskandari, "Histoire de Parti
Toudeh," *Moyen-Orient,* No. 5 (November, 1949), 7.

direct instrument of Soviet diplomacy, the other treating it as an indigenous attempt to seize power by constitutional means and, failing that, by armed revolution.

First Phase: The Nonrevolutionary Struggle

In the first phase the Communist movement assumed the characteristics of a democratic front, dedicated to legally achieving its political goals. Its organizational expression was the Tudeh party of Iran, formed in early October, 1941, by the hard core of the Erani circle, who had been freed under an amnesty for political prisoners in the previous month.[4]

There were a number of sound tactical reasons for disguising the Communist affiliations of the new party. Chiefly, of course, there was the still-existing law of 1931 prohibiting open Communist activity. But it was also in the best interests of Soviet diplomacy to avoid open identification with its ideological system, and the Erani circle has always maintained that it was a Marxist, not a Communist, group. If it wanted to broaden the basis of its support, the new organization could not openly embrace the Communist ideology, since it would be comprehensible only to the limited group of intelligentsia.[5] Instead, the party exploited the prestige of former political and parliamentary leaders of the pre–Reza Shah era. It chose Soleiman Mohsen Eskandari, a veteran of the old Social Democratic party, as the chairman of a "provisional committee of fifteen," which included two of his nephews, Iraj and Abbass Eskandari, and prominent members of the Erani circle.

The provisional statute of the new organization described it as a mass organization based on a union of workers, peasants, artisans, and intellectual democrats; it was a democratic and progressive party seeking major structural reforms and the demo-

---

[4] C. Steiner, "Der Iranische Kommunismus," *Ost-Probleme*, Sept. 30, 1955, p. 1497.

[5] Reza Radmanesh, "Hezbe Tudehe Iran, Hezbe Taraze Novine Tabaghehe Kargar" [The Tudeh Party of Iran, the Modern Type Working Class Party], *Donya*, Vol. II, No. 2 (Summer, 1961), 1.

cratization of economic and political institutions, and an anti-imperialist organization fighting against all foreign intervention and colonialism.[6] To convey an image of legality the party emphasized its adherence to the principles of the constitution and demanded the full implementation of its provisions as a guarantee of democratic freedoms.[7]

As its first task, the party endeavored to eliminate the influence of fascism, which, it believed, had penetrated the ruling class and a considerable segment of the literate middle class. For this purpose an anti-Fascist paper, *Mardom* (People), was created at the end of 1941 under the editorship of Safar Nowii, a former political prisoner and a member of the Tudeh party. Anti-Fascist committees were formed in several provinces, notably in the northern Soviet-occupied region. These committees focused particularly on those intellectuals who, because of a common hatred of British imperialism, believed they had found in national socialism a powerful means of fighting foreign imperialism and British influence. In effect, the party sought to divert the Anglophobic element of Iranian nationalism from a pro-German orientation to an anti-Fascist one. This was not an easy task, particularly in the years when the Nazis were winning on the Eastern and North African fronts. But as the war progressed, political conversion became easier, so that by early 1944 many Nazi sympathizers of the middle class and the intelligentsia were only too eager to rally to the party's banner, particularly since it had succeeded in creating a substantially nationalistic image.[8]

In November, 1941, the Provisional Committee of Fifteen began publishing a journal called *Siyassat* (Politics), by means of which the party organization was to be spread throughout

---

[6] *Assassnamehe Movaghat Hezbe Tudeh* [The Provisional Statute of the Tudeh Party] (Teheren, 1942). Also quoted in Eskandari, "Histoire de Parti Toudeh," *Moyen-Orient*, No. 6, (December, 1949), 9.

[7] The Military Governorship of Teheran, *Seyre Komonism dar Iran* [The Evolution of Communism in Iran] (Teheran, 1958), p. 61.

[8] Bozorg Alavi, *Kämpfendes Iran* (Berlin, 1955), is one example of Communist literature admitting the pro-Nazi background of the party's first recruits.

the country. Concurrently, the task of reorganizing trade unions, banned under Reza Shah, was begun. The veteran trade union organizers, who had joined the party immediately upon release from jail, and the representatives of a small segment of the working population in Teheran formed a new workers' organization, the Central Council of the Trade Unions of Iran.[9]

In the evolution of the party the first provincial conference of Teheran in June, 1942, stands as a landmark. At this conference, attended by 120 delegates representing intellectuals, professionals, and workers, the groundwork for forming a mass party was laid.[10] For the first time the party also made concrete demands on the government. These included the formation of a democratic government representing the broad strata of the population; implementation of the constitutional provisions related to political liberties and human rights; the abolition of Reza Shah's "antidemocratic" laws, notably the June, 1931, act prohibiting Communist and antimonarchical parties; the distribution among the peasants of state lands and large holdings; and recognition of trade unions and the right of collective bargaining.[11]

The provincial conference also adopted a provisional statute for the party based on the principle of democratic centralism. The organizational pattern of the hierarchy was clearly outlined. At the lowest level the party recruits were organized in a cell or *Howzeh*. Next was the local committee elected annually by the conference of cell representatives and functioning as the executive organ of the party in a city or locality. Above local committees were regional or provincial committees, which were elected by regional or provincial conferences and subordinate to their authority. Finally there was the party congress, the supreme organ of the party, which was to be composed of delegates

---

[9] A. Mohammad Zadeh, "Report on the Trade Union Movement in Iran," *World Trade Union Movement* (December, 1949), pp. 30–31.

[10] Radmanesh puts the membership of the party at this time at 6,000, of which 80 percent were drawn from the working class. See "Hezbe Tudehe Iran," p. 4.

[11] Eskandari, *Moyen-Orient*, No. 6, 10.

elected by local conferences. The congress was responsible for the election of the party's Central Committee and other bodies and would enjoy complete discretion in determining their number and composition.[12] With the approval of the provisional statute the conference urged the Teheran provincial committee to proceed with the organization of the party on the basis of decisions adopted and to prepare for convening the first congress, pending which time it was to assume the task of the Central Committee.

This provincial conference marked the party's transformation from what was primarily an anti-Fascist group into a mass political organization working for basic internal social and political change as well as in support of the Allied cause. To effect this transformation, party cadres were organized in the capital and sent to the provinces, particularly to the north, where, because of the Red Army occupation, greater freedom of this type of activity existed.

The party's relatively impressive success in the northern provinces was, in fact, a liability from which it had long suffered, particularly in the eyes of the nationalist elements of the bourgeoisie, who were not as yet reconciled to the Allied occupation of Iran. The party insisted that its success in the north was due more to the inability of the police to control it than to the Red Army's direct support or encouragement.[13] This may indeed have been true up to 1944, when Soviet occupation had not been used as a lever of pressure on the central government, but by the fall of 1943, during the election campaign, and definitely by the fall of the next year, during the oil crisis, the party was unquestionably identified with the Soviet Union and its policies, not merely in the northern occupied zone but throughout the country.

The activity of the party was not, of course, confined to the Soviet-occupied zone. By 1943 it was a nationwide organization with every appearance of a mass party. Its numerical growth was

---

[12] *Assassnamehe Movaghat.*
[13] Eskandari, *op. cit.*, p. 10.

a direct result of its focus on labor. It was particularly successful in Isfahan, the center of the Iranian textile industry, where
it had made impressive inroads by advocating wage increases
and similar measures designed to appeal to the working class
during these years of war and famine. It strove to show the
workers that without organized mass action they could gain no
concessions from the regime. With the party the workers could
not only obtain redress for their immediate grievances but also
become a formidable political force to be reckoned with by the
government authorities. Strikes, collective bargaining, public
demonstration, picketing, and similar tactics were frequently
used throughout 1942–1943 to win the support of labor. And
often these tactics were successful in achieving wage increases,
shorter working hours, and other concessions, which were in
themselves by far the most effective proof of the party's promises.

Gradually, the party's appeal broadened. Its anti-Fascist orientation was less and less attractive to the intelligentsia, who had
a more sophisticated understanding of international developments and their impact on the domestic situation, but the middle and working classes, on the other hand, were increasingly
drawn by its hopeful slogans. "Bread, Health, and Education for
All" became the rallying cry for the party through its extensive
media of communication.[14]

Another outcome of this broadening process was the gradual
decline in political apathy, particularly among the middle and
professional classes. Besides its formal recruits, the party found
many sympathizers and fellow travelers, a reservoir for future
expansion but so far not sufficiently politically minded or ame-
nable to direct participation in the movement. To attract these
elements, the party set about forming a united front "to secure
constitutional liberties and prevent a return of dictatorship."
Since there were no liberal or democratic parties with a common
goal, the model of the European experience of the mid-1930's
could not be emulated. Instead, the Tudeh party found leftist

---

[14] George Lenczowski, "The Communist Movement in Iran," *Middle
East Journal*, Vol. I, No. 1 (1947), 31.

and liberal newspapers, which existed in some numbers, and determined to embrace *their* goals. In early 1943, the party established contact with the editors of more than twenty publications of a liberal-democratic line with the idea of framing a uniform editorial policy. It would take the form of a "Freedom Front" dedicated to two main struggles: (1) against the restoration of dictatorship and its collaborators, and (2) against fascism.[15]

The idea quickly caught on, and the Freedom Front spread to the major provinces, embracing a total of thirty-five newspapers and marking the emergence of a political polarization that lasted until the Azarbayjan crisis of 1945–1946. On the Left stood the Tudeh party and the Front, with a reformist and democratic program which became crystallized during the election campaign for the 14th Majlis in the winter of 1943–1944. Opposed to them were all political groups of the Right, the most important of which was the Eradeh Melli (National Will), headed by Seyd Ziaeddine Tabatabai, a veteran right-wing politician and the co-sponsor of Reza Shah's coup d' état in 1921. This configuration of political forces carried over to the Majlis and characterized the struggle within the parliament as in the country as a whole at a time when a large measure of democracy prevailed.[16]

The 1943–1944 election provided the first indication of the relative strength of the political forces. Although the peculiarities of the Persian electoral system do not allow for an evaluation of the results in terms of party politics, nevertheless, inasmuch as this was the closest approximation to a party election in the history of modern Iran, an analysis of its results could shed some light on the status of the participating parties. Despite the fact that a majority of districts ran independent candidates without firm political affiliations, the Left-Right alignment prevailed in the campaign. The Tudeh party, clearly the best organized party

---

15 Eskandari, *op. cit.*, p. 10.

16 L. P. Elwell-Sutton, "Political Parties in Iran, 1941–1948," *Middle East Journal*, Vol. III, No. 1 (1949), 45–62.

of the Left, sponsored fifteen candidates in the northern prov-inces and in Isfahan. Nine of these were elected, gaining alto-gether 120,000 votes out of a total of 150,000 cast. The numerical strength of the party in terms of the entire Majlis totaled about 200,000 votes, which, though something less than one-fifth the approximate total of one million votes, represented the largest bloc of solid votes for any single party.[17]

In the north alone the party managed to form tentative elec-toral alliances with other candidates opposed to the Right. The Central Committee of the Tudeh party, realizing that it could scarcely defeat the Right with its own candidates in all northern constituencies, decided to back candidates who satisfied at least two prerequisites: opposition to the former regime and the rul-ing class in Teheran and a reputation for advocating friendship toward the Soviet Union.[18] Counting successful allied candi-dates, the party's victory was even more impressive, since about 50 percent of all candidates thus sponsored won a majority of votes in their districts.

The Tudeh parliamentary group was itself limited to a mere eight out of a total of 120 elected members, Javad Zadeh (now called Jaafar Pishevari) having been rejected by the Majlis because of his known Communist background.[19] In addition, it could almost invariably count on the support of at least three other members, and it was friendly to about thirty more in the "parliamentary opposition," men who more or less represented the left of center in the Majlis. The first big test of the relative strength of this alignment came during the bitter controversy

---

[17] Mme H. Carrere d'Encausse, "Le Parti Toudeh" (Mimeographed lecture notes published by Centre des Hautes Etudes d'Administration Musulmane, Paris, 1956).

[18] Four of these were Rahimian and Habib Dorri from Gorgan, Mozzafar Zadeh from Gilan, and Hossein Lankarani from Azarbayjan.

[19] Jaafar Pishevari, as Javad Zadeh, had of course been one of the active members of the Gilan revolutionary movement. A right wing coalition re-jected his credentials, despite an alleged understanding to the contrary between the majority leaders and the prime minister, Ali Soheili, who was responsible for conducting the elections.

over the seating of Tabatabai.[20] Although the alignment was defeated, the Tudeh party showed that its real strength lay in its unprecedented degree of cohesion and discipline. It alone, among the parties in the Majlis, was supported by the best organized mass political party in modern Iran.

Clearly, by participating openly in the parliamentary election and pursuing vigorous party politics in the Majlis — where they had been nonexistent for more than two decades — the Tudeh party advanced its own ends. Not least important, it emphasized the party's claim to its legality of approach and thus in a sense disguised its Communist ideology. Also, of course, it gave the party a chance to participate in the governmental process, and this was to be more important as the party became identified with Soviet diplomatic goals. With parliamentary privileges, the party could carry out its propaganda offensive more intensively — both negatively, as a way of hindering the process of parliamentary government, and positively, by picturing itself as the only genuinely representative party of the masses.

The First Tudeh Party Congress, 1944

By midsummer, 1944, sufficient groundwork had been laid to warrant holding a party congress to make a new attempt at organizational consolidation and doctrinal readjustments. Preparations were completed by the end of July, and the party's supreme organ met in Teheran from August 1 to August 10.

Gathered together were 168 delegates representing a total membership of 25,000, organized in eighty local and twelve regional committees.[21] The method of electing delegates had

---

20 Opposition to the motion in support of Tabatabai's credentials attracted the support of about one third of the total elected membership of 120. An outcome of this vote was a split in the Socialist party, whose two-member delegation was divided on this issue, causing a further weakening of the left-of-center coalition. Elwell-Sutton, "Political Parties in Iran," pp. 45–62.

21 See M. V. Popov, *Amerikanski y imperializm v Irane v gody vtoroy Mirovoy voyny* (Moscow, 1956), Chap. 3, for an account of the First Congress of the Tudeh party.

been agreed upon by the Teheran Provincial Conference in June, 1942. Each delegate represented about 150 card-carrying members and was elected by a local conference of the party committee in each locality. According to the party's first secretary, in terms of social composition, about 75 percent of the membership was drawn from labor, and the remainder represented the intelligentsia and the petty bourgeoisie. But the composition of the party's leading organs elected at this congress suggests that labor's alleged predominance was not reflected in the party leadership, which continued to have an intellectual emphasis throughout this phase.[22]

One of the main tasks of the congress was the final approval of the party statute and action program, until then only provisional. Principle I of the first party program defined it as "the party of the oppressed classes, i.e., the workers, the peasants, the freedom-seeking intelligentsia, and the artisans." Principle II stated that the party advocated Iran's independence and sovereignty and struggled against colonial policies opposed to it. Principle III advocated friendly cooperation with all freedom-loving countries on the basis of equality of all nations and the preservation of world peace. Principle IV demanded the establishment of a national and genuinely democratic regime. Principle V declared that the party had struggled against economic manifestations of the old social order, such as feudalism and the peasant economy, and was striving for a centralized and progressive economic system based on protecting the interests of the entire nation.[23]

The party's legislative program, presented to the 14th Majlis

---

[22] Radmanesh, "Hezbe Tudeh Iran." It must be noted that the party's first secretary attempted to refute the charge of a general inclination toward elitism. His percentages could in fact have been valid for membership of both the party and its affiliate trade unions, but the actual composition of the delegates showed a heavy majority of the intelligentsia and professional class. See Steiner, "Der Iranische Kommunismus," p. 1498.

[23] *Assassnamehe Hezbe Tudehe Iran Mossavabe Kongerehe Avval* [The Statute of the Tudeh Party of Iran Adopted by the First Party Congress] (Teheran, 1944).

some months later by the spokesman of the parliamentary party, advanced these measures as the minimum legislative demands:

A labor law to regulate employer-worker relations.

A law to reconstruct the civil service on the merit system and equal pay for equal work.

A new electoral law to effect reapportionment, voters' registration, and curtailment of polling time.

Legislation to modernize the civil and criminal codes and to ensure an independent judiciary.

Outright distribution of government estates; purchase and distribution of larger private holdings; and a more equitable crop-sharing law.

New laws to reduce taxes for lower income groups and to consolidate the state monopoly of trade and industry.

Formation of local governments by direct elections.

Implementation of the existing law on universal free education.

Laws for reforming the armed forces.

New laws for free medical services for the poor and the rural population.[24]

In the course of the congress, dissension developed, underscoring the absence of agreement on both the party's ideological content and its tactical position. Although the details of the schism became known only after the major party split in late 1946, it was clear at the time that the dissension had to do with the party's attempts to conceal its Communist identity. A number of critical questions were involved: Was the party in truth a mass political organization or was it merely a loose front of numerous factions with only a token common goal? Was it to advocate a gradual nonrevolutionary method of seizing power or must it sooner or later resort to revolutionary means for

---

[24] Dr. Freydoun Keshavarz, "Mozakerat Majlis," *Rooznamehe Rasmi Keshvare Shahan-Shahi* [Parliamentary Debate, the Official Gazette of the Imperial Government of Iran], Vol. I, No. 81 (September, 1945), 322.

achieving its ends? Now that an end to the World War was in sight, was the party to continue supporting the Allies (which, after all, included imperialist Britain as well as socialist Russia) or should it come out in open opposition to the Western powers?

There was great diversity of opinion within the congress about these and similar questions. The Central Committee and the parliamentary group were criticized for opportunistic policies in the previous two and one-half years. Khalil Maleki, the spokesman of the critical faction, was opposed specifically to the party's participation in the election, "which having an undemocratic character could only deceive the masses and weaken their revolutionary zeal." [25] He demanded a purge of "the opportunist elements" within the party and urged more selective recruiting of cadres.

Some of these criticisms had been acknowledged by the leadership both before and during the congress, but despite promises of reform, the leading organs failed to satisfy their critics in the immediate years after the congress. This failure had a pragmatic and practical justification because any submission to the demands of the critical faction would have resulted in a purge, a weakening of the united front, and a legal ban on the party. Therefore, most delegates only paid lip service to criticism, notably regarding party organization. In turn, the leadership accused the critics of unconstructive criticism aimed at weakening the party by disqualifying its most devoted leaders.[26] The old guard's hold on the party was demonstrated by the reelection of the majority of its leading organs, including the Central Committee and its political bureau. Maleki himself was elected to the control commission, which among other things was charged with organizational realignment and ideological stratification. Despite this, he was accused of creating a faction in the commission hostile to the Central Committee and bent on electing him

---

[25] Khalil Maleki, *Do Ravesh baraye Yek Hadaf* [Two Approaches Toward the Same Goal] (Teheran, 1946), pp. 11–12. This was the first publication of the Tudeh Socialist League after its defection from the main party; hereafter cited as *Do Ravesh*.

[26] Eskandari, *op. cit.*

secretary general. For the time being, however, the bone of contention was thus buried at the first congress, though dissension continued.

The congress adopted the concept of collective leadership. Rather than electing a chairman to replace Soleiman Mohsen Eskandari, who had died in February, 1944, three general secretaries from among the Central Committee's eleven members were elected. In addition, a nine-man control commission and a political bureau of five where chosen, in all of which the parliamentary group was heavily represented, thus ensuring unity of action between the leading organs of the party and its representatives in the Majlis.[27]

It was decided that a party congress would meet annually to elect members of the main governing bodies and to effect changes. For the reasons mentioned, no attempt was made to reveal the party's Marxist–Leninist orientation, but by accepting such principles as democratic centralism, the subordination of minority to majority, collective leadership, and strict party discipline, the party reflected at least the organizational expressions of this orientation.[28]

The Party in the Majlis

With the conclusion of the congress, party strategy for the immediate future began to take definite form. Although the party was formally dedicated to supporting the Allies, it was still pos-

---

[27] The three who held their posts until the 1946 reorganization of the party were Dr. Mohammed Bahrami, Nureddin Alamuti, and Iraj Eskandari. Other members were Parvin Gonabadi, Ehsan Tabari, Ardeshir Ovanessian, Ali Amir Khizi, Dr. Reza Radmanesh, Mahmud Boghrati, Abdolsamad Kambakhsh, and Dr. Freydoun Keshavarz. The control commission was composed of Dr. Morteza Yazdi, Dr. Hossein Jowdat, Abdolhossein Nushin, Ali Olovvi, Reza Rusta, Ahmad Ghassemi, Dr. Mohammad Hossein Kiyanouri, Ziaeddin Alamuti, and Khalil Maleki. Altogether the congress elected seven committees, which, apart from those mentioned above, included one in charge of finance and another in charge of political education. *Rahbar* (anniversary issue), Oct. 2, 1946.

[28] Radmanesh, *op. cit.*, p. 3.

sible for it to acknowledge publicly that British imperialism was its main adversary. The chief ammunition was directed at those elements considered to be the agents of imperialism, especially the right wing political groups headed by Tabatabai. To carry out an effective campaign against the pro-British politicians, the party's action program was designed to rally to its support all democratic forces in the name of defending the parliamentary constitutional system, which had provided the party with its sole legal channel of influence.

The parliamentary party was entrusted with implementing this strategy in the Majlis, where the lines were drawn between the majority that supported successive cabinets and a minority that was considered progressive because of its consistent opposition to the governments in power. Outside the Majlis the party increased its efforts to form a common action program with all progressive groups, notably with the Iran party, which was composed mostly of liberal intellectuals of strong nationalistic persuasion.[29]

Meanwhile, the Freedom Front controlling about thirty publications continued to function as a party auxiliary. This front was directed by a council in which the party was heavily represented. Furthermore, to reinforce the appearance of a broad nonparty press coalition, a number of veteran Communists deliberately stayed outside the party to publish an ostensibly independent newspaper for the front.[30] In September, 1944, on the initiative of the party's representative, the Front's managing council issued a resolution inviting the democratic elements of Iran to unite to prevent Tabatabai from taking office and to defend constitutional liberties. The resolution sought to attribute to the Right an alleged plot to seize power, with the aim of establishing a dictatorship and doing away with leftist parties.[31]

The First Tudeh Party Congress had been marked by in-

---

[29] Elwell-Sutton, *op. cit.*, p. 51.

[30] *Azhir*, edited by Pishevari, and *Damavand* edited by M. Fattahi, also of Baku background, were examples of this sort of publication. See Lenczowski, "The Communist Movement in Iran," p. 39.

[31] Eskandari, *op. cit.*, p. 9.

creased indications of the ascendancy of Soviet diplomacy in the form of open intervention in Iran's domestic affairs, far exceeding the limits imposed by the 1942 Tri-Partite Treaty.[32] This treaty had elevated Iran from the status of an enemy to that of a country whose sovereignty was to be respected and whose occupation would be terminated within six months of the end of the war. Allied occupation was to be limited to preserving communication lines to the Soviet Union and to ensuring the safe transport of Lend Lease war materiel to the U.S.S.R. through Iran. In reality, however, the occupying powers went beyond these limitations, treating their respective occupation zones as the territory of a defeated enemy. The security requirements for preserving the communication lines to Russia became an excuse for active Soviet political intervention in the northern zone. And in the capital city itself, although it was declared a neutral zone and was relatively free from foreign intervention, except for the token presence of Allied forces, power politics existed in every major development.

For the first three years of occupation there was a remarkable amount of political freedom in the capital. Newspapers, parties, political groups, and associations of all kinds sprang to life.[33] Not surprisingly, the electoral campaign for the 14th Majlis in the fall and winter of 1943–1944 not only reflected domestic political forces but also indicated the respective influence of the two occupying powers.

The majority of the pro-Soviet deputies were elected in northern Soviet-occupied provinces. Eight of these belonged to the Tudeh party.[34] Elsewhere, except in industrialized Isfahan in

---

[32] Text of 1942 Tri-Partite Treaty in Lenczowski, *Russia and the West in Iran, 1918–1948* (Ithaca, N.Y., 1949), pp. 319–322.

[33] According to the best available accounts, on the eve of the election there were more than fifteen "parties." Many of these were of a sectional and temporary nature, however, and quickly disappeared once the election was over. See Elwell-Sutton, *op. cit.*, p. 35.

[34] These were Dr. R. Radmanesh and Dr. F. Keshavarz (Gilan), Shahabe Ferdose and P. Gonabadi (Khorassan), I. Eskandari (Mazanderan), A. Kambakhsh (Qazvin), A. Ovanessian (Armenians of the North), and T. Fadakar (Isfahan); see *Salnamehe Majlis* [Majlis Yearbook] (Teheran,

the British occupation zone, the candidates of the Tudeh party were unsuccessful. But since the more populous northern provinces accounted for roughly one-half of the 136 Majlis seats, even in the north the Soviets could not be said to have won a great victory. Most of the deputies elected, in all parts of Iran, were pro-Western in social and educational background, but were opposed to both occupying powers. In the Azarbayjan crisis a year after the elections, it became evident that the deputies from the north were not in fact strongly anti-Soviet. There seems no doubt that the Soviets resorted to a number of tricks to ensure the success of the candidates they favored, including outright deportation and pressure on the government to withdraw a nominee.[35]

In the case of the seating of the veteran Communist leader Pishevari, who had been elected from Tabriz, no amount of backstage pressure was successful. During the consideration of parliamentary mandates, traditionally the first trial of strength, since the Majlis is the sole judge of the propriety of the electoral process, the Left suffered its first defeat. Pishevari's credentials were rejected and the pro-Communist faction was thus denied an experienced leader in the initial stage of its political struggle.[36] This test case also indicated what the alignment within the Majlis would be: the Tudeh party, with its thirty-odd supporters, could expect defeat from a Right-Center coalition on major issues involving obvious Soviet pressure.

An analysis of the parliamentary records, especially in the

1945). Pishevari, whose mandate was rejected by the Majlis, was one of the nine deputies elected in Tabriz.

[35] The election of Sheikh Hossein Lankarani from Ardabil in Azarbayjan is a case in point. To ensure his success, the Soviet authorities simply banished his opponent from the city. See Ann K. Lambton, "Some of the Problems Facing Persia," *International Affairs*, XXII, No. 2 (April, 1946), 266.

[36] A number of Center deputies regretted the denial of Pishevari's mandate when he became the leader of the insurrection in Azarbayjan a year later, believing that if he had been seated in the Majlis, he would have been denied a major personal grievance which was behind his involvement in that rebellion. See M. Mossadegh, *Rooznamehe Rasmi*, Vol. I, No. 249 (December, 1945), 381.

later phase of the 14th Majlis, indicates the growing subordination of the Tudeh party to Soviet diplomacy, to the point where, in early 1945, the Tudeh group was little more than a Soviet mouthpiece on major issues. During the procedural debate over the members' mandate, the Tudeh group lined up with the progressive and anti-British elements to oppose the seating of Tabatabai, whom they regarded as a symbol of reaction and an advocate for the restoration of the pre-World War II regime, even though Tabatabai and his party supported the Allied cause and were critical of the former Shah. In their opposition to Tabatabai the Tudeh members were supported by most of the newly elected deputies of nationalist and progressive persuasion, led by Dr. Mohammad Mossadegh and roughly representing the left-of-center faction of the Majlis.

Until the spring of 1945, when at last a cabinet was proposed that had the open blessing of the Soviets, the Tudeh parliamentary group opposed every cabinet. In accordance with the Central Committee's decision, the support given to Morteza Bayat in the spring of 1945 and to Ahmad Ghavam the following winter marked the party's departure from steady opposition. It also underscored a political-ideological problem which the party's subordination to Soviet diplomacy had evoked.

One aspect of this problem was the abandonment of the party's radical line, which until then had kept it from supporting all cabinets whose programs failed to embody the party's minimum legislative demands. Departure from this line created a crisis, especially among the intellectual wing of the leadership, which voiced its criticism at the Second Congress some years later. This wing had already expressed misgivings about participation in the electoral process, which it considered undemocratic and incompatible with the party platform. During the First Congress, as we have seen, dissension on this point nearly caused a breakdown in party leadership. Less than a year later, the party's parliamentary group proposed to go one step further and join with the independents, the progressives, and even elements of the Right to back a government not substantially different from its predecessors.[37] Another aspect of the problem was the implication that the intended policy reversal was necessitated solely by Soviet diplomatic requirements. At a time when the party was seeking support from the nationalistic middle class, the charge of being a tool of the Soviet Union, which by the fall of 1944 had become actively involved in Iranian power politics, was a formidable liability.

The Oil Crisis

Utilizing to the full both the traditional and the revolutionary elements of its diplomacy, the Soviet government waged a serious offensive to obtain an oil concession in the north. It brought unprecedented pressure on the government of Mohammad Saed to force negotiation on the proposed concession, even while the Allies were still occupying the country, and sent an undersecretary of the Soviet Ministry of Foreign Affairs to Teheran to dramatize the Soviet diplomatic offensive. The revolutionary elements of this drive assumed the form of a vigorous campaign by the Tudeh party and its affiliates to overthrow the cabinet that had resisted the Soviet demand.[38] The party and the Freedom Front sponsored impressive demonstrations in the capital and major cities. In some of these Red Army units took an active part, banishing all doubts as to why the campaign was being waged.[39] Walkouts and sitdown strikes occurred repeatedly in

---

[37] Dr. Keshavarz of the Tudeh party told the Majlis: "Our support of the new government stemmed from the party's desire to protect the constitution and democracy; otherwise the prime minister belonged to the same ruling class to which the party was uncompromisingly opposed." *Ibid.*, Vol. I, No. 81 (September, 1945), 322.

[38] The party blamed the government for precipitating the crisis by engaging in exploratory oil negotiations with American oil companies and stubbornly refusing the same to the Soviet Union; Great Britain, of course, already held the major oil concessions in the south. Eskandari, *op. cit.*, p. 10.

[39] A demonstration in the Majlis Square on October 27, 1944, climaxed open agitation in favor of the Soviet policy. See Parviz H. Farboud, "L'Evolution politique de l'Iran pendant la Second Guerre Mondiale," (Doctoral dissertation, University of Lausanne, Lausanne, 1957), p. 192.

important industrial cities, such as Shahi in the north and Isfahan in the center, as well as in the capital, where armed workers
actually assumed control of some major factories.

The Tudeh party, forced to come out openly in favor of the
Soviets, found itself isolated in the Majlis as the only support
for the oil concession demanded by the Soviet Union. As a result,
a new political alignment emerged. The progressive and nationalist elements sided with the Right and the independents. The
breakdown over Mossadegh's motion to prohibit all governments
from entering into oil negotiations while Iran was under foreign
occupation solidified this alignment, which lasted until early
1945.[40]

Saed's cabinet was a victim of this initial setback to Soviet
diplomacy. In the face of continued Soviet pressure, the cabinet
resigned. The Tudeh party promptly hailed the resignation as
an important victory, and it attempted to justify its support of
Saed's successor, Bayat, in January, 1945, as a necessity forced
on it by the Right. According to the Tudeh party, the Right was
planning to form a new government under Tabatabai, whom
they now regarded as the champion of anti-Soviet policies.[41]

It was no secret that the Bayat government enjoyed Soviet
support. In addition to the Tudeh party, a left-of-center coalition also backed it, largely to soothe the ruffled feelings of the
Soviets. In the crisis following Saed's resignation, the official
attitude of the Soviet government toward Iran became increasingly aggressive, and Communist propagandists worked hard at
driving home the point that the era of a predominantly pro-
Western orientation in Iranian politics was approaching its end.

At the height of the oil crisis the Tudeh party developed the
thesis of "the security perimeter of the Soviet Union," according
to which Iran's northern region was to be recognized as essential to the security of the U.S.S.R. and kept clear of British
influence. An oil concession, especially one comparable to that

of the British–Iranian Oil Company in the south, would simply consolidate the region as a security perimeter. It would, in addition, the Tudeh party argued, help the industrialization of a major part of the country and bring about the ultimate economic emancipation of the people.[42]

This policy, according to the nationalist members of the Majlis, notably Dr. Mossadegh, the sponsor of the "no concession" motion, amounted to a "positive neutrality," which sought to restore a balance between Great Britain and the Soviet Union by matching whatever privileges the former enjoyed with the granting of similar favors to the latter. In fact, however, the Tudeh party did not deny that this was its stand regarding Iran's foreign relations: the party propaganda steadfastly adhered to the concept that any policy which opposed the Soviet Union was inherently pro-British.

Numerous party spokesmen justified this pro-Soviet orientation in terms of the broader revolutionary changes in power relationships affecting Iran as a result of the Second World War. One leading member of the party's Central Committee and parliamentary group, Reza Radmanesh, charged that, under the former regime, his country knew nothing of Russia's enormous sociopolitical movement because the regime did not want the people to know of Russia's achievements. He warned that, since the Soviet Union had become a leading world power as a result of its major burden in the anti-Fascist war, this policy could no longer last. Instead, he proposed a balanced policy:

I advocate a balance of power policy, which substantially differs from the present policy and is in sharp contrast to that of the pre-1941 period. We should be an instrument of the balance between the two major powers; we should strengthen it rather than disturb it. Concurrent with this, we should create a social equilibrium inside the country by drastic reforms and serious attempts to eliminate the regime of privilege. If we fail in these our country will move toward a revolution which will ruin the advocates of the present policies.[43]

---

[42] These views were advanced in an editorial in the party's official organ. See *Rahbar*, Oct. 11, 1945. Also quoted in Lambton, *op. cit.*, p. 264.

[43] Radmanesh, *Rooznamehe Rasmi*, Vol. I, No. 77 (May, 1945), 300.

This was typical of public policy statements made by the party shortly before the fall of the Bayat cabinet, which had been more or less an interim cabinet, installed largely to appease the Soviet Union and as an attempt to remove misunderstandings resulting from the oil crisis. The Bayat cabinet fell in mid-April, 1945, after a vote of no confidence that was unsuccessfully opposed by the eight Tudeh members and 37 other deputies out of a total of 90 deputies present. The no confidence vote had, of course, been moved by a coalition of the Right.[44] The new alignment meant a return to the alignment that had existed before the oil crisis, and it continued in roughly the same numerical proportion for some months.

During the prolonged crisis following the defeat of the Bayat cabinet, the Tudeh party used the parliamentary deliberation over cabinet succession to allay popular misgivings about its pro-Soviet stand. One spokesman in the Majlis justified the Tudeh's general support of leftist movements the world over by arguing that Iran's interest demanded the support of all freedom movements, no matter where they developed. Socialism was not a monopoly of the Soviet Union, nor had it originated there, he said. "It is a national and international creed which offers hope and inspiration to many peoples in many lands. But this is beside the point, for our party is not socialistic in any sense. Rather it is a democratic political organization which developed in Iran as a historical necessity."[45] Pursuing the same line, another leading party member denied that he or the party were Communist. "We are interested in basic reforms in Iran," he said. "Our methods are based on the interests of the masses. We want friendly relations with all allies, especially with the Soviet Union and Britain."[46]

The party advanced what it considered to be a major defense in favor of the Soviet Union: that a socialist state could not, by its very nature, follow a colonial policy. A party member put it succinctly: "The Soviet government cannot and will not advo-

---

[44] *Ibid.*
[45] Ardeshir Ovanessian, quoted in *ibid.*, Vol. I, No. 79 (May, 1945), 310.
[46] *New York Times*, March 17, 1945.

cate colonialism, for Russia is a classless society where no exploitation of many by man or by state takes place. Such a society is incapable of pursuing colonial policies. We should know our neighbor better in order to formulate a correct policy toward its government." [47]

There were many who disagreed with this argument, especially at a time when the Soviet Union was showing so much belligerence over the oil issue. The Soviet backing of the party until then could have been partly justified in terms of the practical necessity of offsetting the domination of the pro-British parties of the Right. In fact, the struggle against Tabatabai had a nationalistic emphasis which permitted the party to use the united front tactic. But support of a Soviet oil concession was of a different nature, in that it placed a heavy burden on advocates of pro-Soviet domestic politics. Such arguments as the inherently noncolonial nature of a socialist state were plainly inadequate to offset the burden, and it was on this issue that the seeds of major dissension in the party's rank and file were sown. Several years later a major faction of dissidents set out to prove that the U.S.S.R. was far from lily white in the matter of colonial and imperialistic tendencies, nor was the mere label of a classless society adequate to prevent one major power from behaving like other major powers organized under a different political philosophy. [48]

Generally speaking, the Tudeh party's pro-Soviet orientation had three components: the concept of "positive equilibrium" in relations with the Soviet Union and Great Britain; the concept of the "security perimeter" of the Soviet Union; and the concept of "the inherently noncolonial character of a socialist state." The first concept was used to justify the granting to the Soviet Union of privileges similar to those enjoyed by Great

---

[47] Ovanessian, quoted in *Rooznamehe Rasmi, op. cit.,* Vol. I, No. 79, p. 310.

[48] Khalil Maleki, the leading writer and theorist of the dissident faction, developed the thesis of "Soviet state capitalism" as a corollary to his rebuttal of this notion in numerous writings, such as editorials in *Elm Va Zendegi* [Science and Life], Nos. 1, 3 (Teheran, 1947).

Britain, including the disputed oil concession. Party spokesmen, including the leading member of the party's three-man
secretariat, formulated their attitude toward major powers in
this context:

> We wish for a policy of equilibrium between the Soviet Union and
> the United Kingdom. . . . We wish to improve our political and
> socioeconomic ties with Moscow. . . . I am sure that the Soviet
> Union has no colonial aspirations in Iran or any sector thereof. I
> believe our country should enter into a mutual defense alliance with
> both these countries. Our party favored granting an oil concession to
> the Soviet Union because as a matter of principle we support every
> measure that benefits the masses of people.[49]

The grant of an oil concession was one way of restoring the
balance in favor of Russia. Another method was to give the proponents of a policy of positive equilibrium a more influential
voice in the country's ruling circles. Communist propaganda
decrying the "undemocratic" nature of the Iranian regime made
it clear that the lack of adequate representation in the government was one of the chief Soviet grievances. *Pravda*, for example,
complained that despite the numerical strength of the democratic
forces, they had little voice in the government and consequently
could do little to advance their policies.[50]

The second concept favored a zone of Soviet influence in the
north to ensure the security of the "motherland of socialism."
The rapid and unchecked expansion of the party and its trade
union affiliates in that sector was related to a systematic attempt
to achieve this purpose. Toward the end of this first phase of
essentially nonrevolutionary struggle, the party began organizing in major industrial centers of Mazanderan the so-called self-
defense service, which amounted to armed occupation of these
centers by Tudeh party workers. The use of this clearly revolutionary measure at a time when the party was still committed
to constitutional methods was justified on the grounds of "the
government's inability to protect the victims of Fascist agitation,

---

49 *New York Times*, March 17, 1945.
50 *Pravda*, as quoted in the *New York Times*, July 10, 1945.

which had forced the party to take drastic measures for the support of democratic organizations against the aggression of armed terrorist bands."[51]

The third concept was used to defend pro-Soviet policies in response to the charge of subordination to Russia's interest — a charge which threatened the party with the massive alienation of its non-Communist and nationalist sympathizers. To win their confidence the party differentiated between the foreign policies of Great Britain, representing the capitalist-imperialist camp, and those of the Soviet Union, representing a socialist system.

Second Phase: The Revolutionary Adventure

The fall of the Bayat cabinet in April, 1945, marked the beginning of more radical policies of the Soviet Union toward Iran. One reason for this was the frustration of the Soviet government's expectation that the Soviet-supported cabinet would redress Russia's grievances. Indeed, this experience showed that, irrespective of who headed the cabinet, no rapprochement seemed possible between the two countries as long as the Soviet government pursued its policy of trying to obtain vital political and economic concessions from Iran. The supposedly friendly Bayat cabinet was quite unable to bring about a reversal of the policy of resistance to this concept of power balancing. When the Bayat cabinet fell, the government swung to the right, and the Left was provoked to a more extremist program. The result was the country's most acute crisis in the immediate postwar era.

The trend toward rightist policies culminated in the installation of a new cabinet under Mohsen Sadr. For an entire summer, this cabinet ruled without the customary formal vote of confidence, despite the fact that such a vote was a part of the formal authorization of a new cabinet. The legality of the new cabinet had created a delicate constitutional issue, and a minority of the Left used the traditionally effective "parliamentary

---

[51] Eskandari, "Histoire de Parti Toudeh," *Moyen-Orient*, No. 11 (May, 1950), 9.

obstruction" technique to postpone a vote of confidence, though in so doing it dangerously undermined the machinery of parliamentary government and indeed that of the whole state.[52] Most of this minority, comprising about one-third of the Majlis membership and led by Dr. Mossadegh, was considerably to the right of the Tudeh group politically and ideologically, but tactically it cooperated with it on the grounds than an extreme rightist government at that time could not hope to bring about an easing of tension with the U.S.S.R. If anything, it was feared that such a government would only aggravate relations at a time when Iran needed the cooperation of both the United States and the U.S.S.R. to return to normalcy. At the root of this apprehension was the fear that the Soviet Union might refuse to fulfill its treaty obligation to evacuate its occupied zone by March 2, 1946 — a fear that proved justified.

Inevitably, the rightist trend resulted in an intensification of the Tudeh party's Soviet line. As the Right and Left moved further and further apart, the Communist movement in Iran returned to a policy of open offensive, reminiscent of 1920–1921 and aimed, at the least, at an ending of oil concessions, and, at the most, at the establishment of a pro-Soviet government in Iran. So far as the tactics in the country as a whole were concerned, the hardening of the line meant dumping the still basically nonrevolutionary Tudeh party in favor of a revolutionary organization.

The first characteristic amounted to a reintroduction of traditional Soviet power politics, including the effective use of the Red Army in northern Iran, where it had by this time paralyzed the governmental machinery by constant interference in domestic affairs. The second characteristic was tantamount to a reintroduction of the revolutionary element of Soviet diplomacy, which in the summer of 1945 had assumed unprecedented belligerence toward the Iranian ruling class. The Communist move-

---

[52] The cabinet finally received a vote of confidence of 40 out of the 69 present on September 25, 1945, after the opposition temporarily abandoned its obstructionist technique on the understanding that the prime minister would resign if more than 40 members failed to support him. *Rooznamehe Rasmi*, Vol. I, No. 180 (September, 1945), 596.

ment found another organization expression in the Azarbayjan Democratic party and its junior partner in the Kurdistan province known as Kumeleh. Elsewhere in the country the Tudeh party continued as the primary organizational expression of the movement, but it was definitely abandoned as an instrument of revolution in Azarbayjan and Kurdistan. In effect, during this new phase of Soviet diplomacy, these two branches of the Communist movement in Iran were to serve as separate levers of pressure on the central government. The Tudeh party was to intensify its work in the Caspian province and in Teheran, Isfahan, and Khuzistan, stopping short of an actual armed attempt to seize power. The Azarbayjan Democratic party and the Kumeleh party were to resort to armed rebellion in their own provinces with the declared aim of securing autonomy for their brand of peoples' democracy.

The Tudeh party made no pretense about its increased revolutionary activity in various parts of the country. The targets of its assault were Prime Minister Sadr and his chief of staff, General Hassan Arfaa, whom they accused of drawing up the plans for the systematic annihilation of the Tudeh party and trade union organizations.[53]

In August, 1945, government troops occupied the headquarters of the Tudeh party organizations in the capital city; its newspapers were suspended and orders issued for its branches in provincial towns to be disbanded. A leading Tudeh deputy, Dr. Freydoun Keshavarz, was beaten up in a scuffle with security forces blocking a Tudeh march in downtown Teheran, and later dramatically appeared in the Majlis to plead not guilty to the charge of favoring continued Soviet occupation and to pledge his allegiance to Iran's territorial integrity.[54]

In reaction to pressures on the party in the capital, militant worker groups in Mazanderan and Gorgan in the north occupied major towns, factories, and railroad junctions. The so-called self-

---

[53] Eskandari, *Moyen-Orient*, No. 11, 9.

[54] Dr. F. Keshavarz, *Rooznamehe Rasmi*, Vol. I, No. 180 (August, 1945), 594–596.

defense service assumed control of roads and communication
networks.[55] Attempts by the government to enlarge their security
forces in these areas were blocked when the Soviets refused to
allow troop movements; in some cases the Soviets even denied
freedom of activity to government officials on the grounds that
any civil conflict in the Soviet zone was likely to endanger the
security of their forces. In the summer and fall of 1945 the north
was firmly in the grip of the Tudeh party, which now clamored for a quick general election to increase its parliamentary
representation.[56]

Insurrection in Azarbayjan

Three factors had determined the choice of Azarbayjan and
Kurdistan for an open Communist offensive. First of all, these
provinces, with outspoken minorities, held many antigovernment grievances, not least of which was their proportionately
inadequate representation in the governmental system, notably
in the Majlis.[57] Second, these provinces were easily infiltrated
from across the border, that is, from Soviet Azarbayjan, where
the identical dialect of Azari–Turkish was spoken.[58] Addition-
ally, there was good reason for beginning a fresh revolutionary
drive in a place where the Tudeh had not been substantially
involved and where the refusal to seat Pishevari in the Majlis
could be exploited to the full.

---

[55] Eskandari, Moyen-Orient, No. 11, 9.

[56] Rightly fearing a decline in its power after the evacuation of the
country, the party persisted in demanding an immediate election until the
very end of the Majlis term in February, 1946. Typical of statements to this
effect was a speech by Shahabe Ferdose in the Majlis open meeting on
February 2, 1946. Rooznamehe Rasmi, Vol. II, No. 294 (February, 1946),
1061.

[57] A breakdown of the voting record of the Azarbayjan 19-man delegation
in the Majlis indicates its general opposition to the government. Apart
from the Armenian member, who belonged to the Tudeh group, 14 consistently opposed the successive cabinets based on a right-of-center coalition.

[58] One estimate put the number of Mohajers (immigrants) of alleged
Persian parenthood at 2,500. Rooznamehe Rasmi, Vol. I, No. 148 (August,
1945), 493.

In Pishevari the Soviets found not only an experienced revolutionary leader but a strong-willed Azarbayjani who had adamantly refused to be drawn into the revived Communist movement, which he believed to be neither sufficiently revolutionary nor fully representative of Azarbayjan.[59] His contempt for the Tudeh party was apparent in the high-handed manner in which he forced the dissolution of its provincial branch and its absorption into his new Democratic party. This was done as a fait accompli, without prior negotiation with the Tudeh party's Central Committee in Teheran, which severely criticized the provincial committee for accepting the dissolution on its own.[60] In his memoirs, Pishevari describes the Tudeh party in Azarbayjan as a worn-out, disreputable organization, whose years of struggle had failed to produce any tangible results.[61]

Pishevari's new Democratic party was formed at the end of the summer of 1945, and a communique containing ten articles about its goals was issued on September 3, 1945. It demanded the adoption of Azari–Turkish as the province's official language and autonomy within the framework of Iran's sovereignty. Other objectives called for liberal and progressive reforms of a social and economic character typical of parties organized in postwar Iran.[62] On September 11, the chairman of the province's United Council of Trade Unions, Ahmad Biriya, announced it would join the Democratic party; the Tudeh provincial committee took a similar measure the same day. A few weeks later, at the end of September, the new party's First Congress met as a cross-section of nearly every level of the population, including mem-

---

[59] Some Western authors have attributed the choice of Pishevari to his alleged reputation for religiosity, presumably in view of his advocacy of the province's united front alliance, which rallied to his support a considerable segment of the clergy. See Von Alfred Joachim Fischer, "Hat der Kommunismus Chancen in Persien?" *Die Zukunft* (Wien), No. 3 (March, 1954), 63.

[60] *Seyre Komonism*, p. 67.

[61] Najafgholi Pesyan, *Marg Bud Bazkasht Ham Bud* [There Were Both Death and Retreat] (Teheran, 1947), p. 21.

[62] *Ibid.*

bers of the clergy, merchants, tribal chieftains, intellectuals, Communists, and petty bourgeoisie.[63] Its most important decision was to form a peasants' militia, the Fedayeens (Devotees), and the stage was set for open insurrection.

On November 4 the attempt to seize power by force of arms throughout the province began. The same pattern was successfully followed in the various towns. First, the militia surrounded the military post and issued an ultimatum to the local commander to surrender; when the encircled garrison requested reinforcements, they were blocked either by the militia or by the Soviet garrison;[64] finally, cut off from reinforcements, the garrison was given a chance to disband and the choice of either joining the militia or returning to Teheran.

One after another the major towns and military posts succumbed to the militia. On November 9 and 10, 1945, the Democratic party held an "All-Peoples Grand National Congress" in Tabriz, the administrative center of the province, with 744 delegates purporting to represent 150,000 inhabitants from all over the province. Some of these delegates had been elected in open meetings in public squares, where party emissaries from Tabriz not only addressed the crowd but nominated the candidates and secured their approval by acclamation. Others were elected by petitions circulated by party workers in different constituencies and signed by an alleged majority of the eligible electorate.

The All-People Congress of the new Democratic party, meet-

---

[63] Soviet sources strongly emphasized this apparent broad basis of the new party. *Izvestia* on November 20, 1945, wrote: "The election of different party organs shows that important strata of the population desired to assure the democratic rights of the Azarbayjan people within the framework of the Iranian state" (as quoted in *L'Humanité*, Nov. 21, 1945).

[64] On November 8 a column of the Iranian Army, which had left the capital for Azarbayjan, was halted by the Red Army at Sharif-Abad on the outskirts of Kazvin. Colonel Smirnov, representing the Soviet command in the region, informed Colonel Amjadi, the commander of the Iranian expeditionary force, that failure to abide by the Soviet request would be considered a hostile act against the Red Army. Thus delayed, the reinforcement failed to reach Azarbayjan in time to quell the insurrection at its start. Pesyan, *op. cit.*, pp. 30–31.

ing in four sessions, unanimously agreed to present the central government with the following resolutions of their fundamental rights:

The right to determine the fate of the Azarbayjani people, "who possess distinctive national, linguistic and traditional characteristics."

The right to exercise their national self-determination without endangering Iran's territorial integrity.

Support for Iran's constitutional democracy via representation in the national parliament and payment of just taxation.

The freedom to manage their domestic affairs through democratic and sovereign methods within the framework of Iran's independence.

The right to elect a national Majlis and to form an autonomous government from its membership.

The adoption of Azari–Turkish as the official language "to develop our national culture and education." [65]

The resolution also stated that the congress had assumed the function of a constituent assembly and had elected a 39-man national executive board to carry out the declared objectives of the congress. As to the method of achieving these goals, "peaceful organizational and propaganda work," in preference to hostile acts leading to civil war, was advocated. The central government was warned, however, that any use of force to suppress Azarbayjan's "legitimate" right to national autonomy would be resisted. The national executive board was given the task of securing autonomy for the provinces through negotiation with the central government. [66]

---

[65] Text of Resolution in *ibid.*, pp. 61–63.

[66] Communist sources have vigorously denied the charge that the insurrectionist movement was separatist in nature. One official Soviet source declared: "The reactionary forces throughout Iran have focused their attack on the Azarbayjan democratic movement on the pretext that it advocated separation from Iran. The British reports of Russian intervention

Acting on the resolutions passed by the congress, the Democratic party at once held general elections for an Azarbayjan Majlis. These were held from Dec. 3 to Dec. 8 throughout the province, including the areas still under control of the central government. For the first time in Persia's history universal suffrage was exercised, and as there was no other organized party, the list presented by the Democratic party won an absolute majority. In some cases the ratio of the popular vote for the winning candidate to the opposition stood as high as 200 to one.[67]

While the elections were in progress, the central government, whose composition had changed in mid-October from right-of-center to a more moderate coalition, made a desperate effort to halt the insurrection. Morteza Bayat, the former prime minister of the left-of-center coalition, arrived in Tabriz at the head of a peace mission. Little was achieved, for the Democratic party persistently demanded autonomy and recognition of local language, which the government would not concede on the ground of the implied change in the Iranian constitutional system from a unitary to a federal multilingual type.

The elections provided the Democratic party with a measure of legality used to buttress the claim of popular representation of the province's inhabitants. On December 12 a truce was signed with the army garrison in Tabriz providing for its evacuation and for consolidation of the Fedayeens' control over the town. On the same day the 101 members of the newly elected Azarbayjan Majlis met under the chairmanship of Nezameddoleh Rafii and, after electing its presidium and speaker, voted Pishevari prime minister. The cabinet he presented to the Majlis reflected the popular alliance on which the party was based.[68]

---

there were similarly designed to divert attention from their policies in Palestine, Egypt, and elsewhere." *Izvestia*, Nov. 20, 1945.

[67] U.S. Congress, House Foreign Affairs Committee, *Strategy and Tactics of World Communism*, 81st Cong., 1st Sess. 1949, House Doc. 158, Supp. 3.

[68] Pishevari was also minister of labor. The other ministers were Dr. S. Javid, interior; J. Kavian, war; Dr. Mahtash, agriculture; M. Biriya, education; Dr. Orangi, health; Gh. Elhami, finance; Y. Azima, justice; M. Kabiri, P.T.T.; R. Rasouli, commerce and economy. In addition, Z. Ghiyami and

The Democratic party's principal leaders were included in the cabinet, but the actual power was concentrated in the hands of the party's ruling committee and the militia under its control. The pattern of party hierarchy was similar to that of the Tudeh party: local cells, district committees, provincial committees, and finally a central committee in Tabriz.

Civilian supremacy was assured by the appointment of a political officer to assist the military commander of each unit. At the center this task was given to Gholam Daneshiyan, a veteran Communist agitator from Soviet Azarbayjan, whose official title was political deputy minister of war. To increase the number of military cadres, the regime at once established military elementary and high schools as well as a military and police college. The backbone of the regime's military power was the militia, composed of party members who had been the first volunteers for armed rebellion, many of them at the time of the congress in September. Its leadership was composed of the most militant party members, who formed a kind of military elite exercising great power over the conduct and policies of the regime.[69]

The cabinet's program, unanimously approved by the Majlis, contained the main points of the Grand Congress resolution, in addition to certain reform measures that were to be initiated immediately. The most important of these were the consolidation and strengthening of Azarbayjan autonomy, the election of local councils, the reorganization of the militia into a people's army, the introduction of Azari-Turkish as the official language, free and compulsory education in the native tongue for all children of school age, the creation of a national university, the development of industry and trade, the passage of a labor law and a law regulating peasant-landlord relations, the distribution of state lands among the peasants, the confiscation and distribution of estates belonging to "reactionary" landlords, guarantees

---

F. Ibrahimi were elected chief justice of the Supreme Court and prosecutor general, respectively. Pesyan, *op. cit.*, pp. 123–124.

[69] Such were Kavian in Tabriz, Kabiri in Margheh, Daneshiyan in Miyaneh and Sarab. *Ibid.*, p. 139.

of freedom of conscience and religious teaching for all citizens, and, finally, the protection of equality of rights and duties of every inhabitant of the province, including the minorities.[70]

Immediately after the consolidation of the regime in Azarbayjan, a regular army, known as the Ghezelbash, composed of conscripts, was formed with the help of some Iranian army officers who had defected to Azarbayjan. By the end of the regime's first year, the numerical strength of the Ghezelbash had reached 18,000 enlisted men and 950 officers.[71] There were in addition some 8,000 men and 87 officers in the Fedayeen.

In February, 1946, the counterpart of the revolutionary government in Azarbayjan, a people's republic, was established in Kurdistan under the presidency of the veteran Kurdish leader, Qazi Mohammad. In the same month a treaty of alliance and mutual defense was signed between the two, pledging resistance to the central government and maintenance of autonomy for both revolutionary regimes.[72] With the seizure of power in the two provinces, Soviet diplomacy had thus achieved its immediate goal: a formidable lever of pressure on the Iranian central government to submit to its demands. With this pressure, the Soviets, aided by the Tudeh party, were ready to bring to power in Teheran a government that would enter negotiations for the oil concession denied them the previous year.

While the Azarbayjan insurrection was underway, near the end of October, a moderate center cabinet was installed under Ebrahim Hakimi with the declared intention of reversing some of the previous cabinet's anti-Communist measures. But during the customary debate on the new cabinet it became clear that

---

[70] M. S. Ivanov, *Ocherk istorii Irana*, in *CAR*, Vol. IV, No. 3 (1956), 319.

[71] Government sources estimated that at the time of its collapse, there were 10,000 enlisted men and 870 officers in the revolutionary army. Pesyan, *op. cit.*, p. 140.

[72] For a Western version of the Kurdish revolt see Pierre Rondot, "L'Union Sovietique et les confins Irano-Kurdes du Moyen-Orient," *Politique Etrangère*, Vol. X, No. 3 (1945), and Archie Roosevelt, "Kurdish Republic of Mahabad," *Middle East Journal*, Vol. I, No. 3 (July, 1947). The Communist version is given, among other sources, in Ivanov, *op. cit.*

it would be no more acceptable to the Soviets than its predecessors had been. In a remarkably frank speech, a leading Tudeh representative, Abdolsamad Kambakhsh, informed the Majlis that the occupation forces would not withdraw as long as discrimination against one of Iran's neighbors continued. He charged that Iran's government approximated a fascist dictatorship in view of the suspension of more than forty newspapers and the military occupation of the Tudeh party's headquarters. This, he said, was contrary to Iran's commitment under the United Nations charter, which prohibited member governments from establishing fascist regimes on their soil.[73] When the Tudeh deputies abstained in the vote to confirm the new cabinet, it became evident that Soviet support in this attempt to stabilize the Iranian government would not be forthcoming.[74]

Briefly, the attitudes of the various factions of the Majlis toward the Communist-sponsored insurrection in Azarbayjan were as follows: The Right, uncompromisingly opposed to it, sought the help of the West and the United Nations to bring pressure on the Soviets to enforce noninterference. The nationalist progressive elements, like Dr. Mossadegh and his supporters, acknowledging the long accumulated grievances of the Azarbayjani people, counseled conciliation and compromise. They opposed, however, the Democratic party's most controversial demands for autonomy.[75] The left-of-center, which included the majority of Azarbayjan deputies, criticized the failure of successive cabinets to reach an understanding with the Soviet Union, believing the government had long neglected the Azarbayjan people's legitimate demands.[76]

The Tudeh group, representing the extreme Left, unconditionally supported the Democratic party, despite its high-handed treatment by Pishevari, which had hurt its prestige as the sole

---

[73] Abdolsamad Kambakhsh, speech in Majlis open session, *Rooznamehe Rasmi*, Vol. I, No. 215 (January, 1946), 707.

[74] Of 94 members present, 88 voted for the cabinet. *Ibid.*

[75] Mossadegh, *ibid.*, Vol. I, No. 231 (February, 1946), 870.

[76] Typical of this attitude are speeches by Sadeghi from Tabriz and Mozaffar Zadeh from Gilan. *Ibid.*, I, No. 258 (February, 1946), 943–944.

representative of the radical Left. With the successful seizure of
power in Azarbayjan, this group in parliament became the official voice of the insurrection in the capital, and it used every
occasion to advance its cause. Tudeh deputies countered charges
of Soviet intervention by emphasizing the movement's united
front nature, though they could hardly deny that the insurrection was linked with Soviet diplomacy and were forced to admit,
at least by implication, that the movement had foreign ties. Radmanesh, the secretary general of the party, told the Majlis that
Azarbayjan's problems could not be considered out of the larger
context of general political developments; they would have to
be viewed against the background of past events and the attitude
of the central government. Referring to the charge of Soviet
active support of the Democratic party, he said, "Each revolutionary movement seeks to utilize and take advantage of the
circumstances of time and place as the examples of French, American and even our own constitutional revolution indicate." [77] The
essence of his argument was that because of her proximity to
socialist Russia it was impossible for Iran to preserve a feudal
regime and resist social progress. The Soviet Union, on the other
hand, merely wanted a democratic regime for its neighbor and
had repeatedly disavowed any territorial ambitions in Iran. But
by the same token it could not tolerate in Iran a regime suspicious
of its motives.

Besides the party's general support of the insurrection, the
secretary general also offered the government concrete measures
for solving the Azarbayjan problem. Most importantly, these
were the purge of the ruling class, the enforcement of pressing
domestic reforms, the restoration of democratic freedoms, the
adoption of new electoral laws for local and provincial councils,
the termination of the anti-Soviet offensive, and the amendment
of the constitution to reach a compromise with the Democratic
party.[78]

Another Tudeh deputy, Shahabe Ferdose, also addressed the

---

[77] Radmanesh, *ibid.*, Vol. I, No. 253 (February, 1946), 900.
[78] *Ibid.*, p. 901.

Majlis in support of the insurrection. He urged a policy of positive equilibrium to remove the Soviet and British misgivings
about transforming Iran into a base against either of them, and
he called for a quick and simultaneous countrywide election beginning on March 2, 1946 (the deadline for the Allied evacuation) — which he knew would give the party a larger majority
in the 15th Majlis.[79]

The Crisis in Irano–Soviet Relations

In the midst of the Azarbayjan crisis, in the autumn of 1945,
the Irano–Soviet dispute was at last referred to the UN General
Assembly and Security Council as the first case to threaten the
anti-Axis wartime alliance.[80] The Soviets were determined to
impose their own solution to the Iranian crisis, however, and
proceeded to agitate actively for a new Iranian cabinet under
Ahmad Ghavam, an avowed supporter both of Azarbayjan and
the U.S.S.R. Once the moderate center became convinced that
Hakimi's cabinet could not win Soviet confidence, a new left-
of-center coalition was formed to vote Ghavam into power in
January, 1946. The Tudeh parliamentary group, for the second
time, joined in a vote of confidence for a new cabinet, though
in doing so it raised once again the issue of the party's attitude
toward the ruling class. As in its earlier support of Bayat, the
party was compelled to back a candidate favored by the Soviets,
regardless of his social origins and the nature of the coalition
that voted him into office. This forced the party's Central Committee to justify its stand by arguing that on the eve of the
new cabinet's inauguration the party had only two alternatives —
either to support a government headed by a man who had professed good will and understanding for the Soviet Union and
Azarbayjan or to risk a military dictatorship that would have

---

[79] Shahabe Ferdose, *ibid.*, Vol. I, No. 294 (March, 1946), 1061.

[80] For details of the UN debate on this question, see chaps. 1 and 2 of
Abdolhossain Hamzavi, *Persia and the Powers: An Account of Diplomatic
Relations, 1941–1946* (London, 1947).

meant a return to extreme rightist policies. Furthermore, since
the party itself could not assume and retain power, it would
throw its support to Ghavam and thus gain time to consolidate
"victories already achieved by the people." [81]

The new prime minister at once entered direct negotiations
to secure the evacuation of the Soviet occupation zone by the
treaty deadline, March 2, 1946. The Soviet Union ignored the
deadline, even though Ghavam was himself in Moscow on
March 2, and Red Army units remained in occupation in a major part of the north, including the turbulent Azarbayjan. [82]

This failure to meet the deadline was not unexpected, for
ever since the oil crisis in the fall of 1944, it had been apparent
that the Soviet Union would use every means to gain the oil
concession. The Soviet success in determining the Iranian cabinet showed that both the Tudeh and Democratic parties could
be manipulated for its own ends, and it was now clear that the
Red Army would not be withdrawn until the Soviets got what
they wanted.

Soviet diplomacy at this point showed an evident reliance on
the revolutionary element, which made the fate of the Azarbayjan rebellion and Soviet formal relations with the central government nearly one and the same thing. So far the Soviets were
successful. On April 4, 1946, a draft agreement signed by Prime
Minister Ghavam and the new Soviet ambassador, Ivan Sadchi-
kov, pledged the Soviets to evacuate Iran by the definite deadline
of May 9, 1946, in exchange for, tentatively, an oil concession in the form of a joint Irano–Soviet company to be established in the north and a pledge that the Azarbayjan problem
would be solved peacefully, with due consideration for the
legitimate grievances of the people in the province. [83]

---

81 Eskandari, *Moyen-Orient*, No. 11, 10.

82 For a detailed report on the efforts of the Iranian delegation in Mos-
cow, see Ghassem Massudi, *Mossaferat be Moscow* [Mission to Moscow]
(Teheran, 1946). For an over-all review of the Soviet attitude and goals, see
Raymond Lacoste, *La Russie Sovietique et la question d'Orient* (Paris, 1946).

83 Persian text in *Ettelaat*, April 5, 1946; English summary in *Washington Post*, April 6, 1946.

On its face, the draft agreement satisfied the minimum goals of both nations: the Red Army evacuation on the Iranian side, and the oil concession and pledge of compromise with the Democratic party in Azarbayjan on the Soviet side. However, the main proviso, which in the long run conclusively benefited Iran, was the subjection of the Iranian commitment to approval by the yet-to-be-elected 15th Majlis. By imposing a seven-month deadline for submitting the draft agreement to the new Majlis, the Soviets were given a vested interest in a quick normalization of the situation to pave the way for general elections across the country, including the rebellious Azarbayjan. Thus, while the Soviet government grew impatient for a settlement of the Tabriz–Teheran dispute, the Iranian government gained the upper hand with the withdrawal of the Red Army by May 9, 1946, as the draft agreement stipulated.[84]

Only in the light of ensuing developments did the significance of this agreement to Irano–Soviet relations become apparent. Leftist elements in Azarbayjan and Teheran seemed overjoyed with the apparent concession to their side. The draft agreement clauses on oil exploration in the five northern provinces were favorably compared with the Anglo–Iranian oil concession in Khuzistan. The Tudeh press hailed the agreement as an example of the remarkable advantage that could accrue to Iran from a policy of "honest amity and cooperation toward Soviet Russia."[85] As for the central government, it set out immediately to cultivate Soviet trust and good will by forcibly eliminating the most outspoken anti-Soviet politicians and journalists from the scene and giving every appearance of the desire to fulfill its obligations, however tentatively they were pledged.

The spring and summer of 1946 marked the peak of the Com-

---

[84] Some Soviet sources attempted to credit the Red Army with precisely meeting the withdrawal deadline by referring to the May 9 deadline only and totally ignoring the original March 2 deadline under the tripartite agreement of January, 1942. See Ye. L. Shteynberg, *Sovestko-Iranskiye otnosheniya i Proiski Anglo-Amerikanskogo Imperializma v Irane* (Moscow, 1947), as quoted in *CAR*, Vol. IV, No. 3, p. 323.

[85] Eskandari, *Moyen-Orient*, No. 11, 10.

munist movement's influence and power. May 1 was celebrated
with huge demonstrations sponsored by the Tudeh party and
its trade union affiliates, in which nearly half a million party
members, trade unionists, and sympathizers participated. The
Tudeh party and the trade unions were by now clearly national
organizations, having achieved great success in organizing the
oil workers in Khuzistan. In a series of token strikes in late 1945
these workers had wrested impressive concessions from the
Anglo–Iranian Oil Company.[86]

As a result of delicate negotiations, conducted with the approval of the Soviet Union, a modus vivendi was reached between the Tabriz revolutionary regime and the central government in the form of a fifteen-point agreement signed June 13,
1946. Under the agreement, the central government sought to
satisfy the demand of the Tabriz regime within the framework
of the constitution. The Azarbayjan Majlis was recognized as the
provincial assembly, sanctioned by the Iranian constitution but
never put into practice because of its probable adverse effect on
the heavily centralized government. The minister of interior
in the Tabriz cabinet assumed the role of governor general, and
a ratio of 3 to 1 in favor of the local regime was accepted as the
basis of revenue allocation. A modified version of bilinguality
was adopted, providing for Azari–Turkish to be taught in the
primary and also, along with Persian, in the secondary and higher
schools; Azari–Turkish was also to be used on the official level.

The central government also accepted the revolutionary regime's land-distribution program, but Article 8 of the agreement
provided for compensation to private owners through a joint
commission representing the central government and the provincial assembly. A new electoral law based on universal suffrage was also promised.[87]

---

[86] In these demonstrations the workers demanded labor laws and a pay
raise, while the peasants advanced the slogan of "land to the peasants." On
some occasions even the slogan "People to Power" was used. *Ibid.*

[87] An English summary of this agreement appears in the *New York Times*,
June 15, 1946; a fuller Persian text is in Pesyan, *Marg Bud Bazkasht Ham
Bud*, pp. 150–152.

The Coalition Cabinet

On August 1, for the first time, a coalition cabinet was formed in Teheran with the participation of three Tudeh party members, one from the liberal-nationalist Iran party, and one representing the independent Left.[88] This unexpected "opening to the left" initiated by Prime Minister Ghavam took the Tudeh party by surprise. On June 29 the prime minister had taken a measure that was expected to antagonize the party, driving it into open opposition. This was the formation of a new party, the Iranian Democratic party, to contest the general elections which the Soviets and their supporters were eagerly anticipating. Using the vast resources of the government and the services of some former Tudeh organizers and agitators, the new party soon assumed gigantic proportions, embracing a cross-section of every class, from labor to the bourgeoisie and the aristocracy. This was the first serious challenge to the Communist movement's exclusive claim on the skillful use of the techniques of mass organization and mobilization.[89]

Although the party was doomed to a short life, it was, for a year at least, a thorn in the side of both the Tudeh and the Democratic parties in Azarbayjan. Despite the obvious challenge in the name of the new party, the Tudeh and Democratic parties welcomed this new move, and by joining the coalition cabinet some weeks later, affirmed their unconditional support for the prime minister's party.

Indeed, the offer of participation in the government was so tempting to the Tudeh party that no serious deliberations were made before its acceptance. Years later, the party's central committee attempted to justify its hasty decision. It was an opportunity, it said, not only to safeguard the advantages already gained for the movement in Iran but also to prevent a reversal

---

[88] The Tudeh ministers were Iraj Eskandari, national economy; Dr. Freydoun Keshavarz, education; and Dr. Mohammad Yazdi, health. *Ettelaat*, Aug. 1, 1946.

[89] A summary of the party program appeared in *Journal de Teheran*, July 1, 1946.

of governmental foreign policies; furthermore, the party could thus strengthen the cabinet's leftist trend and neutralize the Court's pressure on the prime minister. The central committee also claimed that this participation had not been unconditional and had been made contingent on the acceptance of a democratic program of agrarian reform, the final solution of the Azarbayjan question, and free elections.[90]

However the party may have rationalized its decision to join the coalition cabinet, it considerably jeopardized its position by departing from the popular front concept. In the first place, the alliance of four parties — the Democratic party in Azarbayjan, the Iranian Democratic party, the Tudeh party, and the Iran party, on which the coalition cabinet was at least theoretically based — did not permit the Tudeh party a vanguard position. The government party, mostly representing the landed aristocracy and the upper bourgeoisie, hardly qualified as a liberal or democratic party with which an alliance could be formed on the model of the mid-1930 European popular front. On the contrary, it strongly aspired to assist the aging prime minister in ridding the country of Soviet influence.

Not least in importance was the fact that in joining the coalition government the Tudeh party sharpened the already noticeable split in its own rank and file. It was the familiar lineup, the radical Left versus the moderate leadership. The left wing of the intelligentsia condemned the participation on ideological and tactical grounds and warned that such a move would nullify the party's revolutionary aspect. There were many, also, who believed that by joining the coalition the party confirmed the impression of being an instrument of Soviet diplomacy prepared to abandon its long-term ideological objectives in favor of the U.S.S.R.'s immediate gains.

Prime Minister Ghavam apparently believed that in inviting the Tudeh party to join the cabinet he would be effectively blocking its customary role as opposition leader, at which it

---

[90] Eskandari, *Moyen-Orient*, No. 11, 10.

had been only too successful. If, at the same time, this partial identification with the ruling class helped to undermine the party's image as champion of the oppressed, so much the better. It was also evident, of course, that in forming a cabinet that represented all organized parties of the Left and Center, the new Iranian Democratic party acquired the status of a genuine party.

There was one further, very sound reason for inviting the cooperation of the Tudeh party: to use its hold on the trade unions as a means of controlling the growing labor unrest that was threatening the government's preoccupation with Irano–Soviet relations. That the Tudeh cooperation could be of utmost importance was demonstrated in the course of a general strike in Khuzistan on July 14, 1946.

The ostensible reason for the strike was to force the Anglo–Iranian Oil Company to fulfill a promise of wage increases and paid holidays, but the avowed objective was to frustrate a company "plot" to destroy the Tudeh-backed unions.[91] In the course of the strike, heavy casualties were inflicted on both sides, and Iran found itself in a major diplomatic crisis. Great Britain dispatched naval reinforcements to the vicinity of Abadan and threatened intervention in case of danger to British lives and property. On the initiative of Prime Minister Ghavam, Dr. Radmanesh, the Tudeh party's general secretary, and Reza Rusta, the first secretary of the United Council of Trade Unions, were dispatched to Abadan, where they very soon persuaded the workers to call off the strike even though their demands had not been met. With the formation of the coalition cabinet a week later, the party undertook not to exploit labor unrest any further, a pledge which was kept through the summer and which fulfilled

---

[91] The Tudeh press claimed a 100 percent response to the strike, which covered not only the working people but the entire population of the oil town (*Rahbar*, July 15, 1946). Anglo–Iranian Oil Company sources admitted that 95 percent of the industry's working population belonged to the Tudeh union. See U.S. Congress, *Strategy and Tactics of World Communism.*

at least one of the prime minister's expectations in inviting the party to join the government.

Reference was made earlier to some of the reasons prompting the party to join the coalition cabinet. The party's expectation from the pending parliamentary election, which had to be completed by November, 1946, should also be mentioned. So far as one can tell from numerous indications of its numerical strength — the May Day turnout, the number of strikers on July 14, and the crowds at the Constitution Day celebration on August 4 — plus the fact that the Democratic party was in full control of Azarbayjan, the Communist movement was rightly hopeful of securing the majority of seats in the 15th Majlis. Therefore, while the Tudeh party was increasingly losing its revolutionary character and thereby alienating the radical Left among the intelligentsia, it was offering the rank and file the prospect of seizing power through nonrevolutionary methods. This prospect by itself had a great psychological impact, as indicated by the large response to party-sponsored public demonstrations.[92]

In anticipation of the election, Communist leaders were at this time enthusiastically engaged in negotiations to form an electoral coalition of parties of the Left and the Center, which was to include not only the three Communist parties — the Azarbayjan Democratic party, the Kurdish Kumeleh party, and the Tudeh party — but also the Iran party and the prime minister's Iranian Democratic party. The plan was to offer a single ticket in all electoral districts and to divide the parliamentary seats by a proportional system. Events conspired, however, to put an end to this plan, or any plan for a left-of-center government, and to topple the coalition cabinet then in office.

---

[92] The best available estimate puts the numerical strength of the Tudeh party and its sympathizers at 50,000 in the capital and an almost equivalent number in the rest of the country, not including Azarbayjan, where the Democratic party was the only Communist organization. Judged by participation in the First and Second Party Congresses, not more than 25,000 of these were card-carrying members eligible to participate in the election of representatives to the supreme party organ. See U.S. Congress, House Committee on Foreign Affairs (Subcommittee No. 5), *Communism in the Near East*, 80th Cong., 1st Sess. 1948.

The Collapse of the Insurrection

The cause of the breakdown was a tribal revolt in the southern province of Fars which broke out on September 24, 1946, when a coalition of major tribes of the area, notably the Ghashghai and Bakhtyari, rose in arms against the central government, demanding autonomy similar to that granted Azarbayjan and the expulsion of the Tudeh representatives from the government. The prime minister skillfully used this new crisis to counteract pressure from the Left. Indeed, his reaction to the tribal uprising and the countermoves which were taken by slow deliberation cast some doubt on whether the revolt was an entirely spontaneous affair.[93]

Whatever the degree of the central government's complicity in this episode, the prime minister at once exploited it in favor of a return to precoalition policies. Fully aware of Soviet interest in the forthcoming general elections, he confidently assumed that a quick move to restore normalcy would not evoke serious Soviet objection. By the same token, he anticipated no radical Soviet opposition to ending the coalition government as a measure for restoring the order necessary for holding elections. His resignation on October 17 forced the ouster of the Tudeh members from the cabinet and the installation of another cabinet without the parties of the Left. The new cabinet appeared to be a caretaker government, and though it excluded right wing representatives, it was made up primarily of the Center's independent and nationalist elements.

This was a serious blow to the Tudeh party, which in a meeting of its Central Committee on October 16 tried to save face by declaring that the conditions prompting the party to join the coalition government had ceased to exist and therefore the Central Committee had instructed its representatives to resign.[94]

---

[93] Tudeh sources cite the fact that leaders of the Ghashghai tribe were among the first to join the prime minister's party as strong indication of Ghavam's complicity in the uprising. See Eskandari, *Moyen-Orient*, No. 11, 10.

[94] *Rahbar*, Oct. 18, 1946.

Eskandari, who held the portfolio of national economy in the short-lived coalition government, reflected the party's disappointment. He wrote that if the party and other democratic organizations had succeeded in imposing a general election on the prime minister at the beginning of 1946, this setback would have been avoided; but by wishfully thinking that Ghavam would honor his commitment under the Iranian–Soviet draft agreement and soon hold elections, and by overestimating the Shah–Ghavam feud, the democratic movement lost a precious opportunity.[95]

The bitterness of this setback grew, as the government followed up the dissolution of the coalition cabinet by a drastic reversal of policy toward the Communist movement, including an unwillingness to tolerate labor agitation as an instrument of pressure on the government. A strike by a Tudeh-sponsored union on November 12 was severely put down, and it provided an excuse for the wholesale arrest of hundreds of trade union and party members across the country. A deliberate policy of copying the Communist methods for mobilizing labor, including the formation of a new government-sponsored union, yielded good results. Not only was it successful in splitting the labor movement's rank and file, but it also served to wrest from the Tudeh party the exclusive claim of championing the workers. This was followed by the formation of a ministry of labor and the passage of a labor code so that the government for the first time could show the workers that it was on their side.[96]

A second, and far more radical, reversal of policy took the form of careful preparation of a formula sanctioning Azarbayjan's military recovery. Confident that Soviet vested interest in an early convening of the new Majlis would prevent Moscow's serious objection to any move in that direction, the prime minister resolved to make the presence of Iranian army units in Azarbayjan province a prerequisite for holding elections. To

---

[95] Eskandari, *Moyen-Orient*, No. 17 (June, 1950), 8.
[96] International Labor Office, *Labor Conditions in the Oil Industry in Iran* (Geneva, 1950), pp. 46–53.

allay Soviet misgivings that the new Majlis might take a hostile attitude toward the April agreement, he endeavored to give every appearance of intending to take an active part in the elections in all constituencies and to win a majority for his party, which would fully support his commitments.

In early December, 1946, preparations were completed for a march into Azarbayjan in accordance with the cabinet decree for "supervising an orderly election." Frantic efforts of Soviet diplomatic representatives to dissuade the government from this move, including an eleventh-hour call on the Shah by Ambassador Sadchikev, failed to forestall the move. Except for token resistance at the fringe of the province, around Miyaneh, the revolutionary regime failed to put up the fight its propaganda machinery had so loudly pledged.[97]

On December 12, a year to the day after the inauguration of the revolutionary regime, the Iranian army entered Tabriz, and within a few days insurrection in Azarbayjan and Kurdistan had ended. The top leaders, including Pishevari and his close lieutenants, managed to cross the Aras River into Soviet Azarbayjan, but most members of the lower echelon were captured. Some of the active leaders, including the rebellious officers of the central army, paid with their lives for the insurrection. Others died in the riots and clashes between royalist tribes and pro-Communist elements between December 9 and 12.[98]

The Communists have advanced a number of reasons for this remarkable collapse of the Democratic party's revolutionary regime in Azarbayjan. On December 10, 1946, the Democratic

---

[97] For details, see Robert Rostow, "The Battle of Azarbayjan, 1946," *Middle East Journal*, Vol. IX (Winter, 1956).

[98] There are no reliable statistics on casualties, but Eskandari mentions the execution of the officers who had defected from the Iranian army and of Y. Azima, a member of the Azarbayjan cabinet, who "with his twenty-six comrades-in-arms appeared before the firing squad singing the 'Internationale'" (Eskandari, "Histoire de Parti Toudeh," *Moyen-Orient*, No. 17, 8). A non-Tudeh source puts the total casualties of the one-year rebellion at 1,500 dead and wounded (Pesyan, *op. cit.*, p. 153). Another source says there were 800 Communist casualties in riots before the troops arrived (*Strategy and Tactics of World Communism*).

party's Central Committee meeting in Tabriz resolved that
armed struggle in Azarbayjan would have provoked direct
Anglo–American intervention and thereby endangered international peace on the immediate frontiers of the Soviet Union.
The committee could see only two alternatives: "(*a*) Resistance
to the government's aggression and risk of foreign intervention,
with the logical corollary of dismemberment of the frontier provinces in favor of Anglo–American interests, as well as an eventual
clash between them and the Soviet Union; and (*b*) a temporary
retreat, and eventual return when the time would be more favorable."[99] When the latter alternative prevailed, the Provincial
Assembly met in the presence of the party leaders in an extraordinary session on December 12 and resolved to issue a cease-
fire order.

The Tudeh leadership, rightly considering this a catastrophe
for the entire Communist movement, reasoned that this decision
was based on "revolutionary logic, extremely rigorous and ema-
nating from an exact analysis of the international situation and
Iran's particular conditions in that phase of the struggle." The
surrender of the revolutionary regime had indeed, it said, fore-
stalled Iran's disintegration, certain to result from civil war. By
this logic, the Communists who had openly launched a move for
self-determination of the Azarbayjani minority now demanded
credit for having served the opposite objective.[100]

Even the text of the Democratic party declaration announcing
the decision to surrender was something of an attempt to turn
defeat into victory. It read in part:

The Democratic party of Azarbayjan has always been a partisan of
sovereignty and independence of Iran. Before the entire world we
have proclaimed that Azarbayjan must remain an integral part of
Iran. Now a group of traitors and reactionaries have attempted to
falsify the real sense of the Azarbayjan movement, while seeking the
realization of their own designs. To prevent the victory of the enemy

---

[99] Eskandari, *Moyen-Orient*, No. 17, 8.
[100] *Ibid.*

of our people, we agreed that government troops might arrive to control the elections.[101]

Nor was this all. The objective condition surrounding the revolutionary experience was also blamed, now that the undertaking had failed. In the opinion of the Democratic party's Central Committee, the necessary condition for successful revolution had not materialized. The peasantry's struggle was disorganized and incohesive, making impossible the alliance with the working class which was vital to successful revolution. Labor, too, despite its rallying in large numbers to the Tudeh party and the trade union movement, possessed as yet neither the organizational cohesion nor the political and ideological strength to enable it to fulfill its vanguard position in the revolutionary movement. Therefore, reasoned the party, the decision to abandon armed resistance did not stem from weakness and a defeatist mentality: "It was singularly motivated by a realistic consideration of the political situation and based on the exact analysis of historic conditions and a deep corresponding sense of true internationalism."[102]

In truth, the party's account of the collapse of insurrection in Azarbayjan was a clear admission that the revolution had been sacrificed to broader Soviet interests. This was hardly a novelty for Iranian Communists, who had been similarly treated in the Gilan episode of 1920–1921. In that affair, the Persian Communist party had used almost identical language to rationalize the collapse of what was the first serious communization attempt in an isolated portion of the country.[103] "Unfavorable objective conditions" were to blame. But in withdrawing the Red Army, the Soviets had ensured the end of the Azarbayjan revolutionary regime, a victim to Soviet diplomacy in the name of the "true spirit of internationalism."

There were, of course, certain unfavorable objective condi-

---

[101] *Azarbayjan*, Dec. 12, 1946.
[102] Eskandari, *Moyen-Orient*, No. 17, 8.
[103] *Ibid.*, p. 9.

tions: the peasants were not, in fact, well mobilized, and the working class was all too evidently not class-conscious and cohesive enough to lead a mass revolution.[104] But too strong an emphasis on the unfavorable objective conditions tends to ignore major subjective factors, such as the Soviets' ultimate abandonment of the movement, despite its earlier policy of linking its fate to normalizing relations with Iran. To many sympathizers, this abandonment cast serious doubts on the alleged solidarity and homogeneity of international communism. Indeed, the Soviet passivity in the decisive showdown with the Iranian government was so marked that some observers wondered whether Moscow had not secretly written off the Tabriz regime.[105]

It has been conjectured that the Soviet failure to back the insurrection may have stemmed from apprehension over the possible impact of an autonomous regime on its immediate frontiers. In the absence of direct Soviet control through its occupation army, it was impossible to determine the future attitudes of the Tabriz regime toward the rest of the Azarbayjani minority residing in the Soviet republic.[106]

There may be some truth in this conjecture, but in the final analysis there seems no doubt that it was primarily a combination of the central government's skillful diplomatic maneuvers and the pressure of the Western powers through UN channels that brought about the ultimate Soviet failure. If these measures had not succeeded in securing the withdrawal of the Red Army, thereby removing the main prop of the insurrection, Azarbayjan would very likely have become the first victim of the postwar Soviet satellization process.

As for the domestic causes of the failure, mention has been made of a lack of a large popular following toward the end of the insurrection. There are, however, strong indications that its

---

104 Significantly, some Soviet sources have claimed that the regime was not sufficiently revolutionary, for the peasantry yearned for more radical measures like the outright land confiscation and distribution among the peasantry. Ivanov, *Ocherk istorii Irana.*

105 *New York Times,* Dec. 17, 1946.

106 Mme Carrere d'Encausse, "Le Parti Toudeh."

land-distribution program, moderate by Socialist–Communist standards, was well supported at first.[107]

Communist sources credit the program with distribution of more than a quarter of a million hectares formerly belonging to the state or to the "reactionary" landlords. Under this measure, more than 200,000 peasants became small holders and began to receive a larger share of the crop under a complicated land-reform regulation adopted by the regime in April, 1946.[108] The accompanying measures for marketing and taxation have been mentioned as sources of the peasants' growing dissatisfaction, to the extent that, when the regime fell, they greeted the entering Iranian army with considerable enthusiasm.[109]

The peasantry's dissatisfaction could very well have stemmed from two diametrically opposed factors. The stiff marketing and production regulations would tend to alienate the newly propertied peasantry, while at the same time the moderate nature of the reform would serve to antagonize peasants not benefiting from land distribution. Communist sources profess that the entire peasant movement had assumed such proportions that a partial solution could not satisfy these grievances. One recent writer has said: "They aimed at a radical change in agrarian relations, at the complete liquidation of the landowner's ownership of water and land, and at the division of the land among the peasants. In many areas the peasants, contrary to the decisions of the government, openly ceased to pay the landlord's share of the crop. In some areas they proceeded to divide up lands not covered by the land reform law." [110]

The failure of the revolutionary regime to adopt more radical policies in domestic fields was clearly due to tactical considerations necessitated by the broad alliance on which the regime was based. Furthermore, as negotiations with the central gov-

---

[107] *New York Times*, Dec. 17, 1946.

[108] Ivanov, *op. cit.*, pp. 371–373.

[109] Western newsmen who arrived in Tabriz twenty-four hours before the central government's army were unanimous in their reporting of the public's welcome of the regime's collapse. *New York Times*, Dec. 17, 1946.

[110] Ivanov, *op. cit.*

ernment continued for a peaceful solution to the insurrection, it became necessary for the regime to dilute certain of its main revolutionary goals which could not be accepted by the central government without drastic changes in the constitutional system. The problem of land distribution alone was a major stumbling block in the Teheran–Tabriz negotiations, and they were not a part of the June 13, 1946, agreement.

As for other domestic measures and their impact on the popular hold of the regime, it should be noted that the revolutionary government did not last long enough to provide a concrete test for success in implementing its program. Such measures as the introduction of an eight-hour working day, labor- and social-insurance legislation, establishment of a national university and a local radio station, and the inauguration of a program of public works were still in the preliminary stage when the regime collapsed.[111] In short, there is little evidence that the revolutionary regime's over-all progressive program in the domestic field contributed to its collapse — although it is conceivable that, apart from the landed aristocracy, some segments of the clergy did not approve of such startling domestic reforms as the extension of suffrage to women.

In any event, the military recovery of Azarbayjan started a new development in the Communist movement. The demise of the Azarbayjan Democratic party left the Tudeh party as the movement's sole political organization. The collapse of this second Communist revolutionary experience produced a severe ideological crisis and organizational disintegration for the Tudeh party which has continued to this day to influence the prospects of communism in Iran.

---

[111] For a non-Communist version of these measures, see Lenczowski, "The Communist Movement in Iran." Ivanov, *op. cit.*, is typical of the Communist versions.

4

THE DECLINE
OF COMMUNISM
IN THE POSTWAR ERA

The collapse of the Iranian Communist movement's second revolutionary experience had a far greater impact on its future prospects than the mere organizational disintegration of the Tudeh party. It raised fundamental ideological issues which had been sidestepped under the pressure of fast-moving events since the party's formation in October, 1941, and it brought into the open the intraparty conflict successfully shelved since the First Congress in August, 1944. Finally, it focused on the nature and content of the movement following the apparent abandonment of its most revolutionary expression by international communism.

This period was, in many ways, different from the previous one, and the existing conditions were far less favorable. For one thing, the Red Army had been withdrawn, leaving Soviet diplomacy without its most effective tool for protecting and facilitating attempted armed insurrection. Conversely, however, the Red Army's withdrawal deprived the Communists' opponents of their most powerful propaganda weapon. The Tudeh party could no longer be dismissed as merely the tool of the Soviets operating under Red Army protection. In fact, the party now assumed a more indigenous character than before. It was now largely on its own and had to continue its struggle against heavy odds without direct outside support.

A second novel element in this period was the government's challenge of the parties of the Left. Prime Minister Ghavam's Iranian Democratic party very quickly assumed the outward characteristics of a mass party on a dimension unprecedented in Iran since the end of the war, and much of its success was due to techniques heretofore the more or less exclusive property of the Tudeh party. Ghavam's party was determined to win a majority in the 15th Majlis, and it proposed to do so by employing the same techniques the Tudeh party had used in the election to the 14th Majlis three years earlier.

A third element, the internal ideological crisis, was the most significant threat to the movement since the collapse of the Gilan republic. This crisis owed its immediate cause to the failure of the Azarbayjan insurrection. The party itself attributed the shock of this failure to a dangerous optimism in the rank and file and among the intellectuals created as a result of past impressive successes. One party leader, Eskandari, has written of this period: "A widespread illusion had haunted the masses of the party as to an imminent victory of revolution in the country. Many were among the cadres and militants of the party who saw this illusion as a reality. This exaggerated optimism had even penetrated the leading elements and organs of the party and trade unions, causing them to neglect alerting the masses against this dangerous state of mind." [1]

The Tudeh Party in Crisis

In the two weeks following the fall of Tabriz, the internal crisis in the Tudeh party became so acute that critics openly demanded the resignation of the Central Committee and its substitution by a seven-man provisional Executive Committee to

[1] Iraj Eskandari, "Histoire de Parti Toudeh," *Moyen-Orient*, No. 5 (November, 1949), 8.

be elected by them. The threat of a mass defection and the clamor for an open discussion of the leadership's past performance finally forced the Central Committee to face the challenge. The normal method of dealing with the crisis would have been to hold the Second Congress, which, under the party statute, was already more than a year overdue. But for reasons that will be examined later, the Central Committee refused to call the party's supreme body into session. Instead, in a secret meeting on December 20, 1946, the Central Committee's entire membership studied the situation and, realizing that at least a segment of its membership could not continue its legal political activity, came to the following decisions: to reject the demand for the resignation of the Central Committee and nomination of the persons suggested by the critics; to delegate its powers to a temporary seven-man executive committee composed of three members of the Central Committee, three of the Control Commission, and one member of the Provincial Committee in Teheran; and to convene a conference of the party activists to explain these changes.[2]

On December 25 the Central Committee's enlarged plenum elected the Provisional Executive Committee (PEC) and in the same week party activists met to hear the report on the decision of the plenum. The fundamental tasks facing the PEC were set forth: reorganizing the party and adapting it to the new conditions of struggle, regrouping the scattered forces, formulating defensive tactics in the face of police action, preparing cadres for work in clandestine organizations while utilizing all legal means, and finally, continuing to struggle against fractionism and ideological deviations.[3] It must be noted that the party was not formally outlawed, because the government did not wish to force it underground at a time when its prestige and appeal were already waning.

---

[2] *Manifeste Hezbe Tudeh* [Tudeh Party Manifesto], Dec. 24, 1946; hereafter cited as *Manifesto*.

[3] *Nashriyehe Heyate Ejraiyehe Movaghate Hezbe Tudehe Iran* [The Publication of the PEC of the Tudeh Party of Iran] (Teheran, December, 1946), pp. 1–2; hereafter cited as *Nashriyeh*.

At this first meeting the PEC elected Dr. Reza Radmanesh as secretary general, hoping to appease party critics by choosing a man who had not been a member of the coalition cabinet and who was not identified with the policies of the previous phase. The same consideration led to the suspension of the old daily newspaper *Rahbar* (Leader), which had been edited by Eskandari, a member of the coalition cabinet and the three-man secretariat of the party. The new daily *Mardom* (People) was to be edited by Dr. Radmanesh.

In January, 1947, the PEC issued a manifesto declaring a general boycott of the forthcoming election. Such an action was justified, it said, because of the "severe persecution of parties and candidates of the Left, which denied the people, and especially the workers, the chance of exercising a free choice."[4] The committee argued that even nominal participation by the Tudeh party would be tantamount to recognizing the legality of a fraudulent election to the 15th Majlis. The manifesto also corrected some political and ideological errors reflected in the earlier statement put out under the influence of party critics immediately after the collapse of the Azarbayjan insurrection. That statement had severely criticized the party and had found the Central Committee to blame for erroneous tactics employed in the insurrection.[5]

Six months after the transfer of executive responsibility to the PEC, the party thought that it was well on the road to recovery. "The task of streamlining the party and restoring its discipline was squarely faced," Eskandari has written; "an energetic purge was conducted; and gradually our network of cadres reappeared in full force."[6] Neither this optimistic appraisal nor the measures taken to cope with the crisis were accepted by the critics as realistic and adequate. The critics, some of whom were represented on the Control Commission by Khalil Maleki, regarded the new organizational setup as merely an attempt to silence

---

[4] *Manifesto*, p. 3.
[5] Military Governorship of Teheran, *Seyre Komonism dar Iran* [The Evolution of Communism in Iran] (Teheran, 1958), p. 161.
[6] Eskandari, *Moyen-Orient*, No. 5, 12.

them without really considering the causes of their grievances. Two of the three members of the Control Commission who now sat on the Provisional Executive Committee, they complained, were not active participants, and the third member was a former cabinet minister of the coalition government known for his consistent support of the original Central Committee.[7] The critics also complained that the party was defensive of its past policies and recent errors. The PEC answered this with the argument that, since the moral and social idiosyncrasies of Iranian society were reflected in the party, a purge of those not strictly following the party line would reduce the party to a small group of purist faithfuls. By encompassing the broad masses, the PEC said, the party inevitably had embraced the major weakness which characterized the vast layers of society.[8]

The critics saw the issue clearly as one of preserving the party's idological integrity as well as its organizational characteristics, both of which had suffered as the movement grew larger. To these critics, the same who in the First Congress had warned against the impact of popularization of the party on its ideological purity, the PEC's defense was obviously unacceptable. They contended that one reason for the failure of the movement was the unplanned and opportunistic growth of its organization. Certainly the movement was expected to broaden its basis as the years went by, but, they argued, the party should have been more selective in its membership and should have conducted at least a limited purge of its governing bodies and rank-and-file membership long before it reached its ascendancy. More specifically, the Central Committee was charged with preventing the Control Commission from carrying out the purge pledged in the First Congress. Had this been done, the party would not have found itself burdened with the social and moral defects the executive board now attributed to society as a whole.[9] The

---

[7] Khalil Maleki, *Do Ravesh baraye Yek Hadaf* (Teheran, 1946), p. 4.

[8] *Manifesto.*

[9] Typical of this line of criticism are the two pamphlets issued by the critics in the wake of the Azarbayjan fiasco, *Do Ravesh* and *Hezbe Tudeh Bar Sare Do Rahi* [The Tudeh Party at the Crossroads] (Teheran, 1947).

party critics apparently agreed on this basic issue, though they differed widely on the specific organizational and ideological reforms.

The party's former leadership, which had largely retained its hold in the new temporary arrangement, denounced the reformist group as an antiparty faction and accused it of regarding the present difficulty as primarily a leadership crisis. It singled out the two publications issued by prominent members of the reformist group, claiming that they were self-seeking intellectuals who after the Azarbayjan episode favored a completely new leadership and later demanded a somewhat vanguard position for their group.[10]

In fact, however, the critics were not confined to this faction, for at this stage several strands of criticism were present among the reformists and other dissident party members.

The Leftist Faction

The first group of critics were those who supported the views of the authors of the mentioned publications and who, in advocating violence and other revolutionary methods, in effect represented leftist tendencies among party intellectuals. A leader of the faction was Dr. A. Eprim, whose pamphlet *Che Bayad Kard* (What Is to Be Done?), published in December, 1946, stated very clearly the main objections of the faction. Their criticism of the party definitely went beyond the confines of a "leadership crisis."

They thought the party's biggest mistake was the emphasis on numerical strength and the resulting decline in quality of membership. Party leaders, they said, showed appalling ignorance of the vital difference between the economic struggle of the trade union movement and the political struggle of the leftist parties; the former needed no qualification other than having a working class occupation, whereas the latter called for an advanced degree of political consciousness and organizational abil-

---

[10] *Nashriyeh*, p. 15.

ity. They further criticized what they said was the reliance of some party leaders on the course of international events to protect the party from severe crises rather than depending on its own strength as an indigenous political force.[11]

Reviewing past performances, these critics acknowledged that the first phase of the movement, generally characterized by public education, propaganda, and agitation, had been fairly successful. The second phase had required a complete realignment of leftist elements and careful preparation to seize power in the third phase; and it was in the second phase, according to these critics, that the party had allowed itself to become weakened. The fundamental defects were the lack of a positive working plan and a weak organization, the leaders of which seemed resigned to the present course of events, hoping it might one day lead to their assumption of power either by the electoral process or through a national uprising.[12]

The organizational structure, these critics said, was too heterogeneous to be effective, and it gave the party the character of a front of democratic and liberal elements without the existence of another party to its left. The result was twofold: the component parts could not achieve a more cohesive organization, and the existing organization could not actively seek power because it lacked the necessary organizational solidarity to lead the front to victory.

To solve the dual problem of organization and action plan, these critics suggested that most militant members must be separated from the main body and organized into a disciplined core capable of playing the vanguard role. To safeguard the party, there must be periodic drastic purges to root out unsavory and opportunistic elements. Further, the party must do all it can to fight the prevalent but false belief that the party was subordinate to the Soviet Union and to prove that the movement was indigenous and nationalist. Along with this, it must work for closer ties with progressive parties and trade unions in cap-

---

[11] Dr. A. Eprim, *Che Bayad Kard* [What Is to Be Done?] (Teheran, 1946).
[12] *Ibid.*, p. 5.

italist countries, so as to underline its independence of the U.S.S.R.[13]

According to these critics, the party's two main shortcomings — the lack of a vigorous political theory and the lack of a compact organization — were closely related. A militant, revolutionary party, they contended, should have definite and practical long- and short-range programs to meet every contingency. It should always be on the offensive, creating and initiating events rather than reacting and adapting to them, an achievement impossible without a scientific and comprehensive political philosophy. Such a philosophy would have as its essence the recognition of the rich ruling class as the principal defender of the status quo, which could not be radically altered in favor of social justice and economic progress without the formation of a regime representing the masses of the oppressed people.[14] It would be understood as an element of party ideology that the ruling class would not permit the party to seize power without a struggle. Even if the party could win in elections, the ruling class would resort to force and eliminate political democracy in the name of maintaining peace and order. Therefore, to cope with such a contingency, the party should be prepared to use violence when needed. To assure success, reliable cadres and the support of the progressive forces of the country were needed.

Elaborating on their plan for organizational realignment, the intellectual left wing proposed that the contemplated popular front, called either the "Progressive" or "Democratic" front, should encompass all the present party members and organs as well as other affiliated progressive elements; it should continue to advocate the present Tudeh party program, which embraced the broad goals of social justice and public welfare. But, they said, the vanguard party to be established within this front and called the "Socialist Party of the Democratic Front" should maintain an independent identity and use maximum care in its recruitment process.

The tasks of this vanguard, elitist force should be to carry

---

13 *Ibid.*, pp. 9–10.
14 *Ibid.*, p. 12.

out the policies adopted by its Central Committee, to occupy most and even all sensitive positions in the popular front, and to seize and retain the leadership of all progressive forces by direct or indirect, secret or open, methods. In short, the vanguard should be the brain of the leftist forces and the source of their power. Another vital task of the vanguard should be to purge the party of dubious members, keeping constant watch against the dilution of the popular front by opportunists.

This elaborate plan was believed to be capable of being carried out clandestinely in case of government persecution. "The vanguard will go underground if persecuted; it will regroup and reemerge again and will continue to do so until power is seized and a government based on the masses and their common interests is formed."[15]

Finally, the leftist critics recommended that, concurrent with the formation of the vanguard, the illiterate and religiously fanatic masses, whose support was indispensable for seizure of power, should be mobilized. The condition of society was not viewed as a serious obstacle to the application of these reforms, for the existing working class and intelligentsia were regarded as sufficiently large, politically conscious, and responsive. Likewise, the huge class of "oppressed and exploited" peasantry, despite ignorance and illiteracy, was believed ripe for systematic political education.

These recommendations were rejected by the "old guard" as unacceptable and deviating from the correct concept of a mass party. Their proponents were called elitist and "vanguardist" and had to defect from the party shortly after the publication of the first PEC communique, which, as noted earlier, accused the critics of having created a leadership crisis to pursue personal gain.

The Moderate Faction

The second and numerically largest group of critics was led by Khalil Maleki, a former Control Commission member who

---

[15] *Ibid.,* p. 18.

organized the Tudeh Socialist League of Iran and publicized its criticism of the party leadership and past performance in a lengthy essay entitled *Do Ravesh bavaye Yek Hadaf* (Two Approaches to the Same Goal). This publication was in effect a rebuttal to the PEC communique, which had dismissed the entire reformist group as Dr. Eprim's followers.

Maleki's essay took the former leadership to task for failure to create cadres of the party's best elements and to offer them participation in the leadership apparatus, although this failure had more or less been acknowledged even before the collapse of the Azarbayjan insurrection.[16] There were now several major strands of thought in the party in the wake of the Azarbayjan defeat: The leftist opportunists, who were taken by surprise by the party defeat and left the party's leading organs in dismay; the rightist opportunists, who, like the Tudeh members in the coalition cabinet, had lost their status within the ruling class and decided to rely more on party organization; the genuine reformists, who strove for a regrouping of the rank and file at the time when morale was at its lowest; and finally, the wavering elements who at first advocated an immediate split and then joined the old guard with the formation of the temporary executive board.[17]

Maleki's faction claimed to represent the party's constructive critics. Denying that they advocated a total purge of the former leadership, they demanded the immediate convening of a Second Party Congress, at which policy-making machinery could be overhauled from within, without risking open dissension in the rank and file. Party members, they declared, had been denied their democratic right to a congress for more than three years, and in refusing to convene a congress the old guard showed how much they feared open criticism as a threat to their hold on the party organization. They also questioned the legality of the PEC,

---

[16] A party document has referred to unimaginative and incompetent members who, "aided by a few corrupt and adventurist persons, blocked the popular demands for serious reforms." *Nashriyeh*, p. 15.

[17] *Do Ravesh*, p. 73.

which had assumed control with the implied promise of convening a Second Congress within three months and electing a permanent executive board. Their negligence in this matter, in addition to the fact that there had been only one congress in more than five years, was proof, they said, that the leadership had ignored the membership's democratic rights. They accused the PEC of deliberately postponing the calling of a new congress lest the reformists influence its decisions: the leadership was merely marking time, awaiting the voluntary defection or a large-scale purge as a means of removing its most serious critics. (This last charge was substantiated by later events.) As for the PCP's appeal to party discipline and to respect for the principle of centralization of authority, the faction argued that centralization was an accepted party principle only when it was combined with the democratic principle of the popular election of its governing organs from the bottom to the top.[18]

The left wing's criticism of overreliance on international developments was also voiced by the moderate faction. It particularly objected to the party's having used "international obligations" as a reason for supporting Ghavam's government. The old guard was "simply trusting the course of international power politics to determine Iran's destiny without making use of the tremendous democratic forces of the Tudeh masses." This was a subtle way of raising the problem of subordination to Soviet diplomacy, which the faction did not wish to evoke publicly, since it hoped to continue its political existence within the broader context of the socialist Left.

Maleki's faction presented its ultimate decision to defect as a carefully considered and constructive measure. Before doing so, it had looked to two sources for party reform: (1) the "wavering" elements of the leadership who had advocated drastic reforms, and (2) the elected bodies (such as the provincial conferences and party congresses), through which public opinion could force reform on the leadership. Their hopes had not been fulfilled. The

---

[18] *Ibid.*, p. 16.

three wings of the leadership had joined their less serious critics to oppose the reformists, who had a clear majority in the Teheran Provincial Conference, and together they had opposed the immediate call for a congress, half of whose membership was to represent the Teheran Provincial Party Conference.[19]

The moderates' defection stemmed not only from the failure of these hopes, Maleki's faction explained, but also from the more fundamental question of the party's role in Iran's political development. This role could be looked at from two points of view — one, that of an exaggerated sense of historical determinism, which led the party to act in a purely defensive way; and the other, that in which the party was considered a determining factor, a mass party which must be the initiator of events.[20]

The majority of the Provincial Committee of Teheran and a number of party activists, who had lost hope of carrying on their struggle inside the party, joined in the defection of the moderates, but it was the Tudeh Socialist League of Iran, representing the Maleki faction, that bore the brunt of the party's opposition. One reason for this was the numerical strength of the faction. If it were permitted to continue separately, the faction might seriously challenge the party's claim of exclusively representing the socialist Left. Propaganda pressure was so formidable that the league shortly declared itself out of existence, after it became convinced that its separate path would neither be tolerated by the Tudeh party nor condoned by the Soviets. An editorial in a Soviet newspaper condemning the faction as traitorous to the socialist cause sealed its fate and thereby reaffirmed the Tudeh party's recognition as the sole party of the pro-Soviet Left.[21]

---

[19] *Ibid.*, p. 25.

[20] *Ibid.*, p. 32.

[21] Some Soviet sources have put the blame for intraparty strife on British agents: "[They] managed to secure a measure of schism in the Tudeh party in the defection of Maleki with a small group, but the failure of this provocation was so obvious that within nineteen days the group of traitors was forced to announce its own dissolution." See M. N. Ivanova, "The National Liberation Movement in Gilan Province in Persia in 1920–21," *Sovetskoye Vostokovedeniye*, No. 3 (1955); English summary in *CAR*, Vol. IV, No. 3 (1956).

Other Dissidents

Besides these two factions representing the principal strands of criticism inside the party — the liberal intellectuals and the Maleki group — there were several other splinter groups whose political tendencies only became known long after their defection. One of these, which was third in numerical and ideological importance, centered around Anvar Khamei, a leading intellectual who had been a member of Dr. Erani's Marxist circle. Several years after defecting from the party his followers emerged as a small faction known as *Jamiyate Rahai kar va Andisheh* (The Society of Liberation of Deed and Thought), which published a weekly newspaper directed mainly at left wing intellectuals.[22]

The ideological line reflected in the writings of this group was strongly Marxist–Leninist in tone, and it challenged the right of the loosely ideological party to represent the international Communist movement in Iran. In its stand on international and domestic problems it was, in fact, considerably left of Dr. Eprim's leftist faction, for it advocated closer ties and unreserved subordination to the Soviet Union. It, too, however, attributed the failures of the Tudeh party to its leadership, but it denounced the Maleki faction as nationalist revisionist. Its attack on this group became more outspoken after Tito's expulsion from the Cominform, since this action, as we shall see later, put Maleki's group in the new so-called "nationalist Communist" category.[23]

Not surprisingly, the Khamei faction was violently anti-American. It denounced alleged American assistance to the Iranian government in coping with Soviet diplomatic pressure, hoping to prove its unqualified support of international communism.

Needless to say, only the most articulate of the defectors expressed their grievances and criticisms so precisely. But they

---

[22] The group was most active in the first phase of the nationalist movement in 1950–1952.

[23] Maleki, who had earlier anticipated Tito's expulsion, became the chief proponent of the concept of the "separate roads to socialism," which was later adopted as the slogan of a new non-Communist nationalist party known as the Third Force. See C. Steiner, "Der Iranische Kommunismus," *Ost-Probleme*, No. 39 (Sept. 30, 1955), 1497.

were by no means the only ones to defect. The Azarbayjan failure had in fact resulted in a mass defection of party sympathizers, apparently for a multiplicity of reasons that could not be ascertained because of the unorganized and unsystematic manner of defection. That party sympathizers and fellow travelers were disillusioned was all too apparent. But of the many reasons for their disillusionment, the most significant was probably associated with the overriding patriotism of the middle class.

This patriotism had been challenged time and again — beginning with the way in which the Tudeh party had shown itself to be subordinate to the Soviet Union during the oil crisis. The insurrection in Azarbayjan had placed further strain on the party, for its support of the revolt in a minority region had aroused the hostility of at least some of the middle class, which was traditionally suspicious of the motivation of any minority movement.[24] The persistent demand of the Azarbayjan Democratic regime for autonomy and a separate language did not help to ally this suspicion, notwithstanding the alleged attraction of the principle of self-determination for the native population.

Then there were other sympathizers who were disappointed for the quite opposite reason that the revolution had been confined to Azarbayjan. Many had supported the insurrection in Tabriz in the belief that it would soon spread to the capital in a fashion reminiscent of the revolution of 1907, when constitutionalists led by veteran Azarbayjani revolutionary leaders, Sattar Khan and Bagher Khan, marched to Teheran and saved the newly won constitution from the Shah's tampering pen.[25] As the revolutionary regime continued to pursue its separatist policies and refused in effect to nationalize the insurrection, many disillusioned sympathizers turned their backs on the party. Some of these even joined the government Iranian Democratic party after December, 1946. Finally, there was simply the psychological appeal of success and the disillusionment of defeat, which

---

[24] Mme. H. Carrere d'Encausse, "Le Toudeh Iranien," _Revue Militaire d'Information_ (February–March, 1957), p. 58.

[25] See Edward G. Browne, _The Persian Revolution of 1905–1909_ (Cambridge, Eng., 1911).

in this case, as in most other mass political movements in the country, tended to inflate and deflate the movement in rapid succession.

The Impact of Defection

So far as the mass defection of sympathizers was concerned, party leaders were undismayed. They viewed this as a relatively insignificant phenomenon and expressed confidence that, with a minimum freedom of political activity, the party could easily regain its mass appeal and win back most of its sympathizers.[26] About the loss of some of the most militant cadres, however, they were seriously concerned. They well knew that the party faced a serious challenge, and as a consequence the Tudeh party underwent several important reorientations, all designed to show that the party alone was the Iranian representative of international communism. Increasingly, the party identified itself with Marxism–Leninism, and it borrowed from the vast experience of foreign Communist parties, notably that of the Soviet Union, to find answers to its critics. Much of its literature of this period quotes copiously from international Communist sources dealing with the organizational and ideological questions.

Thus, rejecting the charge of "lack of a concrete plan of action" to face various contingencies, Ahmad Ghassemi, a party theorist, retorted: "There can be no universal prescription for a social undertaking of mass dimensions, for, as Lenin has aptly remarked, only a charlatan could attempt to invent for the proletariat a formula for the solution of all eventualities and a guarantee that the revolutionary proletariat would never face setbacks. As for the leftist faction's proposal for the formation of a separate vanguard inside the party, Ghassemi denied that a mass party could splinter itself. This would be tantamount to giving in to "intellectual individualism," which, Lenin had warned, would be detrimental to the proletariat's interests: "This intellectual individualism proves with abundant clarity

---

[26] Ehsan Tabari, "Konferance Baraye Faaline Hezbi" [Address to Party Activists in Teheran], *Mardom*, Vol. II, No. 11 (August, 1948), 5.

the need for absolute centralism and the strictest discipline as an essential condition for the proletarian victory over the bourgeoisie."[27]

Ghassemi charged the critics of the left and center with bourgeois intellectualism and sought to isolate those elements of the party from the rest of the membership. The majority of the party, he said — especially its working class elements — distinguished between constructive criticism and sabotage, between democratic principle and anarchical chaos, and he quoted Lenin to defend the party's attitude at the time of crisis. In his opinion, Ghassemi said, the crisis besetting the Tudeh party in the wake of the Azarbayjan defeat and the crisis of the Russian Social Democratic party following the defeat of 1905 were comparable: "The Tudeh party was subjected to similar pressures from two directions, the persecution by the government and the clamor of some party members for the total revision of the party composition. But the critics have belied this claim by their open defection, for it is an undeniable social tenet that ideological affinity must be cemented with tangible and practical unity of proletarian organization to achieve victory."[28]

According to Ghassemi, Tudeh leaders had learned from the Russian experience not to appease the critics, just as Lenin had opposed Plekhanov's counsel of lenience toward the minority critics after the Second Congress of the Social Democrats. Similarly, Tudeh leaders had rejected the left faction's demand for an inner party of militants, on the authority of Lenin, who had dismissed the idea of a party divided between "privileged" members exempt from organizational discipline and the "unprivileged" subject to the severest party discipline.[29] In sum, the party continued to regard centralized hierarchy, unified leadership, and a single constitution, in addition to the strictest discipline, as the essential requirements for the successful leadership of working class organizations.

---

[27] Ahmad Ghassemi, "Dar Sarashibe Ensheab" [On the Brink of Split], *ibid.*, Vol. II, No. 5 (March, 1948), 17.

[28] *Ibid.*, p. 23.

[29] *Ibid.*, p. 21.

Although the Tudeh leadership refused to accept the major criticism of the defecting left and center factions, it did not completely ignore some of the main points raised by them.[30] Even before the defections became final at the end of 1947, the leadership in its new guise as the PEC had begun to reappraise the entire concept of party organization. Acknowledging that the extraordinary inflation of the party in 1945 had contributed to the loss of organizational solidarity, it set out to assure against the recurrence of past mistakes. The task was made somewhat easier by the fact that, with the defection of a large number of sympathizers and fellow travelers, the party now contained only card-carrying members who had been recruited before the expansion of 1945. Thus it could focus on the hard core of activists, most of whom, threatened by the defection of a considerable number of intellectuals, suffered from low morale and acute despair.

The task of reorganizing and indoctrinating the faithful was given to the young and dynamic leader of the party's youth league, Ehsan Tabari. Tabari had had nothing to do with the leadership's past mistakes, and party intellectuals trusted him. Like other party theorists, he relied heavily on Marxist–Leninist literature and the actual experience of the Russian Communist party to instill the idea that, despite appearances, the Tudeh party was an integral part of the world Communist movement.

Addressing a conference of party activists, he defined the concept of a political party and party struggle in Marxist terms. The anticapitalist struggle, he said, was the essence of party struggle, which was neither an incidental and temporary phenomenon nor one that could be eliminated as long as the class society existed. Accordingly, the Tudeh party had rejected the capitalist view of a loosely organized liberal party and the fascist notion of a leader-dominated dictatorial party, for both were anachronistic to a modern working class party. Tabari added

---

[30] In a resolution the PEC even paid lip service to demands for reprimanding the old leadership, after careful examination of their past errors. *Nashriyeh Hezbi* [party publication] (Teheran), No. 28 (Jan. 5, 1948).

that the Tudeh party's solution to the dual task of organization
and unity was democratic centralism, which required obedience
to the democratically elected leadership. The party should not
assume an elitist character, he emphasized, but should rely ultimately on the masses, though without giving in to their emo-
tionalism and neglecting their political education.[31]

The party was aware of the air of defeatism among intellectuals
and students, and Tabari warned students against the many
different "deviations" threatening the party, ranging from dogmatism to nihilism and liberalism.[32] But apathy and noninvolve-
ment in the political process were also criticized. Intellectuals
who advocated purism were rebuked for avoiding the facts of
social and political struggle and harboring the illusion that,
given the state of things in Iran, a social movement could be
undertaken without risking mistakes and setbacks.

In short, for the Tudeh party the two years that followed the
failure of the revolution in Azarbayjan were marked by soul-
searching in an effort to root out the causes of the movement's
decline and to prescribe solutions to the ideological and organizational questions that threatened future prospects. It was not
until the Second Congress in May, 1948, that the party finally
recovered and reemerged with clear political and ideological
conceptions.

During these two years, developments in the country were
rapidly moving toward a consolidation of the central government's power. Having successfully discredited the leftist parties —
and aided by the Tudeh boycott of the elections and the lack of
organized support for the new opposition led by Dr. Mossadegh
— the government party (the Iranian Democrats) won nearly 90
percent of the seats in the 15th Majlis.[33]

The new parliament convened in July, 1947, and after the
preliminary debate on parliamentary mandates and investiture

---

[31] See Ehsan Tabari, "Hezb Chist?" [What Is Party?], *Mardom*, Vol. I,
No. 9 (May, 1947), 1–10.

[32] Tabari, as reported in *ibid.*, Vol. II, No. 3 (February, 1948).

[33] L. P. Elwell-Sutton, "Political Parties in Iran, 1941–1948," *Middle
East Journal*, Vol. III, No. 1 (1949), 60.

of the new cabinet under Prime Minister Ghavam, the deputies got down to the business at hand — the draft treaty for the formation of the joint Iranian–Soviet oil company. This was presented in late September, and it was a foregone conclusion that it would be defeated, despite the prime minister's apparent support. Even so, the overwhelming passage (102–2) of a motion declaring his pledge to the Soviet government null and void came as something of a surprise to the regime's supporters and opponents alike.[34]

The rejection of the oil agreement by the Majlis was an anticlimax to the Soviet postwar diplomatic offensive in Iran. It represented a total failure for both the traditional and revolutionary elements of Soviet diplomacy in one of its first trials of strength since Russia's emergence from the Second World War as a major power. Neither the revolutionary experience of aiding the indigenous Communist movement nor the use of traditional diplomatic pressure had succeeded in extending Soviet influence into Iran.

This apparent defeat of Soviet diplomacy did not, however, mark the conclusive decline of the Iranian Communist movement. For though the sovereignty of the country was finally restored and the power of the central government consolidated, the objective conditions that had nurtured the emergence of the movement's renewed expressions had not fundamentally altered. Within a year after the collapse of Azarbayjan, the Tudeh party began to show signs of revival, which led to the convening of the Second Congress in April, 1949. If anything, the party manifested every indication of increased militancy and a marked shift toward the leftist radicalism from which it had previously shied away.

The Second Tudeh Party Congress, 1948

The issue of holding annual party congresses to reelect leading organizational bodies and to reformulate policies was a bone of contention which had strongly alienated those critics who sin-

---

[34] The two deputies who opposed the motion were known for their pro Soviet sympathies. *Journal de Teheran*, Oct. 23, 1947.

cerely believed in reforming the party from within, rather than by hasty and irreversible formal defection.

The moderate critics of the Maleki faction hoped that by convening the congress in the aftermath of the Azarbayjan failure, an honest evaluation of past errors could be made and new personalities elected to guide the strife-torn party through this crisis. The leadership, on the other hand, was convinced that convening a congress when defeatism was rampant in the party could only result in a total overhauling of the leadership apparatus and its takeover by critics of the Left and Center. The leadership had refused to call the congress into session in the summer of 1946, while the coalition government was in power and the revolutionary regime in Azarbayjan was seemingly well established; it had reasoned that holding a congress then would merely have alienated the nonparty elements of the Left and Center with whom the party had formed the five-party coalition as a prelude to participation in general elections. In addition, the leadership further contended that at the height of success there was no need for a congress.

In February, 1946, the Central Committee had prevented the Second Teheran Provincial Conference from electing the capital's representatives to the Second Tudeh Party Congress, as required by its statute.[35] Those calling for the immediate convening of the congress believed that in the last six of the eighteen months since the First Congress, the party had emerged from a serious phase of struggle into a new era. For the first time it was actively participating in the ruling class and was even being recognized as a major factor in the rapidly developing events in Iran. All these considerations made it imperative for the party's supreme organ to meet and examine the present and future party stand.

In response to this pressure, the Central Committee promised in March, 1946, that the Second Congress would definitely be held on the following June 22, and, to prepare for it, proposed to reconvene the old Teheran Provincial Conference instead of

---

[35] *Do Ravesh*, p. 27.

holding a new one in accordance with the party statute. A meeting of party activists and cell leaders in May overwhelmingly rejected the Central Committee's proposal.[36]

The latter, in turn, reacted by dropping plans for the Second Congress until its authority was transferred to the Provisional Executive Committee in December, 1946. The PEC immediately promised a congress in three months, but failed to take action. Finally, in August, 1947, the Third Teheran Provincial Conference convened and unanimously demanded a new congress. The PEC thereupon promised a congress in two months, but more than three months later resolved that it should be indefinitely postponed because the general political situation did not allow either a clandestine or a public congress. Furthermore, it reasoned, open debate in congress would only aggravate party turmoil, nor could the congress be in any degree nationally representative, owing to the dissolution of a number of provincial party organizations.

None of these reasons satisfied the reformists. An advisory meeting in December, 1947, attended by fifty members of the Teheran Provincial Conference unanimously objected to the PEC's proposal for indefinite postponement, forcing it to withdraw the resolution and to promise a congress in March–April, 1948.[37] Within days, however, the split had become a reality. In a strongly worded resolution in January, 1948, the PEC condemned the defection of the Maleki faction as an act of treason. The PEC's propaganda machinery waged a massive campaign to discredit this group, which included the core of fifty intellectuals who earlier had held a majority in Teheran's Third Provincial Conference. The Central Council of the Unified Trade Union movement, the formal labor organization affiliate of the party, came out in support of the PEC and condemned the defection, "at a time when reaction and imperialism have united against the freedom-loving worker organization and have re-

---

[36] *Ibid.*

[37] *Nashriyeh Hezbi* [party publication] (Teheran, December, 1947), pp. 2–4.

sorted to every means for undermining the democratic development of our country."[38]

With the defectors thus out of the way, the leaders were ready
to go ahead with the long-postponed Second Congress, and it duly
convened in Teheran on April 25, 1948, with 118 delegates, representing almost every part of Iran, in attendance. The opening
report, by Dr. Radmanesh, the secretary general, unconditionally
supported the party's attitude on domestic and international
developments during the forty-four months since the First Congress; but the real business of the Congress was to make plans
for the future. Six separate study groups took up various aspects
of party life and recommended a series of resolutions. These were
summed up in an account in *Mardom*, the party journal:[39] (1) a
new party statute which reinforced the principles of democratic
centralism and division of labor in addition to giving a narrower
definition to membership by extending the candidacy period
from three to six months;[40] (2) approval of general policies of
the party in the past, with the due acknowledgment of the former
leadership's tactical errors; (3) careful examination and condemnation of the split motivated by leftist "avant-gardist" and
"centrist" factionalism.

Owing to the absence of several former party leaders, some
because of their involvement in the Azarbayjan insurrection and
others to satisfy critics of the old guard, some reorganization in
the party structure was necessary. The revised statute gave the
Central Committee nineteen members, who, together with fifteen alternates, were to constitute the general session of the Central Committee's plenum. This plenum was to function as a supreme council and was to meet every three months to examine
the past record and approve the future policies. The alternates,
functioning in an advisory capacity, would participate in these

---

[38] Bozorg Alavi, *Kämpfendes Iran* (Berlin, 1955), pp. 100–101.
[39] Ehsan Tabari, "Kongerehe Dovom" [Second Congress], *Mardom*, Vol.
II, No. 9 (May, 1948), 1–8.
[40] Alavi, *op. cit.*

deliberations but would have no vote.[41] The statute required that upon the election of the Central Committee and its alternate advisory members the first plenum should meet to elect from the Central Committee members an eleven-man executive board and a five-man control commission. The executive board, primarily responsible for the execution of the Central Committee's decisions and policies, was in turn divided into a political bureau and an organization bureau.[42] In addition to the post of general secretary, to which Dr. Radmanesh was elected, there were a second and third secretary representing the political and organizational bureaus.[43]

One innovation motivated by past experience was the election of a much smaller control commission from among the Central Committee's membership by the plenum rather than by the congress, as had been the case under the first party statute. As mentioned earlier, the inclusion of some of the reformist elements, notably Maleki, on the commission had been an annoyance to the Central Committee because of their pressure for a purge and for holding the Second Congress at the prescribed time. Under the new arrangement the voting members of the plenum — namely, the full membership of the Central Committee — were responsible for the election of the control commission, but it was in effect the choice of the eleven-member executive

---

41 The 19 members of the Central Committee were Dr. Reza Radmanesh, Ehsan Tabari, Dr. Hossein Jowdat, Dr. Freydoun Keshavarz, Dr. Gholam Hossein Forutan, Dr. Mohammad Bahrami, Dr. Morteza Yazdi, Ahmad Ghassemi, Mahmud Boghrati, Dr. Mohammad Hossein Kiyanouri, Ali Ollovi, Reza Rusta, Abdolsamad Kambakhsh, Nader Sharmini, Samad Hakimi, Ali Amirkhizi, Abdolhossein Noushin, Iraj Eskandari, and Mohammad Babazadeh. The 15 alternate advisory members were Amanollah Ghoreishi, Jahangir Afkari, Morteza Ravandi, M. Hossein Tamaddon, Ali Mottaghi, Shandramini, Seydashrafi, Sadegh Ansari, Shabrang, Bozorg Alavi, Ghazi, Mahzari Farahi, Emamvardi, Sayad Nejad, and Maryam Firuz. *Seyre Komonism*, p. 199.

42 The first 11 members of the Central Committee as listed in n. 41 comprise the executive board.

43 Tabari and Dr. Keshavarz were elected, respectively, as the second secretary in charge of the politbureau and the third secretary in charge of the orgbureau. *Mardom*, Vol. II, No. 9 (May, 1948), 8.

board, since they constituted a clear majority of the nineteen-member Central Committee.[44] Notably missing from the new executive board were Eskandari, Kambakhsh, and Rusta; the first two had left the country following the Azarbayjan collapse, and Rusta, who was in charge of the trade union affiliate of the movement, was omitted because of his preoccupation with that post. He, too, however, subsequently fled the country as government pressure on the union mounted.

The Central Committee wielded vast authority over party organization and activity. Its powers included the right to dissolve a provincial committee, even though it was an elective organ chosen by the provincial party conference. Theoretically this right was subject to the election of a new committee by the next congress, but since neither a new congress nor the plenum of the Central Committee met regularly, in practice it gave the former the power of life and death over the party's provincial branches.[45]

The new statute reflected an attempt to incorporate definite Leninist principles into the party organization, aimed at moving it further toward a cohesive working class party. One section dealt specifically with the duties of members, under a tight central organization. Members were required to observe strict discipline and enforce the decisions of the majority, to comply with the decisions and orders of the higher party organs, and to recognize the right of the party to appoint officials and assign duties.[46] To enforce the fulfillment of these duties and to ensure organizational unity, elaborate provisions were made for reprimanding negligent members. These measures were also designed to prevent the recurrence of factionalism, ever a threat since the First

---

[44] The members of the Control Commission, reduced from nine under the original statute to five in the revised statute passed by the Second Congress, were Nader Sharmini, Samad Hakimi, Ali Amirkhizi, Abdolhossein Nushin, and Mohammad Babazadeh. *Seyre Komonism*, p. 200.

[45] *Ibid.*, p. 204.

[46] *Assassnamehe Hezbe Tudeh Iran* [Statute of the Tudeh Party of Iran] (Teheran, 1948), pp. 19ff.

Congress and finally responsible for the defections at the end of 1947.

After the Second Congress, the party set out to implement the new resolutions and to rebuild its organization with tighter controls and well-trained new cadres. Commenting on the significance of cadres, the new statute had echoed Lenin's views that, although a correct political ideology was most essential for a modern working class party, it would be inadequate in the absence of trained cadres. Accordingly, the entire party apparatus was to join in training new cadres of devoted, well-disciplined, class-conscious, and dependable members.[47] At a general assembly of party activists convened in July, 1948, by the Teheran Provincial Committee to hear the first quarterly report under the new statute, Tabari, now the political second secretary of the Central Committee, noted that the training of cadres was the party's most heavy burden because Iranians in general were not used to collective political or social action and even workers and intellectuals had relatively little experience in this field.[48] Nevertheless, he said, the party believed that Iranian society was capable of developing and evolving sociopolitical movements, primarily because of "the absolute deprivation that people suffer at the hands of imperialism and its local agents."[49] As in the past, when even a minimum degree of freedom of political activity had enabled the party to reach the politically conscious strata, now too the party was confident of its ability to combat the prevailing mass lethargy.

Throughout this period of ideological purification which prevailed after the Second Congress, the party seemed aware of the dangers of elitism and of a loss of its populist character. The activists were cautioned against the "avant-gardism" of leftist defectors, which, if permitted to penetrate the party, would pervert it into a sect, instead of a modern working class organiza-

---

[47] *Ibid.*, p. 31.

[48] Ahmad Ghassemi, "Tarbiyate Kadrha" [Training Cadres], *Mardom*, Vol. II, No. 10 (June, 1948), 59–71.

[49] *Ibid.*, Vol. II, No. 11 (August, 1948), 1–5.

tion.[50] They were also reminded of the difficulties which the party had faced as a result of the absence of a large industrial proletariat. In a fashion reminiscent of the PCP's reaction to the failure of the Gilan insurrection in 1921, the Tudeh party, two decades later, also blamed the country's young and insufficiently proletarized working class for its recent setbacks.[51]

Nor was the problem of mobilizing other classes any easier. As the party saw it, the vast peasantry was backward and politically apathetic, and the middle class was largely poor and underdeveloped.[52] The small progressive intelligentsia, on the other hand, had a pronounced revolutionary zeal but shied away from revolutionary action because it did not correctly comprehend its meaning and obligations. With such raw material, the party proposed to reconstruct its membership. Quite obviously, it was a job that became doubly difficult outside the confines of the capital and other major cities, in the backward and illiterate rural areas.[53]

The response of the working class to the party in the past had been satisfactory. Indeed, during most of the party's existence, its rank and file was drawn mainly from labor; it was only after the Azarbayjan demise that the party lost its hold on labor. This defection had, of course, been in part the result of a general falling off after defeat and disappointment, but it was also a result of Prime Minister Ghavam's active and systematic attempt to win working class support and even allegiance to the government, a policy pursued also by succeeding cabinets with fairly impressive success. Even so, many of the working class continued to support the Tudeh party, and the party still had a hard core of labor organizers whose skill in mobilizing the working class was unrivaled by any other union. The party's success in winning over labor was an important factor in the evolution of the Communist movement.

---

[50] *Ibid.*

[51] *Ibid.*, p. 4.

[52] A comparison with previous pronouncements indicates the consistency of Communist interpretation of that important issue. See p. 42.

[53] *Mardom*, Vol. II, No. 11 (August, 1948), 5.

The Trade Union Movement

The struggle to win the working class, as potentially the most suitable source of recruitment for the movement's various organizational expressions, had, of course, been one of the most consistent accents of the Communist movement. The most convincing proof for this assertion is the fact that all political parties representing the movement in the past four decades have measured their success and failure in terms of their relations with the working class and in proportion to the degree of its political consciousness. Both the Adalat Committee, which pioneered in organizing working class elements in Baku in 1918, and the Persian Communist party, which carried on the labor drive on Persian soil, first in Gilan and later elsewhere, have evaluated their performance in terms of working class response and loyalty.

Similarly, the Tudeh party has measured its rise and fall by the degree of influence over the working class throughout its existence since 1941. The party, which attributed its very formation to the drastic change in the objective condition of Iran as a result of the relative industrialization and numerical growth of the working class under Reza Shah, claimed the exclusive loyalty of more than 300,000 workers at the height of its strength in the summer of 1946. Conversely, it has blamed the same phenomenon for the decline of communism after the Azarbayjan failure.[54]

By the same token, when the party was subject to the criticisms of leftist reformers in 1947–1948 and again after it was forced underground in 1949, the challenge to its ideological affinity with communism was met by the emphasis on its working class basis as the ultimate measure of its doctrinal purity.[55] Labor has always

---

[54] Mohammad-Zadeh, "Report on the Trade Union Movement in Iran" (Nov. 20, 1949, session of the Trade Union Conference of Asian and Australian Countries held in Peking, Nov. 16–Dec. 1, 1949), *World Trade Union Movement* (December, 1949), pp. 30–31.

[55] Radmanesh, "Hezbe Tudehe Iran, Hezbe Taraze Novine Tabaghehe Kargar" [The Tudeh Party of Iran, the Modern Type Working Class Party], *Donya*, Vol. II, No. 2 (Summer, 1961).

figured prominently as an integral part of the movement, and it is likely to continue as such as long as communism's doctrinal foundations evolve around the championing of labor's interests.

The historical development of the trade union movement in Iran can be traced to the end of the First World War, when for the first time a regular trade union was set up by the printers in Teheran. In the following decade the movement gradually spread to other industries, and by 1927, according to some accounts, there were six unions in the capital and an oil workers' union in Khuzistan.[56] The consolidation of Reza Shah's power in 1928, which was accompanied by strict measures against all political opposition, ended this period of growth of the union movement; not until the overthrow of Reza Shah's regime and the restoration of democratic freedoms in 1941 was a revival of the movement possible.

With the new regime the Provisional Committee of the Tudeh party quickly set out to reorganize the trade unions. In October, 1941, with the amnesty extended to the Reza Shah's political prisoners, several Communist trade union organizers were released from jail, along with the members of the Erani group. Some of these experienced men started to organize various trades into unions independent from the Tudeh party. By 1944, there were four major independent union centers in Teheran, with a total membership of about 10,000.[57] All these centers were led by experienced Communist elements, who remained outside the Tudeh party for reasons having to do with the uncertainty of party-union relations. Some of this independence was sheer tactical restraint occasioned by the Allies' objection to the political infiltration of labor, which they feared might undermine the early war effort. In fact, the Tudeh union claimed credit for

---

[56] "Central Council of Unified Trade Unions in Iran," in *Report of Activity of the World Federation of Trade Unions* (presented to the Second World Trade Union Congress, Milan, June 29–July 10, 1949), pp. 165–170; hereafter cited as *Report of WFTU Activity.*

[57] *Zafar* [Organ of the Tudeh Trade Union Movement], anniversary issue, May 1, 1946.

preventing labor unrest in war industries as an indication of its kinship with the Soviet Union.[58]

By 1944, with a certain relaxation of Allied control as the war progressed, these considerations no longer limited the trade union movement. The election of the 14th Majlis in 1943–1944 had convinced the Tudeh party of the advantage of labor's organized support, and, in addition, the party had gradually assumed the characteristics of a mass organization, dependent for its strength and influence on the working and professional classes. It had already taken some measures to found a unified trade union organization, including the formation, in early 1942, of the Central Council of the Trade Unions of Iran,[59] which included labor organizers and workers' representatives. On May 1, 1944, this nucleus of the Communist organizers in Teheran managed to bring about the unification of the four independent unions in a new organization called the United Central Council of the Unified Trade Unions of Iranian Workers (referred to as the United Council). The United Council immediately established ties with the leftist World Federation of Trade Unions (WFTU), which accepted it as an affiliate on the grounds that it represented more than 200,000 workers brought together by the freely negotiated May 1 agreement.[60]

By the summer of 1945 the United Council was undoubtedly the major nationwide union in Iran. In the twenty-seventh session of the International Labor Conference held in Paris in October–November, 1945, it challenged, unsuccessfully, the right of the delegation sent by the Persian government to the conference as representative of three other non-Tudeh unions. The United Council was represented in the Iranian delegation in an advisory capacity only, both the full delegate and his alternate

---

[58] *Tarikhchehe Mokhtasar* [Brief History of the Movement], as quoted in *Seyre Komonism*, p. 309.

[59] Eskandari, "Conditions of the Working People in Iran," *World Trade Union Movement*, No. 2 (January, 1951), 35–52.

[60] See the International Labor Office's report, *Labor Conditions in the Oil Industry in Iran* (Geneva, 1950), esp. chap. 7, "The Trade Union Situation."

being representatives of the non-Communist unions.[61] This episode inaugurated a long series of bitter feuds between government authorities and the United Council, during which the WFTU dispatched several missions to Iran to observe labor conditions and to investigate Tudeh union complaints of government persecution and the latter's countercharge of political subversion.

The period between May 1, 1943, and December 13, 1946, marked the gradual rise of the United Council as an open and formally recognized trade union. The ascendency of the United Council corresponds with that of the Tudeh party, which after 1943 publicly claimed the leadership of the working class, even though the United Council still maintained its separate organizational identity.

The unions encompassed by the United Council were organized on a territorial basis and controlled by the central council through provincial and local trade councils that were more or less the counterparts of those in the Tudeh party.[62] The constituent body was a congress composed of delegates of the affiliated unions; it was required to convene annually for elections to the leading organs and a general policy review. The administrative structure of the member unions was based on a regional system whereby the trade unions in each city elected their own administrative officers at the same time that they elected their representative to the city council. Delegates of various city councils formed the area council, above which was the provincial council. The highest organs were a council of forty-five members, elected by the annual congress, and an execu-

---

[61] These non-Communist unions were the Central Council of Workers and Agricultural Laborers of Iran, claiming 153,000 members; the Trade Unions of Workers and Peasants, claiming 10,000 members; and the Trade Union of Workers and Handicraftsmen of Iran, claiming 35,000 members. *Record of Proceedings of 27th Session International Labor Conference* (Paris, 1945), pp. 317–321.

[62] At the end of this period there were 186 such unions purporting to represent nearly 300,000 workers throughout the country, including 70 percent of the labor force in the oil industry. Mohammad-Zadeh, *op. cit.*, p. 31.

tive committee of fifteen elected from among the council's membership. The executive committee in turn designated three secretaries, one of whom was chosen secretary general.[63]

The United Council claimed a membership of 200,000 by the end of 1945 and of approximately 400,000 by the end of 1946, when it added to its ranks the unions of artisans, thereby inflating the movement at the time when Communist prestige and power were at their zenith. Membership dues were one percent of each member's monthly income, of which half was given to the union's central fund and half to the local councils.[64]

Political control of the union by the Tudeh party was assured by the presence of the leading members of the Tudeh party's Central Committee on the union's executive committee. Thus, in addition to the three secretaries of the fifteen-man executive committee of the central council, all of whom were simultaneously members of the Tudeh party Central Committee, more than 60 percent of the membership of the union also belonged to the Tudeh party's leading organs elected in its First Congress in the summer of 1944. To ensure coordination of policy and action of the union and the Tudeh party Central Committee, leading members of the latter were appointed as liaison officers with the movement. The veteran party organizer, Ardeshir Ovanessian, was in charge of ideological problems between the party and the union, and Iraj Eskandari, until December, 1946, the leading member of the three-man secretariat of the party's Central Committee, was a political adviser to the United Council's executive committee. The union had its own publications, including the daily newspaper *Zafar* (Victory), which was practically identical to the Tudeh party organ in its editorial policies and coverage.[65] By far the most powerful man in the union was

---

[63] Before the ban on the union and the Tudeh party, these secretaries were Reza Rusta, Dr. Hossein Jowdat, and Mahmud Boghrati. *World Trade Union Movement* (March, 1950), pp. 34–35.

[64] *Report of WFTU Activity*, p. 167.

[65] Ovanessian's *Tashkilate Hezbi* [Party Organization] (Teheran, 1943), was used as a doctrinal guide for party and union organization. See *Seyre Komonism*, p. 309.

Reza Rusta, whose prestige at the height of the movement's rise in the summer of 1946 rivaled, if not surpassed, that of the Tudeh members in the coalition government.

This period of ascendency of the United Council was marked by the successful and systematic use of collective bargaining, which by itself constituted the most effective source of the movement's rapid growth. In a detailed report to the Second World Trade Union Congress sponsored by the WFTU, the Iranian delegate listed the following as the most important strikes in terms of securing immediate objectives across the country: the strike in Teheran of the construction union engaged in government public work projects in 1942–1943; the strike of the municipal workers in Teheran in 1944; the strikes of textile workers in Teheran, textile and leather workers in Azarbayjan, and textile workers in Mazanderan in 1943–1944; the mass strike of 20,000 textile workers in Isfahan in the fall of 1944; the series of successive strikes in the oil industry in Kermanshah in 1945, in the Abadan and Aghajari oil fields in May, 1946, and finally, the largest and most successful in terms of participation, on July 14, 1946, in Abadan.[66]

Some of the union's success in organizing various trades was due to deteriorating living conditions in the war years. Whereas the cost-of-living index increased almost sevenfold compared with the base year of 1941, the over-all wage increase for labor by the end of 1946 did not exceed 70 to 80 percent. Therefore, regardless of whether the strikes were politically motivated or not, they were always presented to the workers as the only effective means of securing concessions from the ruling class. Even a meager degree of success in the endeavor constituted a powerful weapon for winning labor's support.

Another reason for the union's success was that, like the Tudeh party, until 1946, it, too, was working in a political vacuum. Although there were attempts to compete for the loyalty of the working class, until that year only the United Council could

---

[66] *Report of WFTU Activity*, p. 168.

claim to be a nationwide working class organization. There were too few experienced labor organizers in the non-Communist parties to challenge the United Council, not to mention the general reluctance of other parties to welcome labor with open doors.

Naturally, the Tudeh union exploited this exclusiveness, and when it was threatened by the government and the parties of the Right, it recruited the active support of the WFTU. As a result of a disagreement over the Iranian representation to the WFTU and the rejection of the statements of the United Council to the WFTU congress held in Paris on October 7, 1945, the WFTU proposed to send a delegation to Iran to investigate the real nature of trade union organization there. The task of the proposed commission of inquiry was to verify the accuracy of the declarations of the United Council concerning membership and viability of its organization; to ascertain the independent and democratic nature of its organization; and to examine the possibility of achieving total unity of the trade union movement.[67]

Louis Saillant, the general secretary of the WFTU, presented a report on the trade union situation in Iran to the first session of the executive bureau of the WFTU, meeting in Paris on December 22, 1945, but the dispatch of a commission of inquiry was postponed until the next meeting, June 22–27, 1946, in Moscow. In the interim, the United Council's general secretary, who was eager to secure international recognition for his union, sent a series of communications to the WFTU executive bureau complaining about the police action and government interference with free labor union activity in the country. Finally the executive bureau in its meeting in Moscow authorized Saillant to visit Iran and report to the bureau in its next meeting scheduled for September 20–24 in Washington, D.C.

Saillant arrived in Iran on July 20 to witness the Tudeh party and the union at the peak of their influence. Impressed by the gigantic union-sponsored demonstrations and firmly convinced

---

[67] *Ibid.*

of the close Communist ties of the union, he recommended to the WFTU executive bureau that the United Council be formally admitted into the WFTU and that it be granted the right to be represented in its general council thereafter by Reza Rusta, secretary general of the Tudeh union. In December, 1946, the general council, meeting in Prague, adopted a resolution approving Saillant's recommendation to declare the United Council as "the only democratic trade union in Iran to be recognized as such by the WFTU."[68]

Needless to say, Saillant's mission fell short of fulfilling the task outlined for it by the council's executive bureau in its earlier decisions concerning the verification of the genuine organizational independence of the Tudeh union. For, as related earlier, the union's leadership was closely linked with the party's highest executive organs. The First Tudeh Party Congress had already publicized the composition of these organs, and it was common knowledge that the two were controlled by the same men. If further evidence were needed, it was supplied in the Abadan strike on July 14, 1946, when the United Council was obliged to subordinate its objectives to party interests by calling off the strike and refraining from any labor agitation that might have impeded the impending participation of the Tudeh party in the three-party coalition government formed on August 4, 1946.[69]

The issue of the Tudeh party's infiltration of the United Council was again raised when the council sought the intervention of the WFTU following the collapse of the Azarbayjan insurrection. Encouraged by the sudden and overwhelming decline of the parties of the Left as a result of this event, the government stepped into the field of trade unions. Early in 1947,

---

[68] *Ibid.*, p. 169.

[69] The leading member of the Central Committee of the party, Dr. Reza Radmanesh, who was simultaneously a member of the central council of the union, played a dominant role in settling the strike as the union representative on the Mixed State Commission for resolving the dispute between the workers and the Anglo–Iranian Oil Company. Alavi, *Kämpfendes Iran,* p. 103.

with the support of the newly formed ministry of labor, a new organization called ESKI (an abbreviation of the Persian name for the union of Iranian workers syndicates), was formed as an affiliate of the government party, the Iranian Democratic party. It sent a delegation to the thirtieth session of the Labor Conference meeting in Geneva that year, claiming to be the only professional and nonpolitical trade union.[70] The formation of the new union was accompanied by several measures to curtail the activity of the United Council on the grounds that it had been involved in the Azarbayjan insurrection and that, as a branch of the Tudeh party, it was primarily a political rather than a trade union organization.

To counteract these measures the United Council once again appealed to the WFTU. The WFTU promptly sent a three-man commission of inquiry to Iran, but during its visit, from March 18 to April 22, 1947, it became divided as to the nature of the union movement.[71] The British delegate, E. P. Harries, thought the government's actions against the United Council were justified because of the council's identification with the Tudeh party, which he regarded as a revolutionary organization seeking to overthrow the government by force. In his view, some members of that union were arrested because of their active membership in the Tudeh party and not because of their exercise of legitimate trade union rights.

Needless to say, these views were not accepted by the commission's Communist members, who in a detailed report to the WFTU reflected the complaints and testimonies of Rusta and other leaders of the United Council. The British delegate signed the report with reservations and made his own evaluation of

---

[70] *Labor Conditions in the Oil Industry in Iran*, p. 52.

[71] The members of the commission were Mustefa El-Aris, the Lebanese Communist member of the WFTU's executive council, P. A. Borisov of the Soviet Automobile Workers Union, and E. P. Harries of the British Trade Union Council; A. Malfettes, a Frenchman, acted as secretary of the commission. See U.S. Congress, House Foreign Affairs Committee, *Strategy and Tactics of World Communism*, 81st Cong., 1st Sess. 1949, House Doc. 158, Supp. 3, p. 9.

Iran's trade union problem in a separate report some months later.[72] It was his judgment that the union's position was complicated by the existing political association with the Tudeh party, which gave to most union activities, such as the strikes in Isfahan and Abadan, a purely political character. Despite this involvement in political activity in 1946, he noted, both the party and the union continued to function; and in fact, the United Council was the only union represented on the High Council of Labor by three leading figures in the party's hierarchy.[73]

As for Communist infiltration of the union and its link with foreign Communist parties, Harries' report referred to the political background of its secretary general, Rusta, and quoted from documents found in his house to show that his union sought to recruit French Communists to advise the Iranian government on labor organization. Permission for their engagement had been secured during Saillant's visit to Iran a year earlier on the understanding that they would be neutral nonpolitical labor experts. But Harries revealed that, on Rusta's request, two of the Communist officials of the French ministry of labor working with the Communist deputy prime minister, Maurice Thorez, had been nominated by that ministry to these posts.[74]

The Iranian government's refusal to grant visas to the nominees of the French Communist party was one of the major complaints of the United Council brought to the attention of the commission. As a result of the violent disagreement among its members over this and similar issues raised by the union and in the face of Harries' threat to file a separate minority opinion, the commission had to modify its original all-out support for the Tudeh unions.

The revised report recognized that the United Council de-

---

[72] E. P. Harries, "W.F.T.U. Delegation to Iran," *Trade Union Congress* [mimeographed confidential monthly report of the British delegation prepared for the Labor party] (London, May 29, 1947).

[73] These were Taghi Fadakar, Dr. Reza Radmanesh, and Dr. Hossein Jowdat, all represented in the Central Committee, the first two in the parliamentary group of the party in the 14th Majlis. *Ibid.*, p. 3.

[74] An exchange of letters between Rusta and a Communist agent in Paris revealed their names to be I. Amiot and A. Floch. *Ibid.*

fended the rights of the workers through legal channels; that it
had striven to secure good understanding between workers and
employers; and that it did not conspire to overthrow the established regime. Significantly, the paragraph denying the government's claims about the union's past revolutionary plans against
the regime was eliminated. The report proposed, however, that
the union continue to be recognized by the WFTU; that the
Iranian government be urged to release innocent workers and
reinstate others who had been dismissed; that the headquarters
of the United Council be returned to the union; and that the
future election of local and central councils of the union take
place according to democratic principles and under the supervi-
sion of the WFTU.

Notable for their absence in the final version were recommendations to the Iranian government for the exclusive recognition
of the Tudeh union as the sole labor organization, dissolution
of government-sponsored unions in Isfahan and Abadan, abolition of martial law in labor centers, reinstatement of Reza Rusta
as union secretary general, and, finally, a threat that the Iranian
case should be appealed to the United Nations, "if the present
situation resembling those under a Fascist regime continued."[75]

The British delegate, in a reservation accompanying his en-
dorsement of the revised draft, sharply disagreed with major
parts of its contents. There had, of course, been wholesale arrest
and dismissal of union members, but, he pointed out, these did
not result from trade union activity but from participation in
civil revolts organized by the Tudeh party in various industrial
centers. In his opinion, since the union had become indistin-
guishable from the Tudeh party, the imprisoned workers should
have been regarded as primarily political prisoners and only
incidentally as trade union members.[76]

The attempt to deny the Tudeh union's predominantly political nature failed to convince the government. The United
Council leaders were subjected to the same pressure that the

---

[75] *Ibid.*, pp. 6–7.
[76] *Ibid.*

party suffered after the Azarbayjan demise. Having failed to secure government recognition as a professional and nonpolitical organization, its leadership abandoned further pretense of separate identity and joined the Tudeh party's old guard in the crisis of 1947–1948. It fully supported the party's leadership in its struggle against the critics and defectors, and a year later, during the Second Tudeh Party Congress, reinforced its ties with the party by reelecting its secretary general, Reza Rusta, and two other secretaries to the Tudeh party's enlarged Central Committee.

The WFTU, which by early 1948 had assumed an increasingly obvious Communist orientation, continued to recognize the Tudeh union as its sole affiliate and unconditionally supported its struggle against the Iranian government. Accordingly, in July, 1948, as authorized by its executive committee meeting in Rome in May, it intervened on behalf of the United Council at the seventh session of the UN Economic and Social Council.

Reporting on the general topic of trade union rights, Saillant referred to the Iranian government's measures against the Tudeh trade union and echoed its complaint against the official encouragement of workers to join the rival progovernment union.[77] It was apparent from the tone of these complaints that the Tudeh leaders were worried about the government's attempts to win over labor, which had faced a crisis similar to the party's after the Azarbayjan failure. A split had occurred in its leadership, and a sector of its rank and file had deserted the union, some joining the progovernment syndicate and others staying away from trade unions altogether.[78]

As a challenge to the leftist union's claim of representing labor exclusively, the government permitted the ESKI to hold the only authorized May Day demonstration in 1948 and to send

---

[77] Iraj Eskandari, "Federesione Jahani Sandikaha va Nehzate Kargari Iran" [World Federation of Syndicates and Iranian Labor Movement], *Razm*, Vol. II, No. 6 (December, 1948), 9.

[78] The splinter group called the "Reformists of the Central Council" included some former Tudeh members like Yousef Eftekhar and Abass Shahandeh. *Ibid.*, Vol. II, No. 6 (December, 1948), 18.

delegations to various labor conferences thereafter. At the end of 1949 the ESKI joined the newly formed International Confederation of Free Trade Unions, thus bringing to completion the process of identification with anti-Communist trade unionism of the world.[79]

Meanwhile, the rival WFTU continued to give the Tudeh union its unconditional protection. In the eighth session of the UN Economic and Social Council, the WFTU once again complained of the government's attitude toward its affiliate in Iran, charging that the government-sponsored union was a creation of the Ministry of Labor and as such was determined to prevent the freedom of genuine trade union activity.[80] These protests no longer bothered the government, however, and it continued to tolerate the Tudeh union so long as its influence could be held in check.

The Ban on the Party

After the Second Tudeh Party Congress in April, 1948, the party and the union managed to regroup some of their scattered forces. Once again an attempt was made to form a united front of the antigovernment forces. At the end of summer, a new and curious alliance emerged which consisted of the extreme Right and Left, as well as some politicians from the Center who were represented in the now discredited Iranian Democratic party. The prospect of the election for the 16th Majlis in 1949 had produced a rallying cause for these forces left out of the ruling circles in the preceding Majlis. The Tudeh party joined the supporters of its former archenemy Seyd Zia Tabatabai in organizing an Antidictatorship Front, which was later joined by a segment of the Iranian Democratic party. The new front, like the earlier Freedom Front, was in effect an alliance of a score of leftist and rightist newspapers and publications supporting

---

[79] *Labor Conditions in the Oil Industry in Iran*, p. 52.
[80] "Report on Violation of Trade Union Rights, Submitted by the W.F.T.U.," *World Trade Union Movement* (Special Appendix No. 26), pp. 385-386.

former Prime Minister Ghavam's party and having an undercurrent of antimonarchism.[81]

It was largely owing to the activity of this alliance that the government of the allegedly monarchist Prime Minister Abdolhossein Hazhir was brought down in November, 1948, on the grounds that it intended to undermine the parliamentary system. The Communist movement seemed by then to have recovered from its disastrous defeat earlier.

The Tudeh party celebrated its seventh anniversary in October, 1948, in a solemn but considerably more optimistic mood. Reviewing its past struggles, Tabari, still the party's second political secretary, told the general conference of party activists that what had distinguished the party from all other political movements was its international outlook based on scientific theories. The Tudeh party, he said, remained the one and only party with a class foundation and trained militant cadres capable of leading that class. He also used the occasion to reiterate the party's principal features and to identify it with international communism in terms not publicly acknowledged before. He pictured the Tudeh as the vanguard of the working class, imbued with a deep sense of internationalism stemming from its interest in the world struggle against imperialism, "without whose defeat the liberation of our country will be most difficult." [82]

The party's continued loyalty to the Soviet Union was demonstrated in its outright denunciation of Tito's break with the Cominform [83] and a restatement of the belief in the nonimperialistic feature of Soviet policy, which, in the words of another party

---

[81] Dr. Freydoun Kashavarz, a secretary of the Tudeh party's executive board, characterized the program of the Front as generally democratic and liberal, aimed at preventing the degeneration of parliamentary government into an authoritarian regime reminiscent of Reza Shah's rule. From a press conference, *Mardom*, Aug. 22, 1948.

[82] Ehsan Tabari, "Haft Sal Mobarezeh" [Seven Years of Struggle], *Razm*, Vol. II, No. 4 (September–October, 1948), 1–4.

[83] In terms identical with the formal denunciations of the Yugoslav Communist party in the Cominform organs, the Tudeh press accused Tito of betraying revolutionary Marxism and endangering the unity of world communism. *Ibid.*, pp. 26–32.

spokesman, was demonstrated by Iran's wartime occupation. "The behavior of the occupation forces during the war proves," he said, "the essential difference between the Soviet and Imperialist policies in our country and underscores the continuation of the beneficial and friendly attitude which has characterized Soviet policies since the October Revolution." [84] Similarly, the party credited the presence of the Red Army in the country with frustration of Britain's alleged antifreedom activities in support of the ruling class and against the interests of the masses.

The defense of Soviet policy in Iran was made considerably easier for the party in view of Russia's more restrained attitude following the nullification of the draft oil agreement in October, 1947. Since there was no longer any obvious Soviet pressure on Iran, the party could now claim that it was an indigenous movement supporting the political ideology it considered best suited to the country's sociopolitical condition. This propaganda theme became more effective as it became evident that the Tudeh party was the only significant political group, working to solve the deeply rooted social and economic ills that seemed beyond the powers of the current regime.

In concentrating on the training of new cadres, party leaders carefully sought to avoid the past errors that had caused dissension and defection. The cadres were recruited mostly from the younger intellectual elements, whose youth and lack of political sophistication permitted their rapid indoctrination and mobilization. By 1948–1949 it was calculated that up to 50 percent of the politically active university students had either joined the Tudeh-sponsored student association or supported its platform and candidates. Most of these students were in their first or second year of college and in many cases were novices in politics to whom no other avenue of political expression was offered. The effectiveness of party work among the students was demonstrated in a number of incidents, including the student strike

---

[84] Dr. Mohammad Hossein Kiyanouri, "Siyasate Shoravi va Siyasete Ampriyalizm dar Iran" [The Soviet and the Imperialist Policies in Iran], *ibid.*, Vol. II, No. 5 (November, 1948), 12–16.

of November 12, 1948, protesting a university decree banning on-campus political activity, all of which marked a gradual weakening of government authority.[85]

Another characteristic of the period following the Second Tudeh Party Congress was the leadership's scrupulous adherence to the new party statute. As provided therein, in mid-July, 1948, the second and in mid-October the third plenum of the Central Committee met to review the quarterly report of past activity and to reelect members of the executive board and other party organs.[86] Although no significant changes occurred in the party's political direction, observance of these regulations did a good deal to strengthen the morale of the membership and to impart the impression of steady progress toward a revival.

The extent of the party's success in restoring itself to a position of prominence after more than two years came into view when a commemorative rally was organized at Dr. Erani's grave on February 4, 1949. The estimated 10,000 to 30,000 party members and sympathizers who participated were indicative of the party's renewed strength. Aided by the Antidictatorship Front, the party seemed likely to play a decisive role in the next election scheduled for the summer of 1949.[87]

However, the opportunity for that trial of strength did not arise, for at the time of the Tudeh rally, an attempt was made on the life of the Shah, while he was attending Charter Day ceremonies at Teheran University. The government at once outlawed the Tudeh party and the United Council and prohibited Communist and antimonarchist political activity. In a lengthy statement in the Majlis, Interior Minister Dr. Manouchehr Eghbal produced documents to prove the assailant's membership in the printer's union affiliated with the United Council and to justify the proposed measure for outlawing these organizational expressions of the Communist movement.[88]

---

[85] *Ibid.*, p. 28.

[86] *Ibid.*

[87] Partisan sources estimate the attendance at 30,000 (Alavi, *Kämpfendes, Iran*, p. 105). Government sources put it at 10,000. *Seyre Komonism*, p. 108.

[88] *Journal de Teheran*, Feb. 6, 1949.

The Majlis approved the government's policy statement, and thereupon followed a proclamation of martial law, the large-scale arrest of party and union leaders, suspension of their newspapers, and occupation of their headquarters in Teheran and elsewhere. The top leaders managed to escape arrest and ultimately found their way to Soviet Russia and other Communist bloc countries, but eight members of the party's Central Committee and most of the Tudeh union's central council were arrested and tried by a military tribunal. Thirteen of the fugitives were condemned to death in absentia, and others who were caught and tried drew five- to ten-year prison terms and banishment to islands in the Persian Gulf.[89]

These measures drove the party and its affiliates underground, thus beginning a new era in the Communist movement which has continued to the present time. The extent of the effectiveness of these measures in curbing the movement and mitigating its ideological attraction will be one focus of the following chapter.

---

[89] The names of the deported party and union leaders were listed in the letter sent to the Iranian premier by Louis Saillant, the general secretary of the WFTU, on March 4, 1950 (*World Trade Union Movement*, March, 1950, pp. 34–35). In another resolution adopted by its executive committtee meeting in Budapest, May 15–24, the WFTU appealed to the Iranian government for the release of both the party and union prisoners, termed "the imprisoned leaders of the Iranian working class." *Ibid.* Supp. to No. 6 (June, 1950).

5

COMMUNISM DURING THE
NATIONALIST MOVEMENT

Since the outlawing of its organizations in February, 1949, the Communist movement has gone through several stages, each characterized by certain distinctive features. Thus, the period corresponding with the rise of the nationalist movement from late 1949 is clearly distinguishable from the one following the overthrow of Dr. Mossadegh's National Front government in August, 1953. Similarly, the process of de-Stalinization in the mid-1950's and the subsequent modification — even reversal — of some of the doctrines of Soviet communism concerning revolutionary Marxism in underdeveloped areas and future relations with the national bourgeoisie have left their marks on the post-1955 phase; so have the Soviet diplomatic rapprochement with Iran after 1953 and its reversal when Iran joined the Baghdad Pact in 1955.

Along with these differentiating factors, several general characteristics provide a continuity during this period. First, the movement remained formally outlawed, under old anti-Communist law of June, 1931. Second, it continued to identify itself openly with Soviet communism. Third, the period after 1949 once again emphasized the significant correlation between the availability of even a minimum of democratic freedoms and the growth of the Communist party as the best organized political force in conditions of socioeconomic underdevelopment. Finally, events in that period served to demonstrate the futility of over-reliance on objective conditions for the ultimate success of native Communist parties without due regard for subjective factors extending beyond the confines of the country into the control of international communism.

The present chapter discusses the first phase of this period, which was characterized by rapid rise and abrupt decline in the development of the movement. The significance of this period lies in the introduction of new elements in the Communist struggle for acquisition of power and the continuous pattern of trial and error throughout this endeavor.

The Party Underground

One of these new elements was the application of front-organization tactics while the party itself remained underground. The party's remarkable success in this respect demonstrated the in-effectualness of democratic and formalistic methods of coping with a Communist movement in a country where no tradition of liberal democracy existed. Conversely, this phase underscored the difficulty for the Communists of trying to wrest the initiative from a nationalist movement with a large following among the bourgeoisie. In fact, the correct assessment of the role of the Iranian bourgeois nationalists posed for the Tudeh party a problem which could not be successfully tackled before the collapse of the nationalist movement in 1953 and without substantial doctrinal modifications finally effected by the leadership of international communism in the mid-1950's.

During the year following the unsuccessful attempt on the life of the Shah, the government made a serious effort to stabilize the regime by consolidating governmental authority and by passing a series of restrictive measures designed to ensure the continued suppression of the outlawed organizations of the Left.

In pursuance of the first aim a Constituent Assembly formed in March–April, 1949, substantially increased the Shah's power and authorized the introduction of bicameralism as a check on the power of the notoriously uncontrollable unicameral Majlis.[1] In addition, the traditional practice of ascertaining the Majlis' preference before the designation of a new prime minister by the sovereign was abandoned, thereby denying the assembly an important prerogative restored to it after the fall of the Reza Shah and partly responsible for chronic cabinet crises ever since.

Another development related to this general trend was the strengthening of the security forces, for which the active support and participation of the United States government had been solicited as early as 1947.[2] In fact, American involvement in this attempt and its growing identification with Western endeavors to contain Communist expansion had introduced into Iranian politics the novel element of the American presence, and this had weighed heavily on the Communist movement. For some months the army and military administration in the capital and the provinces worked hard at the task of enforcing an effective ban on the Tudeh party and its affiliates. A series of trials before military tribunals were held and heavy sentences meted out against party and union leaders, temporarily, at least, depriving the underground organization of its experienced leadership.

A year after the banning of the movement, the first sign of recovery appeared in the form of a clandestine issue of the old party organ, *Mardom*.[3] No real recovery, however, was possible until there was some change on the governmental level, and this appeared, in two ways, toward the end of 1949. One of these

---

[1] This amendment provided for a 60-member Senate, one-half of whom were elected and the other half appointed by the Shah, who was also vested with the right to dissolve parliament. It also authorized future constitutional changes by both houses sitting as a special joint congress. Helen Miller Davis, *Constitutions, Electoral Laws, Treaties of States in the Near and Middle East* (Durham, N.C., 1953).

[2] The Jam-Allen agreement of October, 1947, set in motion a long-term program for modernization of the army, provision of arms, and the services of advisory missions.

[3] The first clandestine issue, a single sheet, appeared in October, 1949. See Military Governorship of Teheran, *Seyre Komonism dar Iran* [The Evolution of Communism in Iran] (Teheran, 1958), p. 35.

was the matter of the revision of the Anglo–Iranian oil concession, which had ramifications not only for Anglo–Iranian relations but also for all Iranian ties with the West. The other was the prospect of the parliamentary election for the 16th Majlis scheduled to convene at the beginning of autumn. These two issues soon became major sources of political agitation, seriously undermining consolidation of governmental authority and rousing the Communist movement from its enforced dormancy.

In the summer of 1949, shortly before the end of its term, the 15th Majlis was given the draft of a supplementary agreement with the Anglo–Iranian Oil Company. Although this draft included better terms than the 1933 concession, it fell short of satisfying Iran's demands for substantially increased oil royalties and participation in the management of the industry.[4] The question of parliamentary ratification at once polarized the country's political forces, and within the Majlis the controversy engendered a debate so heated that the legislature was jerked out of the dormancy into which it had fallen with the strengthening of executive and sovereign powers.

Before this debate, the pattern in the Majlis had been confused. The old lineup, of sides for and against the former Prime Minister, Ghavam, had melted away following the successful rebuff to the Soviet diplomatic offensive and Ghavam's subsequent ouster. Although Ghavam's personal following did not completely disappear, what was left of his Iranian Democratic party ceased to be represented in the Majlis because of mass defection. Some of its more leftist elements continued to be active first in the Tudeh-sponsored antidictatorship press coalition and then in the struggle to oppose amending the constitution to effect bicameralism and augment the Shah's power.

With the injection of the oil issue into Iranian political and parliamentary life, the 15th Majlis acquired a new lineup, in which a small minority of four deputies, enjoying the tacit support of a much larger segment of the membership, transformed

---

[4] Text in J. C. Hurewitz, *Diplomacy in the Near and Middle East, A Documentary Record: 1914–1956* (New York 1956), II, 305–308.

the issue into a major political controversy going far beyond its economic and financial confines.[5] The parliamentary opposition, which successfully filibustered debate on the agreement until the end of the Majlis term in late summer, became the nucleus for the emergence of a new political formation of essentially nationalistic and center political persuasion. The new organization, called the National Front and led by Dr. Mossadegh, was dedicated to entering the elections for the new Majlis on a platform of open opposition to the supplementary oil agreement and a tacit objection to the augmentation of the authority of the sovereign and the executive branch of the government.

The very intensity of its electoral campaign compelled the relaxation of repressive measures against political freedoms, and from this the Communist movement, still the best organized political force, tended to benefit the most. During the prolonged campaign, which ultimately involved the annulment of the election of twelve Teheran deputies because of fraud, the outlawed Tudeh party and its affiliates found the first opportunity to resort to front-organization tactics for regrouping their scattered forces.

With the inauguration of the new Majlis in February, 1950, the National Front opposition, representing a loose coalition of nationalist and progressive forces of the left-of-center, gradually rallied a large majority of the bourgeois nationalists to its struggle against British political and economic influence. This development was of some benefit to the Communist movement in that it created conditions favorable to its reactivation, but it also posed some serious problems, which were to plague its leaders throughout this period.

Foremost of these was the National Front's challenge to the movement as the best representative of the oppressed lower and

---

[5] For a comprehensive Persian treatment of the oil dispute, see Mostafa Fateh, *Panjah Sal Nafte Iran* [Fifty Years of Persian Oil] (Teheran, 1956). L. P. Elwell-Sutton's *Persian Oil; A Study in Power Politics* (London, 1955) is an example of primarily political treatment of the issue; Alan W. Ford's *The Anglo–Iranian Oil Dispute of 1951–1952; A Study of the Role of Law in the Relations of States* (Berkeley and Los Angeles, 1954) provides an essentially legal and juridical examination of the case.

middle classes in the current struggle for Iran's political and economic liberation. For the first time since the Second World War, a genuine popular movement was gathering momentum independently of the Communist movement, heretofore the sole organized political opposition to the established regime. The competition for the loyalty of the discontented assumed an added dimension as the National Front encompassed forces other than the bourgeois nationalists, such as the non-Tudeh leftist section of the intelligentsia and even some segments of the working class. In attempting to reach these elements, the Front was encroaching on sources of recruitment the Communists had jealously regarded as their exclusive domain.

The formation of the Toilers of the Iranian Nation party was the first attempt at organizing the non- and even anti-Communist Left. If this had been successful, it could seriously have undermined the Communist movement's claim to this exclusiveness. That the new party, formed in early 1951, rallied a majority of the moderate Tudeh party defectors belonging to Maleki's group and a score of other leftist intellectuals, who had not rejoined the Communist movement since 1945 either from conviction or fear of government reprisal, was another development the Tudeh leaders could not ignore.[6]

The Toilers party, representing the non-Communist Left in the wide spectrum of the National Front, actively vied for the loyalty of the politically articulate intelligentsia, which since the ban on open Communist organizations had withdrawn into political apathy. The attraction of the new party was not merely that it, too, was a modern cadre party armed with the scientific ideology of non-Communist socialism; it also had patriotic appeal, holding promise of mobilizing the masses in an important national struggle.

The Communist Left thus found itself facing a formidable problem: it was no longer working in a political vacuum in

---

[6] Dr. Mozaffar Baghai, a member of the National Front parliamentary group, was the leader of the Toilers party; Maleki and his followers served as the main core of trained cadres.

which it could speak as the sole advocate of a scientific ideology; it was no longer challenged merely by parties of the Right, which traditionally supported the political status quo and extreme nationalism; and its internationalism was being challenged by the demands of an integral nationalism represented by a government which did not hesitate to cultivate American support at a time when international communism was uncompromisingly opposed to the United States. How, in the face of all these, was it to maintain its exclusiveness? What answers was it to make to the challenges? The solutions were slow to come.

The clandestine Tudeh party and its affiliates at the end of 1950 were contemptuous of the chances for success of the fast-developing nationalist movement. In their opinion, it was chiefly a product of internal contradictions within the ruling classes, the framework within which, ever since their own downfall in 1946, they had tended to view all Iranian internal political developments — the reflection, they believed, of the inherent rivalry in the world imperialist camp. To them, the successive cabinets since the fall of the Azarbayjan revolutionary regime either represented American and British interests or reflected the rivalry between different segments of the ruling class, notably the royal court and the reactionary Right.[7]

They looked on the struggle for oil nationalization at first as bounded within this narrow framework — not merely because it fitted their formula but also because they were simply unable to recognize that there could be any other organized popular movement capable of seriously challenging the basic structure of Iran's power relations. There was no denying that the National Front's struggle represented such a challenge, for by endeavoring to impose on the parliament and the ruling class its own radical solution to the oil dispute, the Front was threatening the regime's Western ties and conceivably its entire power basis — which was, after all, not really secure despite the recent consolidation measures.

---

[7] *Razm*, Vol. II, No. 6 (December, 1948).

Not until the National Front's following became too large to ignore and the initial success of the oil nationalization campaign clearly evident were the Tudeh leaders convinced that the new development was more than a passing phase. At that point, a revision of old formulas and policies was undertaken.

Organizational and Ideological Reconstruction

With the gradual strengthening of their conviction that the nationalist movement was a force to be reckoned with, the Tudeh leadership, backed by the members, embarked on a twofold policy: taking maximum advantage of the relaxation of government measures against political activity, and using front-organization tactics, the party would mobilize old sympathizers and draw new converts; underground, the party would be reconstructed on a more solidly Communist and revolutionary pattern. The movement ultimately achieved considerable success in pursuing this policy throughout this period, though there still remained, as matters for preoccupation, other aspects of the problem caused by the rise of bourgeois nationalists and the acquisition of power by their political organization, the National Front.

The first use of the front-organization tactic began in the spring of 1950, when, along with the publication of the first issue of the clandestine Tudeh newspaper *Mardom,* a peace offensive in the form of the Iranian Society of Peace Partisans was launched.[8] This society was a loose left-of-center alliance started by non-Communist public figures, including several members of the national Front parliamentary group and scores of literary and journalistic personalities, some of whom had publicly opposed the Tudeh party in the past. Gradually, as the

---

[8] *Besooye-Ayandeh* was the leading organ of Tudeh front organizations between April, 1950, and August, 1953. *Mardom* continued as the organ of the underground party though its publication was quite irregular, depending on the seriousness or success of police efforts to enforce the ban on the party.

society became increasingly identified with the Communist-sponsored international peace movement, its leadership passed into the hands of Tudeh members or sympathizers.[9]

Its platform echoed such goals of the international peace movement as a treaty among the five major powers, total disarmament, dissolution of Western military alliances, and a ban on atomic weapons. The society's official organ and other publications supporting its goals were careful to conceal their Communist ties in order to attract as broad a following as possible.[10] Its activity was coordinated with other front and clandestine Communist organizations by a member of the executive board of the Tudeh party's Central Committee, who in effect exercised the over-all control of the society, although the latter had formed its own hierarchy corresponding to that of the party in Teheran and elsewhere.

Toward the end of 1950, when the campaign for nationalizing the oil industry reached its climax, the party formed another front organization solely to embrace party members and sympathizers, many of whom were simultaneously active in its clandestine organizations. But by early spring, 1951, the new organization, the National Society for Struggle Against the Anglo–Iranian Oil Company, had undergone several changes in its official goal, since the oil industry had been nationalized, largely through the efforts of the National Front.

In a congress held that spring it changed its name to the Society to Struggle Against Colonial Oil Companies; but, realizing that this limited goal had already been achieved with the enactment of the nationalization law and the assumption of power by Dr. Mossadegh, it changed its name again — to the National Society for Struggle Against Colonialism — at another congress held in early summer. For all practical purposes, this society, which a year later organized the Tudeh youth into the Demo-

---

[9] Abolhasan Haeri-Zadeh and Dr. Ali Shayegan were among the National Front personalities who left the society once its domination by the Tudeh party became obvious. *Seyre Komonism*, p. 339.

[10] The society claimed to have collected over two million signatures on its petition for peace in 1951–1952. *Ibid.*

cratic Youth Club, became the Communist movement's public organization until the fall of the nationalist regime in August, 1953.[11]

Simultaneously with the formation of these front organizations, the clandestine party also underwent organizational and ideological changes. The ban on the party and its affiliates had, as we have seen, cost the movement nearly all its top leaders. Some of the more prominent members of the nineteen-man Central Committee had left Iran as early as December, 1946, fearing prosecution in connection with the Azarbayjan insurrection. When Communist organizations were declared illegal in February, 1949, others went into hiding and then escaped to Soviet bloc countries. Six members of the Central Committee's executive board, along with two members of the control commission and one alternate member of the Central Committee, were imprisoned and tried by military tribunals, leaving only two members of the executive board free in the country.[12]

On December 15, 1950, through the careful preparation of the party's military network, the nine imprisoned Tudeh leaders, along with Khosro Ruzbeh, who was in charge of the officers' network, managed to escape from prison. For a while the six members of the executive board who had escaped joined the two who had remained free in actively coordinating the clandestine party's operations. But in early 1952, three left the country to participate in the Nineteenth Congress of the Communist Party of the Soviet Union. This left party leadership in the hands of five executive board members until total elimination of the leadership through arrest or escape was accomplished by the end of 1955.[13]

---

[11] Other front organizations were the Society for the Protection of Children, the Society of Freedom of Iran, representing pro-Tudeh tradesmen, and the Organization of Iran's Women. *Ibid.*, pp. 334–341.

[12] The six members of the executive board were Dr. Jowdat, Dr. Kiyanouri, A. Ghassemi, M. Boghrati, Dr. Yazdi, and A. Olovvi. *Ibid.*, p. 20.

[13] The division of labor among the five was effected in this fashion: (1) Dr. Jowdat in charge of the Teheran organization and trade union, (2) Dr. Bahrami as secretary of the C.C. in charge of youth and peasant branches,

The five-man directorate in this phase of clandestine activity immediately set out to reconstruct the party. By mid-1952 the publication of the organ of the underground party became more regular and a number of daily and weekly newspapers representing various front organizations had settled on a fairly consistent ideology and policy.[14]

Along with the party reconstruction, its trade union affiliate also was reorganized. Since most of the former leaders had either escaped abroad or had been arrested, a new five-man central board was elected in which the party's Central Committee was well represented.[15] The United Council continued to be recognized by the WFTU, which acted as an effective organ of international propaganda on behalf of its Iranian affiliate. Most of its former members joined the front organizations, thus supplying the movement with a fairly large cadre of militant workers during the critical developments surrounding the campaign for oil nationalization.

By early spring, 1952, the movement had largely recovered the numerical strength it had had before it was banned in 1949. The best available accounts, based on such factors as newspaper circulation, participation in public demonstrations, and returns of the incomplete election to the 17th Majlis in the winter of 1951–1952, put the total membership and sympathizers at about 50,000 in Teheran and about the same in the provinces.[16] Of these, the clandestine party claimed about 10,000 members in Teheran and an equal number in the provincial centers; these members, together with more than 5,500 members of the Tudeh Youth League, constituted a hard core of party cadres and the back-

---

(3) Olovvi in charge of provincial organization and finance, (4) Dr. Yazdi in charge of information and front organizations, (5) Dr. Kiyanouri in charge of party instruction and propaganda. *Ibid.*, p. 204.

[14] In 1953 there were numerous Tudeh clandestine and cover publications, of which twenty appeared regularly in the capital. *Donya*, Vol. II, No. 1, p. 33.

[15] They were Dr. Jowdat, Babazadeh, Shandarmeni, Yaghoobzadegan, Dr. Razavi, and M. Azimi. *Seyre Komonism*, p. 316.

[16] *Ibid.*, p. 317.

bone of the movement until the National Front era came to a close.[17]

The Tudeh Military Network

The most significant achievement of the movement was its successful infiltration of various branches of the armed forces at a time when, owing to a decline in governmental authority, military morale was low and discipline lax. The military had not been totally impervious to Communist infiltration and the party had succeeded in recruiting from among the army's lower echelon a small but influential core who had played an active part in the Azarbayjan insurrection. In addition to that experience, the small Tudeh officer core had participated in several isolated attempts at armed insurrection; these had failed in their immediate objective, but they served to underscore the susceptibility of the military to the appeal of communism and to active indoctrination by party workers.[18] The discovery in the summer of 1954 of an extensive Tudeh network in the army — some 600 officers, ranging from junior noncommissioned officers to colonels — reemphasized this factor.[19] It also demonstrated the party's accelerated transition toward a more revolutionary posture.

The decision to infiltrate the armed forces seems to have resulted from careful consideration of social and political developments after the 1949 suppression of the movement. In 1952, when Tudeh party leaders took definite steps to abandon the pretense of noncommunism by drafting a new revolutionary program, a corollary scheme for recruiting and training military cadres on a much wider scale was launched. The immediate cause prompting the party to focus on the military was the up-

---

[17] These figures are based on trial records of Dr. M. Bahrami, a secretary of the clandestine party, arrested in 1956. *Ibid.*, pp. 235–264.

[18] The Military Governorship of Teheran's *Ketabe Siyah* [Black Book] (Teheran, 1955) gives a full account of the network's activity after its formation in April, 1942.

[19] For a journalistic account of this discovery, see "The Anatomy of a Red Spy Ring," *Life*, Nov. 21, 1955.

rising of July, 1952, in which the Communists joined the nationalist militant groups to reinstate Dr. Mossadegh to power. This violent incident and its subsequent events brought home to the Tudeh leadership the ultimate importance of the military in seizing power under the conditions of public disorder and political chaos.

During the final stage of that day-long civil revolt against the army and the conservative ruling class the Tudeh party came closest to capturing power. Had it been armed with even a small disciplined military core willing to use violence, it could have exploited the situation of an almost total vacuum which had resulted from the withdrawal of army units. Instead, as soon as the common goal of the tacit Communist–Nationalist alliance was achieved, the Nationalist forces turned on the Tudeh elements and shortly restored the order and authority of the reinstated National Front government in the capital.[20]

The lesson of this incident was undoubtedly instrumental in shifting emphasis to the training of military cadres in the second phase of the National Front regime, and the Tudeh leadership attacked the problem with great vigor. When the entire membership and leadership of the Tudeh military network were arrested and tried in the summer and fall of 1954, it was revealed that more than three-fourths of the cadres had been recruited in late 1952 and early 1953, when the Tudeh drive was at its height.

In accordance with the bylaws of the military network, adopted by the party Central Committee in April, 1953, the three basic principles of total centralization, rigid discipline, and maximum secrecy were carefully observed in recruiting members and conducting activity.[21] To ensure strict adherence to these principles, the bylaws contained detailed instructions governing every aspect of its operation.

Candidates would be accepted on a tentative basis after an elaborate screening process which included a "character report" dealing with the most personal aspects of their lives and beliefs.

---

[20] *The Times* (London), July 20–23, 1952.
[21] *Ketabe Siyah*, p. 75.

They would then go through a six-month apprenticeship during which they would have to display irrefutable evidence of their loyalty to the party and its ideology.

The hierarchy of the network, aside from minor differences necessitated by observing the principle of secrecy, was analogous to that of the party itself. At the bottom was a cell with a minimum of three members led by a leader who was required to have been a member of the organization for at least two years. Above this was the leaders' cell, composed of at least three leaders of member cells and responsible for conveying the party's instructions to the rank and file. At a higher level was the committee of the officer organization, composed of the secretaries of the leaders' cells and other members appointed by the party Central Committee. This committee, in turn, elected from its membership the secretariat, which performed the committee's functions in the interval between its sessions and was responsible to it and to the party's Central Committee.[22]

The control of the military network by the party's civilian leadership was assured by the provision that the secretariat's decisions were to be adopted in the presence of the representative of the party's Central Committee. In effect, a member of the Central Committee's executive board, who functioned as a liaison with the secretariat, exercised full power over the secretariat's decisions, particularly on the major issue of resorting to armed insurrection.[23]

To assure secrecy, the network developed an elaborate code in the form of trigonometrical equations containing the identity, rank, party status, and other characteristics of its members. From the outset, the network was engaged in Communist indoctrination, exposing the recruit to a systematic process of political in-

---

[22] Until August, 1953, it had seven members: Col. E. Siyamak, Lt. Col. M. Mobasheri, Ex-Capt. K. Ruzben, Maj. J. Vakili, Capt. E. Mohaghegh, Lt. M. Mokhtari, and the civilian Dr. Jowdat, the party's liaison officer. Thereafter, it was reduced to the first three. *Ibid.*, p. 83.

[23] Each of the seven members of the secretariat was in charge of a separate branch of the armed forces. *Ibid.*

struction designed to transform him into a party militant in the revolutionary Marxist–Leninist tradition.[24]

Until August, 1953, the military network was primarily engaged in organizational expansion and doctrinal consolidation, but it also carried on intelligence activities which enabled the Tudeh leaders to keep remarkably well informed about political and military secrets. After the overthrow of the National Front government in August, the network began preparing for an armed insurrection.

The New Draft Program

Throughout much of the period of the National Front, the Tudeh party was changing from a Communist-oriented party to a genuine Communist party. A new draft program prepared by the Central Committee and secretly distributed among its membership in mid-1952 sought to effect this transformation by abandoning all pretense of any adherence to democratic and constitutional principles.[25]

Just how radical a departure this new draft program was can be seen by comparing it in detail with the statute adopted by the Second Tudeh Party Congress in 1948. Fundamentally, the statute defined the party as being composed of the four oppressed classes: workers, peasants, artisans, and freedom-seeking intellectuals. The draft program defined it as the party of the working class, "which was armed with the powerful weapon of Marxism–

---

[24] The principal works used were the *Communist Manifesto* and the *Principles of Communism*, Dr. Erani's works on the *Foundation of Marxism* and *Elementary Principles of Philosophy*, the *History of the Russian Communist Party*, major Soviet literary works, notably by Maxim Gorki, and a host of Tudeh literature (*Ketabe Siyah*, p. 43). For a review of the political thinking of the leader of the network, see "Pages from History: A National Hero," *World Marxist Review*, Vol. V, No. 10 (October, 1962), 94–95, based on the final defense plea of Khosrow Ruzbeh, who was executed in early 1958.

[25] *Barnamehe Hezbe Tudeh Baraye Marhalehe Konuni az Takamole Ejtemaiye Keshvare Ma* [Draft Program of the Tudeh Party for the Contemporary Stage of Our Country's Social Evolution] (Teheran, 1952); hereafter cited as *Draft Program*.

Leninism and sought to emulate the experience of those nations which have constructed socialism in their countries by applying this ideology." [26]

The party's foreign policy, defined in the first document as favoring friendly cooperation with all freedom-loving nations based on their equality and the preservation of world peace, was given a new outlook and new aims in the draft program: "The total break with the camp of imperialism, war and aggression, sincere political and economic cooperation with countries struggling to preserve world peace, and membership in the world front of peace and democracy at whose vanguard stands the Socialist Soviet Union are the major goals guiding the party in its international outlook." [27]

Another revolutionary change was related to the party's attitude toward the Iranian constitution. In the provisional statute in force before the First Congress in 1944, the party had given full support to the constitution. The statute adopted by the Second Congress in 1948 contained no reference to the constitution, but a party publication which interpreted its provisions glorified the constitution and described the party's reliance on its provisions as a fundamental condition for ensuring a democratic regime. [28] The new draft program, however, demanded a "democratic" constitution, which, while granting the people democratic rights, would also ensure their fulfillment in a specific and practical manner. It regarded the existing constitution as "possessed of basic defects and totally incapable of securing us freedom, peace, and national independence." [29] It thus appeared that, with the formal adoption of the Marxist–Leninist ideology, the party found continued acceptance of the constitution inconsistent with its support of such principles as secularism and the right of self-determination for Iran's various minorities.

Accompanying this reevaluation of the constitution was a

---

[26] *Ibid.*, Title III.

[27] *Ibid.*, pp. 27–28.

[28] Ahmad Ghassemi, *Hezbe Tudeh Che Miguyad va Che Mikhahad?* [What Does the Tudeh Party Say and Want?] (Teheran, 1944).

[29] *Draft Program*, p. 14.

similar reappraisal of the 1905–1909 constitutional movement, of which that document was the outcome. During its legal existence, the party had repeatedly glorified the early constitutional movement and had in effect attempted to credit Russian Social Democracy with having played a decisive role in its evolution and success; now it revised these old views.[30] Imperialism was blamed for "meddling with the constitutional movement and preventing it from producing a democratic constitution free from the reactionary and antinational features of the present constitution."[31]

The draft program went considerably beyond the renunciation of the constitution, however, in actually demanding the overthrow of "the feudalist monarchical regime and the establishment of a republican regime of the people's democracy headed by a president."[32] The demand was justified by "an analysis of the class origins of the ruling oligarchy, without whose total elimination a genuine regime of the people's democracy could not be established." The violent overthrow of the constitutional regime was also advocated as a definitive progressive measure, made necessary by the established regime's traditional and reactionary features and its stubborn resistance to any change in the prevailing power structure.

Another innovation incorporated in the draft program concerned Iran's territorial integrity. Although the previous party statute had paid lip service to this concept, it was only now that a federal pattern of territorial division of power with a corollary concept of national self-determination was openly advocated as "motivated by a genuine concern for the national characteristics and equal rights of all people united in a single country on the basis of free cooperation."[33]

The party's attitude toward private ownership was also fully revised. The old slogans of land distribution through state compensation to large landlords were dropped in favor of outright

---

[30] Ahmad Ghassemi, "Marahele Enghelabe Mashruteh" [Phases of the Constitutional Revolution], *Razm*, Vol. II, No. 7 (January, 1949).
[31] *Draft Program*, p. 14.
[32] *Ibid.*, Title VII.
[33] *Ibid.*, Title XI.

confiscation of "lands and means of agricultural production owned by the royal family, feudal lords, and owners of large properties." [34]

Finally, in what amounted to an unconditional acceptance of Lenin's dictum on revolutionary seizure of state power, the draft program advocated the destruction of the state apparatus through armed action. "The antinational security forces should be abolished and replaced by local and national guards under the control of people of each locality, thus ensuring the transformation of the security arm of the state from a tool of the reactionary classes against democratic freedoms into a means of protecting these rights and freedoms for the people." [35]

These radical changes terminated the controversy over the Tudeh party's true nature. They did not, however, bring the party into the open as a unified Communist organization. Rather, the party pursued its activity in a dual capacity. With the publication of the new draft program, its clandestine network set out on the course of transition toward a more genuine Communist party. Its front organizations, on the other hand, sought to continue their legal existence under conditions increasingly analogous to those prevailing before the party was outlawed.

As the nationalist movement centering on nationalization of the oil industry gathered momentum, the concomitant relaxation of restrictive measures against political activity greatly augmented the Tudeh party's freedom of action to the extent that a mere legal ban on the party became almost meaningless. The party of course benefited from these favorable conditions, but it also faced certain difficult tactical and ideological problems, which it never fully solved during the course of the nationalist movement.

Attitude Toward the Bourgeois Nationalists

One of these problems was the attitude toward the bourgeois nationalists. At first, despite certain misgivings, the Communists

---

[34] *Ibid.*, Title XX.
[35] *Ibid.*, Title XXI.

welcomed the nationalist movement, primarily because it served as a catalyst for the revival of the party's clandestine and cover organizations. This revival was only incidental to the gradual improvement of conditions for political activity, however; what was of more significance in the recovery of the Communist movement was the pervading nationalistic aspect of the oil nationalization campaign, which made it possible for all political elements of importance, including the Tudeh party, to give a patriotic coloring to their activity.[36]

By pretending to support a national struggle whose avowed goal was Iran's political and economic liberation, the Communist movement hoped to regain some of its former influence with the nationalist-minded bourgeoisie, which had almost completely lost sympathy for the movement after it showed itself subordinate to Soviet interests. The Communists believed themselves justified in this support by reason of two important characteristics of bourgeois nationalism, both of which were an inescapable part of the particular setting of Iranian life: on the one hand, its conflict with British influence and the conservative wing of the ruling class, essentially an anti-imperialist struggle amounting to a revolutionary undertaking; on the other hand, its failure, owing to its "inherent weakness," to break all political and economic ties with Great Britain.[37]

This analysis of the nationalist movement was said to be fully in accord with Marxism–Leninism. Mao Tse-tung's characterizations of the weaknesses of the bourgeoisie during the Chinese revolution also applied to the Iranian case, the party believed, and should be accepted as the guiding principle for the Communists in their relations with the nationalist movement.[38] Similarly, on the authority of Lenin, the Communists accepted the notion that the bourgeois nationalism of every oppressed nation had a general democratic content, inasmuch as it was directed

---

[36] Joseph M. Upton, *The History of Modern Iran: An Interpretation* (Cambridge, Mass., 1960), pp. 95–96.

[37] *Mardom*, Oct. 11, 1952.

[38] Mao Tse-tung, *Selected Works*, III (London, 1956), 162.

against the oppression of the established social and political order. By pledging support for the movement's popular basis and attempting to broaden its goals into definite demands for radical changes in power relations, the party could exploit this content to its maximum advantage.[39]

Recognition of the democratic content of bourgeois nationalism did not, however, imply unconditional support for the nationalist movement, for it was simultaneously held that only the proletariat could lead a national liberation movement to its ultimate goal. This was so because of the inherent weaknesses of the bourgeois nationalists and their alleged lack of devotion to the bourgeois democratic revolution. In the words of a Tudeh theorist: "The national bourgeoisie is concerned mainly with its narrow class interests, and strives to keep the revolution within the framework of these interests. That is why when confronted with such tasks as the elimination of the imperialist influence, the feudal survival of political institutions, the solution of the agrarian problem, and the winning of democratic liberties, it begins to vacillate, may abandon the revolution, hinder the liberation movement, and lead it to defeat."[40]

These concepts armed the Tudeh leadership with theoretical guidance, but their practical application proved difficult, in varying degrees, during the course of the nationalist movement. Most of the difficulty, however, was the result of the party's own conviction of the dualistic and contradictory nature of the bourgeois nationalists, which demanded at every turn a correct assessment and balanced evaluation. These continual reviews took much time and thought, and the result was that the party never arrived at a consistent policy. In Communist terms, this failure amounted to a left wing sectarian deviation, "which is manifest when the working class leaders overestimate the conciliatory

---

39 *World Marxist Review*, Vol. V, No. 9 (September, 1962), 79.

40 Mohammad Hossein Kiyanouri, "The National Bourgeoisie, Their Nature and Policy," *World Marxist Review*, Vol. II, No. 8 (August, 1959), 64. This is a summary of a seminar on "bourgeois nationalism and the liberal movements in Asia, Africa, and Latin America held by the Leipzig Institute of World History in May, 1959.

character and underestimate the anti-imperialist, antifeudal character of the national bourgeoisie. As a result the working class becomes unable to persuade the masses of the correctness of its policy, to isolate the bourgeoisie from the masses of the working people, and, consequently, to create the condition for its leadership."[41]

In retrospect, the failure to cope with this problem seemed due as much to a confusion about the national bourgeoisie's role as to a lack of comprehension of its social composition. Presumably, because of the absence of a current doctrinal interpretation concerning relations with the national bourgeoisie since the Comintern's Sixth Congress, and under the pressure of the rapid pace of political developments, the Tudeh leadership had failed to formulate a sufficiently clear idea of the bourgeoisie's characteristics. So much was later acknowledged:

> During the struggle for nationalization of the Iranian oil industry, for example, we did not support Mossadegh, who undoubtedly represented the interests of the national bourgeoisie. We thought along these lines: Mossadegh is fighting for the nationalization of Iranian oil. But the American imperialists are backing this movement, which means that they are guiding it. And so we drew the incorrect conclusion that the Communists should not support the nationalization movement, thereby isolating ourselves from the masses who followed the bourgeoisie, and not our party.[42]

At the outset, the Tudeh attitude toward the organizational expression of the nationalist movement, the National Front, suffered from equal misconceptions of fact and confusion of roles. The party stubbornly refused to distinguish between various political trends represented in the Front, and except for the few occasions when tactical necessities demanded otherwise, it renounced the Front as inherently incapable of achieving Iran's economic liberation.

The Front encompassed a broad alliance of the Iranian social strata, representing several distinct elements in terms of goals

41 *Ibid.*, p. 65.
42 Iraj Eskandari, "What Do We Mean by the National Bourgeoisie?" *World Marxist Review*, Vol. II, No. 8 (September, 1959), 72.

and social composition. At the center were the middle and petty bourgeoisie, the traders, the white collar intelligentsia, and a large segment of the religious hierarchy and the like who, under the leadership of Dr. Mossadegh, viewed the oil naturalization compaign as primarily a political struggle to secure liberation from British influence, and thereby to consolidate national independence. Vaguely related to this goal was some conception of a democratic and constitutional system of government and social reforms thought to be obtainable only after the elimination of British political and economic influence.

Although the National Front's center was averse to the formation of political parties in a modern sense, viewing them as basically divisive and harmful to national unity, several small political and professional organizations, such as the Iran party and the Merchant Association of the Bazaar, were identified with it. To the right of the Front were rallied splinter extremist groups such as the Islamic fundamentalist Fedayeen Islam (Moslem devotees) and the Pan-Iranist party composed largely of urban petty bourgeois elements having no very clear political goals except perhaps all-out support for the Front's more extremist policies.

The Toilers party and other loosely organized elements of the non-Communist Left constituted the Front's left wing. The Toilers party and its associated labor groups represented the only cadre party with a definite program and ideology in this broad alliance.

This political configuration more or less consistently represented the organizational development of the nationalist movement. Communist leaders, however, following their orthodox conception of the nature of the national bourgeoisie, saw it as differently composed. They viewed the sector of the Front which cooperated with "the party of the working class" as its true left wing, regardless of its social composition or political goal. In practice, this led to the Tudeh party's endorsing some of the tribal chieftains and Moslem clerics who for reasons of their own had joined the Front.

Conversely, they considered the right wing of the national

bourgeoisie to be the minority which refused to cooperate in a broad anti-imperialist front and thus allied itself with the enemies of the people. This means that the Toilers party and other splinter groups of the non-Communist Left were on the right. Significantly, these groups contained a majority of Tudeh defectors, many of whom had neither abandoned their ideological affinity for socialism nor had lost any of their social and class characteristics.

Following the collapse of the nationalist movement in 1953, Tudeh leaders belatedly realized how wrong they were to have neglected the National Front's center and spurned its non-Communist true left wing. The mistake, they said, had been due to the influence of left wing sectarianism:

This incorrect assessment of the National Front must be attributed to a lack of a clear understanding of the Iranian society and its revolutionary characteristics as much as to a leftist sectarianism which had befallen the party as a result of victories in the struggle for reviving our movement. Together these factors prevented us from cooperating with the anticolonial forces, utilizing the reservoir of revolutionary forces, and exploiting various internal contradictions of the society. It is now obvious that we should have strongly advocated the slogan of the united front of all anti-imperialist forces, and persistently urged the National Front as the political representative of the national bourgeoisie to adopt this slogan on the basis of a commonly accepted platform.[43]

Near the end of the first phase of the National Front regime, and definitely after the reinstatement of Dr. Mossadegh in July, 1952, the Tudeh leadership attempted to correct some of these mistakes. A party theorist, modifying an earlier evaluation of the Front, based the doctrinal foundation for cooperation with the national bourgeoisie on the two concepts of unity and struggle. According to these concepts, the working class party was expected to draw the national bourgeoisie, especially its cen-

---

[43] Central Committee of the Tudeh Party, *Hezbe Ma Va Jonbeshe Enghelabiye Salhaye Akhir* [Our Party and the Revolutionary Movement of Recent Years] (Teheran, 1955), p. 14.

ter and left wing, into a united front. But in doing so, it should guard against the attempt of the national bourgeoisie's right wing to water down the policies of the united front and to isolate the working class. The party of the working class, therefore, while cooperating with the national bourgeoisie, would in turn try to isolate its right wing from the rest of the anti-imperialist forces.[44]

These revisions did not, however, identify the components of different segments of the Front. Moreover, because of a breakdown of communication between the two factions of the Tudeh party leadership, that is, the exiled wing encompassing most of the Central Committee members and a reduced executive board remaining in Iran, they had little real effect on the party's attitude toward the National Front.[45] Despite some evidence of at least an academic interest in these concepts, the leadership never fully visualized what was later acknowledged as "the ability of the national bourgeoisie to lead a considerable part of the anti-imperialist forces, especially the petty bourgeoisie sections, in town and countryside."[46] The prospect was perhaps foreseen, but no practical conclusions seemed to have been drawn from it.

These, in brief, were the Communist evaluations of the national bourgeoisie and some of the problems Tudeh leaders encountered in attempting to apply them to the nationalist movement. It must be noted, however, that great though these problems were, after an initial period of indecision, the party's policy toward the Front became more decisive.

An analysis of its attitude toward the Front indicates that this policy was geared to a realistic evaluation of the political situation and to a pragmatic assessment of the relevant domestic and

---

[44] Kiyanouri, *op. cit.*, p. 63.

[45] A case in point was the opposition of the left wing element in the Tudeh youth organization led by Nader Sharmini to the proposed changes of tactics toward the National Front, embodied in a pamphlet entitled, *Tafsiri az Ozaye Siyasi va Ejtemai Iran* [A Commentary on the Sociopolitical Condition of Iran], written by Dr. Kiyanouri from his East European exile. *Seyre Komonism*, p. 275.

[46] Kiyanouri, "The National Bourgeoisie," p. 66.

international factors. If the outcome fell short of the acquisition of power or even a part in the government, the failure was not to be explained simply in terms of leadership blunders or a lack of determination to utilize all the forces at its command.

The Tudeh leadership, once having come to a decision, persistently pursued what it saw as its best chance of attaining its own goals: isolating the National Front from other sectors of the ruling class, and at the same time trying to undermine Iran's Western ties. It hoped that the Front's eventual isolation from the ruling class, on which it was imposed, would force the bourgeois nationalists to turn to the Tudeh party as the sole organized political force capable of retaining it in power. It expected that severance, or at least gradual undermining, of Iran's Western ties would leave the alternative of alignment with the Soviet Union as a more attractive and an ultimately inevitable choice of policy.

Thus, on the one hand, the party campaigned for a total transformation of the nationalist upsurge into a revolutionary challenge to the established order through skillful exploitation of the gradual decline in governmental authority, while on the other it systematically attempted to intensify the anti-Western content of Iranian nationalism. These two emphases characterized the Communist attitude toward the specific issue of oil nationalization and the government of the National Front which acceded to power in the spring of 1951 to resolve that issue.

The Party and the National Front Government

For reasons already discussed, the Tudeh party believed that the period between its ban and the inauguration of Dr. Mossadegh's government was one of rivalry between Britain and the United States over the political and economic control of Iran, notably by means of its seven-year development plan.[47] Reflecting a complete identity with Soviet views, the party's now clan-

---

[47] Iraj Eskandari, "For Bread, Peace, and National Independence," *World Trade Union Movement*, No. 9 (May, 1951), p. 6.

destine newspaper, *Mardom*, cited the *New Times* magazine to prove that the main theme of the post-1949 developments had been a gradual American ascendency in this alleged struggle. "The Americans have succeeded, first, in having the supplementary agreement rejected by the Majlis, second, in launching Iran's seven-year development plan through the American corporation of Overseas Consultants, and third, in concluding a military agreement with Iran during the Shah's visit to the U.S."[48]

The party was also convinced that the nationalization project was essentially an American reaction against General Ali Razmara, whose premiership from June, 1950, to March, 1951, had tipped the balance in Great Britain's favor. Consequently, it reasoned that the National Front, which championed the struggle for the implementation of this project, was merely serving the imperialist interest through exploitation of the appeal of nationalization slogans. Despite these convictions, the party was soon compelled to join this struggle in full force, thereby, one might say, helping the United States to achieve the very goal it was alleged to have.

Once a reversal in policy in favor of oil naturalization was made, the party organizations, front and otherwise, began to take an active part in the popular agitation that swept across the country, including a massive strike in Abadan on March 24, 1951, which it later credited as the decisive factor in forcing oil naturalization on a reluctant Majlis and a hostile ruling class.[49] With the assumption of power by Dr. Mossadegh, the Tudeh leadership became more specific in what it expected the government to do. Putting aside any concrete alternatives, it urged an unconditional reliance on international communism, which it referred to as the "Bloc of Peace and Democracy," and called on the prime minister to "take advantage of the tremendous power of the partisans of peace led by the U.S.S.R. and the sympathy of the masses of the colonial and semicolonial countries because the

---

[48] *Mardom*, July 7, 1951.
[49] *Tarikhchehe Mokhtasar*, p. 21.

only chance of success lay in following the inclinations of the masses and securing help from world democracies." [50]

As soon as the government, faced with a real crisis in Anglo–Iranian relations, showed any cooperation with the United States, the Communist movement turned its attack on the National Front. Thus, for example, suspecting that the acceptance of President Truman's offer of mediation would either lead to a compromise solution or would replace British economic influence with American, the movement organized a mass demonstration, on July 14, 1951, to coincide with the arrival in Teheran of the President's special envoy, Averell Harriman.

The resulting riot and bloodshed sharply emphasized the seriousness of the government's problem with the Communist front organizations — a problem, simply put, of trying to sort out the real Communist front organizations from other radical and leftist but essentially non-Communist organizations. It was a problem that finally led to a complete cutting off of the Front from non-Communist forces. In this case, however, the government reacted swiftly and forcefully to the Communist challenge, not only putting down the anti-American demonstration but also suspending known Tudeh publications and front organizations. The party's reaction was equally forceful, at least in words, when it denounced the government "for having betrayed the revolutionary struggle in the interest of the imperialists with whom a compromise was contemplated." [51]

To emphasize its fears of conciliation with the West, the party waged a series of strikes and demonstrations, which increased in intensity in direct proportion to its assessment of the government's intentions for solving the oil problem. The fact that these moves, at least temporarily, aligned the Communist movement with the extreme conservative opposition to the National Front seemed of little concern so long as they were successful in blocking a possible compromise with the West.[52]

---

[50] *Mardom*, July 7, 1951.

[51] *Ibid.*, July 27, 1951.

[52] On December 5, 1951, a Tudeh column, in open defiance of the government's ban on street demonstrations, started a march toward the Majlis

Meanwhile, the 16th Majlis, still saddled with the problem of the radical nationalist oil policy, was approaching the end of its session. Upon his return from the UN Security Council's debate on the Iranian problem, the prime minister decided to announce elections for a new parliament, perhaps confident of a larger National Front bloc in the 17th Majlis. The immediate issue of the oil dispute was temporarily put aside, therefore, in the winter and spring of 1951–1952, while the National Front campaigned, this time on a platform that went considerably beyond that of nationalizing oil.

This temporary lull in the oil dispute somewhat modified the Tudeh organization's antigovernment attitude. Concurrent with drafting the new program, its Central Committee decided to participate in the election for the 17th Majlis. By doing so, it hoped to secure the freedom of its front organizations and increase its infiltration of non-Communist forces.[53]

Except for isolated cases, the party did not seriously consider applying the tactics of the united front electoral alliance. A suggestion to this effect from the party's Central Committee was quickly rejected by the National Front's leadership, as a result of which the Communists opposed the front in a majority of constituencies. In a score of districts, where conservative-royalist candidates were nominated, a tacit alliance was formed with the Front, but in most of these, as it turned out, no election was held.

In the election Tudeh candidates failed to win a single seat, though results showed they were the second largest vote getters and the best organized party participating in the election.[54] In-

---

Square. The resulting police intervention and the widespread rioting in the capital brought together the extreme Right and Left opposition to the government in a violent attack on the prime minister and his policies. *Journal de Teheran*, Dec. 6–7, 1951.

53 The members of the board of directors of the Iranian Society of Peace Partisans and an assortment of "neutralist" personalities who had supported the peace movement in one way or another constituted the bulk of Tudeh candidates in these elections. *Maslehat* (Teheran), Jan. 17, 1952.

54 There is no complete data on the electoral returns. In the balloting for the twelve-member constituency of Teheran, Tudeh front organizations received about one-third of the more than 100,000 votes cast; the vote in

deed, apprehension about their success in important industrial
centers like Isfahan and Abadan and some northern constituencies was in part the reason for the government's decision to
suspend the election, almost halfway through, in early spring,
1952. The major cause of the suspension was the conviction that
candidates representing the conservative and royalist opposition
to the National Front would win the remaining constituencies
and tip the balance of the membership in their favor.

The outcome of the incomplete elections produced a new pattern of political alliance at the end of spring. The three major
forces in this configuration were the National Front, the Communist Left, and the conservative Right. The first, represented by
the government and a majority of the 79-member rump 17th
Majlis, had clearly failed to consolidate the rule of the nationalist
movement, despite apparent victory at the polls. In the face of
effective opposition of the conservative Right, the attempt to
transform popular support into actual political power through
a general election had fallen short of its goal. The conservatives,
though deprived of their control of the formal machinery of
government, were still firmly entrenched in power and maintained control of the court, the army, and the landed aristocracy,
some of whom were represented even in the new Majlis.

The Right feared that the full control of the Majlis would
perpetuate the Front's rule, wherein lay an inherent challenge
to the regime's existing power structure. The toleration of the
Communist movement and the possibility of Communist infiltration of the Front on a pattern of Eastern European countries,
where Communist-sponsored popular alliances had succeeded,
simply strengthened this conviction.[55] The temporary surrender
of formal governmental power to the Front, therefore, did not

---

the capital normally reflects 50 percent of the numerical support for the
party throughout the country. *Journal de Teheran*, Feb. 12–20, 1952.

[55] Some opposition newspapers frequently cited the experience of Eduard
Beneš to warn Mossadegh against permitting the National Front to become
a ladder for the Communist ascendency to power through the successful
employment of tactics used in Czechoslovakia in 1948. *Shahed* (Teheran),
Dec. 4, 1952.

indicate the regime's unconditional resignation to the Front's continued rule. Rather, it was a tactical retreat partly necessitated by the fear of a premature alienation of the still wide public support for the Front and its cause.

The July Uprising

The conflict of interest between these forces came to its logical conclusion in the cabinet crisis of mid-July. Its immediate cause was Prime Minister Mossadegh's attempt to wrest a further concession from the regime: the extension of governmental authority to the army, traditionally under the Shah's control. Experience in the electoral process of the previous months, during which the army had shown considerable allegiance to the Court, had convinced Mossadegh of the indispensability of this control. His simultaneous demand for plenary power enabling him to rule by decree and to adopt reform measures in times of economic crisis, pending parliamentary approval, also contributed to the crisis.

The Shah's objection to the first move and the Majlis' initially unfavorable reaction to the second prompted the prime minister to resign, forcing a showdown with the opposition. His replacement by a new prime minister, Ahmad Ghavam, led to a radical, if temporary, modification of the political lineup. A tactical alliance of all forces opposed to the conservative Right and the court emerged to force the resignation of Ghavam and the reinstatement of Dr. Mossadegh. The bloody uprising that brought this about cost many lives on all sides.[56]

The Communist movement aligned itself not only with the National Front's center but also with its right wing, which was represented by a conglomeration of religious fanatics and ultra-nationalistic groups, some tribal leaders, and the middle bourgeoisie trade organizations. The party's overtures for the formation of a tactical alliance were readily accepted by representatives

---

[56] See the author's extensive dispatches on this phase of political development in *The Times* (London), July 23, 24, 1953.

of these groups, including Mullah Kashani, a leader of the Shia clergy whose part in the agitation for armed resistance to the new government and to the army was of considerable significance.[57]

Paradoxically, the only component of the National Front that showed genuine apprehension about this development was the non-Communist segment of the Toilers party, which, despite its active role in the July 21 uprising, moved in time to break up the alliance after its immediate goal was achieved. It was largely because of their apprehension that the Shah accepted the National Front's pledge to restore order in the capital and quickly ordered the withdrawal of the army from the scene of mob action.

With the reinstatement of Dr. Mossadegh, the alliance for all practical purposes ended with the same speed that it had been formed. Although the Communist Left, which suffered most of the casualties in the day-long riots, did not secure practical concessions from the National Front, its help in forcing a definite setback on the conservative right was welcomed. In the months following the Front's return to power the Tudeh organizations sought to carry the government stand against the Shah and the army even further. But the apparent rapprochement between the prime minister and the monarch and the persistent warnings of the non-Communist Left against continued toleration of Communist activity resulted in a hardening of the government's attitude toward the party, at least for a while.[58]

At this time the Tudeh leadership made a tentative attempt to revise its attitude toward the National Front. As noted before, a document prepared by a party theorist sought to reevaluate the role of the national bourgeoisie as a whole, and that of the

---

[57] In a statement to the press Kashani gave an affirmative answer to a question by Rahim Namvar, the editor of *Shahbaz*, the leading organ of the Tudeh front organization, about his readiness to cooperate with that organization "for the annihilation of Premier Ghavam." *Keyhan* (Teheran), July 20, 1952.

[58] To counter Tudeh agitation against the Shah, a royal visit to the nationalized oil fields was arranged by the government in mid-November with customary pomp and publicity. *Ettelaat*, Nov. 25, 1952.

National Front government specifically. Among other things, it recommended a fuller recognition of the democratic element in the national bourgeoisie and a more serious appeal to its center for a tacit, if not a public, consent for the formation of a broad alliance of democratic forces against imperialism.[59]

The deterioration of Iran's relations with the West, the prolonged oil dispute culminating in the severance of diplomatic relations with Great Britain, and the rejection of the renewed American effort at mediation strengthened the Communists' belief in the accuracy of their reappraisal of the role of the National Front.

Early in 1953 there appeared concrete evidence of the uneasiness of the Shah–Mossadegh compromise, with the result that a new and drastic realignment of political forces took place. First of all, several important splits occurred in the Front's rank and file. Mullah Kashani and his followers — who because of their earlier acceptance of Tudeh cooperation were regarded as its left wing but who, from the standpoint of social background and political goals were in truth its right wing — deserted the Front and went over to the conservative opposition. A similar split took place in the leadership and rank and file of the Toilers party, with one group, led by Dr. Baghai, joining the opposition and the other, led by Maleki, remaining in the prime minister's camp.

This realignment was fully evident in the crisis of February 27 over the proposed departure abroad of the Shah. Among other things, it formally ended the uneasy truce between Mossadegh and the Shah and rallied to the Court the forces of the Right, both inside and outside the Front.[60] This period, in many ways anticipating the outbreak of the full crisis and the royalist-military uprising in mid-August, 1953, could be characterized as one of a gradual emergence of another alliance of Tudeh

---

[59] Dr. Kiyanouri, the sponsor of the new line, became the principal critic of the party's alleged left wing sectarianism based on the "wrong assessment of the role of the national bourgeoisie," in the post-deStalinization era. See "The National Bourgeoisie."

[60] *The Times* (London), Feb. 28, 1953.

organizations and the center of the National Front, prompted by the power struggle between the government and the conservative oligarchy.

That this alliance was tacit in nature and limited in goals was evidenced by the center's refusal to accept some of the Communists' fundamental demands. The government, which continued to toy with the possibility of enlisting American support in the struggle for economic survival, refused to take any measures that could in any way be construed as acquiescing to persistent Communist demands for the end of U.S. technical and military aid.[61] Indeed, some elements of the Front's leadership, represented by the breakaway segment of the Toilers party, remained uncompromisingly opposed to communism. This faction was numerically weak, but it exercised considerable influence in preventing total alignment with the Tudeh party at a time when the Front had been almost deserted by its initial following and was struggling to survive.

Despite these considerations, the practical identity of the National Front and Communist policies on the one hand and the measures taken by the Tudeh organizations to support these policies on the other, made the controversy over the deliberate or incidental nature of the alliance an academic issue. To pursue its goal of the Front's total isolation from the ruling class, Tudeh leadership actively supported the government on such important controversies as the constitutional interpretation of the Shah's power over the armed forces, the government's objection to the Shah's land reform program, its attempt to enforce the so-called oil-less economy, the extension of the prime minister's plenary power for another year, and, finally, the controversial issue of dissolution of the paralyzed Majlis through a referendum, which culminated the power struggle in mid-August, 1953.

While its front organizations publicly supported the government on these issues, the clandestine party's leadership urged

---

[61] William E. Warne, *Mission for Peace: Point 4 in Iran* (Indianapolis, 1956). See chaps. 9 and 17 for a firsthand account of Tudeh anti-American agitation and the government's unsuccessful efforts to prevent it.

the prime minister to adopt even more radical policies. The party's Central Committee, in a series of communications to the prime minister, appealed for the creation of an anti-imperialist front and demanded legalization of the Tudeh party, a release of all political prisoners, an end of martial law in the southern oil fields, the expulsion of the U.S. military mission to Iran, the rejection of foreign military aid and cancellation of the 1947 Iran–U.S. agreement, nationalization of the American-owned Bahrein oil fields, and recognition of the People's Republic of China.[62]

Demands of a similar sort were publicly voiced in an impressive demonstration on July 21, 1953, commemorating the first anniversary of the 1952 uprising. If clear evidence of the Tudeh recovery from post-1949 disintegration and its success in regrouping its scattered forces was needed, it certainly came in this demonstration. According to the best available information, 50,000 members and sympathizers of the clandestine party and front organizations participated.[63] Emboldened by the brightening prospect of a total break between the prime minister and the ruling class, these organizations joined the Front in support of a referendum to formalize dissolution of the Majlis in early August.[64]

The Demise of the Communist–Nationalist Cause

In the final crisis of mid-August, 1953, which owed its immediate cause to the dispute between the prime minister and the Shah

---

[62] These demands are listed in an open letter of the Tudeh Central Committee dated March 25, 1953, printed in *Mardom*, same date. An English summary is given in George Lenczowski, *The Middle East in World Affairs* (Ithaca, N.Y., 1962), pp. 166–167.

[63] Dietrich Geyer, *Die Sowjetunion und Iran: Eine Untersuchung zur Aussenpolitik der U.D.S.S.R. in Nahen Osten, 1917–1954* (Tübingen, 1955), p. 116.

[64] The official figure of about 2,000,000 "yes" votes represented almost 98 percent support for the government's stand (*Journal de Teheran*, Aug. 10–11, 1959). For a more recent comprehensive treatment of the rise and fall of the National Front regime, see Richard Cottam, *Nationalism in Iran* (Pittsburgh, 1964).

over the legality of the referendum, the Communist movement became, for all practical purposes, the backbone of support for the government. Thus the crisis was, in effect, the result of the power struggle between the Front and its Communist supporters on the one hand and the Court and the conservative opposition to the government on the other.

The showdown was precipitated by an unsuccessful attempt to replace the prime minister by royal decree. The Shah's flight as a result of the initial failure of this attempt plunged the country into what was essentially a revolutionary state. The National Front, including its non-Communist left wing, reacted to this development by advancing a number of demands so drastic that they put themselves to the left of the Communist movement. One segment of its leadership advocated the proclamation of a republic, since the sovereign had left. Another segment contemplated a new referendum to effect proposed changes in the monarchical system. The prime minister himself appeared to be uncertain about the best measure for dealing with the gravity of the crisis.

In the confused state of affairs between August 15 and 19, the Communist movement seemed to be the only organized political force with some notion of its immediate and long-range goals. Abandoning all pretense of observing the still legally enforced ban on its political activity, its press gave maximum publicity to an urgent appeal of the Tudeh party's Central Committee for a rapid transition to a republic and elimination of American influence from the country: "The party demands the immediate establishment of a democratic republic, for as long as the monarchy is not eliminated, the herd of traitors remain and will further create other traitors. . . . In the struggle against the colonial system, the slogan must be, Down with monarchy, long live the democratic republic. The American advisors should leave the country, the U.S. consulates and other American espionage nests should be closed." [65]

---

[65] Full original text in *Mardom*, Aug. 18, 1953; also in *Pravda*, Aug. 19, 1953, and cited in "Der Umsturz in Teheran," *Osteuropa*, Yearbook, Vol. III, No. 6 (December, 1953), 471.

Significantly, the party did not advocate the immediate establishment of a people's democracy or even participation in the now isolated National Front government. Instead, it offered its full support to the Front in the form of an anti-imperialist and antimonarchist alliance; if this alliance had been successful in achieving these immediate goals, it would conceivably have prepared for the transition to a people's democracy.[66]

The anti-American tone of the Tudeh agitations and its intensive campaign against American technical aid and military advisers greatly embarrassed the government, which had no desire to abandon these last tangible ties with the West. These agitations also increased American anxiety, apparently to a point somewhat beyond mere expressions of concern by responsible authorities.[67] To this day the exact nature of American involvement in the episode remains obscure and extremely controversial, but there is no doubt that the United States was apprehensive about the turn of events in Iran and alarmed that the crisis would aid the Communist movement to achieve its declared goal. The prime minister was warned that if he did not guarantee the security of American personnel and advisors, Washington might recall them.[68]

Not surprisingly, in the confusion surrounding these events it was no longer possible to distinguish the attitudes of various nationalist elements toward the declared Communist aims. In retrospect, however, it can be posited that those of moderate tendencies in the Front opposed the more revolutionary Communist demands. Dr. Mossadegh himself has denied ever intending to yield to the Tudeh pressure for abolition of the monarchy.[69] The attitude of some of the leadership's extremist

---

[66] Stella Margold, "The Streets of Teheran," *The Reporter*, Nov. 10, 1953, p. 15.

[67] Eisenhower's speech in Seattle on August 4, 1953, containing a serious warning against cooperation with the Communists was followed by State Department statements to the same effect. *New York Times*, Aug. 5, 1953.

[68] On the CIA's alleged involvement see, among others, Andrew Tully, *C.I.A.: The Inside Story* (New York, 1962).

[69] *Mohakemeye Tarikhi* [Record of the historic trial of Dr. Mossadegh

elements, on the other hand, indicated that such restraint was not the rule. Paradoxically, Maleki's splinter group of the Toilers party, which until then had systematically endeavored to frustrate the Communist infiltration of the Front, was now actively competing with the Communists in advancing the most revolutionary slogans.[70]

Undoubtedly, the fast pace of events and the manifest breakdown of governmental authority were partly responsible for the apparent indecision of the Front's leadership. At the crucial turn of events, however, the government displayed a measure of resolution which proved to be its own undoing. Refusing the Communists' demand for armed resistance to the counterrevolution, it instead ordered the army to repress the Tudeh rioters in the capital city. In the course of doing so, the army turned against the government, thus playing the decisive part in the day-long rioting and bloodshed which ended with royalist-military victory.[71]

This victory was not altogether unexpected, inasmuch as past experience had shown that the government could not retain power for long without at least a tacit acquiescence of the Shah, to whom the army had largely remained loyal. What was not expected was the Communist failure to resist the counterrevolution more determinedly, knowing as it did how successful its infiltration of the armed forces had been. The full extent of this infiltration became known only a year later, during the prosecution of some of the leaders and active members of the party by the newly established military government, and at that time some light was thrown on the party's planning in relation to this abrupt turn of events.[72]

According to government sources, having failed to act de-

---

and his close colleagues before a military tribunal in the fall of 1953] (Teheran, 1954), pp. 39–40.

[70] *Nirouye Sevvom*, Aug. 17, 1953.

[71] Henry C. Ateyo, "Political Development in Iran, 1951–1954," *Middle East Affairs*, Vol. V, Nos. 8–9 (1954).

[72] Walter Z. Laqueur, *The Soviet Union and the Middle East* (New York, 1959), p. 278.

cisively to thwart the counterrevolution, the party contemplated armed counteraction a few days after the overthrow of the National Front government, but it abandoned the plan as suicidal in view of rapidly changing developments favoring the royalist forces.[73] Instead, some months later a staff combining the party's civilian and military leaders was formed to consider the possibility of guerrilla warfare in the Caspian provinces. In preparation for this, about 2,000 reliable cadre members were selected and divided into twenty-man groups to receive training from the party's military corps.[74] But this plan, too, was abandoned, as the Communists continued to shy away from armed insurrection of any kind against the established order.

Various explanations have been advanced for this reluctance despite the seemingly favorable conditions during the National Front's stormy rule. A lack of a will to power, stemming from the unpreparedness of the Tudeh leadership to seize power, has been mentioned as one reason: "Granted that the party sought the destruction of the established order or at least creation of chaos designed to strengthen Iran's anti-Western sentiments, this was hardly adequate for acquisition of power, because mob action unless quickly channeled cannot be maintained at a high emotional pitch or be directed for the national purpose."[75]

It is of course conceivable that a slackening of the tempo of mob action was partly responsible for the Communists' quick reversal of plans, but sounder reasons for their failure to act must be sought in their attitude toward the nationalist movement and the problem of trying to coexist with the latter's political organization without losing their own Communist character.

Some ramifications of this problem have already been ex-

---

[73] *Seyre Komonism*, pp. 354–355.

[74] *Ibid.*, p. 256. The members of the planning staff were K. Ruzbeh and Col. Mobasheri, representing the military, and Dr. Jowdat, Dr. Kiyanouri, and A. Olovvi, representing the party's civilian leadership.

[75] N. Marburg Efimenco, "An Experience with Civilian Dictatorship in Iran: The Case of Dr. Mossadegh," *Journal of Politics*, Vol. XVII, No. 3 (August, 1955), 404.

amined. The absence of any doctrinal interpretation of the postwar national liberation movements, which left the Communists ignorant about the Cominform's views on Iranian developments, must also be mentioned. Apart from a continual insistence on the struggle for oil nationalization as due to Anglo–American rivalries and an over-all emphasis on the peace offensive to rally the non-Communist and democratic Left to the Communist cause, there were few clues to the Cominform's interpretation of the Iranian nationalist experience. As a result, the party persisted in applying the orthodox views to the changing situation as best it could.

It has been suggested that, since its leaders were trained in the most rigorous techniques of Marxism, they could not conceive of a revolution except by the working masses, well organized in militant cadres and capable of acting in line with the classic tactics of the proletariat struggle against the established power — that is, by strikes, sabotage, and terrorism. As one writer has put it: "Although such action could overthrow a power already condemned by a major sector of the population, it would be inadequate in the face of a solid army, which, as was the case in Iran, was still submissive to the regime. In addition, any successful attempt at overthrowing the regime had to combine the organization of the working masses into cadres with a simultaneous mobilization of the rural population and its active involvement in the revolutionary process." [76] The Tudeh party could hardly claim to have satisfied these prerequisites. Despite some attempts at mobilizing the peasantry, the party continued to represent the urban classes and the petty bourgeoisie in composition and political orientation alike. This was true of both the civilian and military clandestine organizations. The latter, which could have played a decisive role in an armed revolt against the regime, was particularly representative of the urban middle class, as an analysis of its composition indicates beyond doubt. [77] Although

[76] Mme Carrere d'Encausse, "Le Toudeh Iranien," *Revue Militaire d'information* (February–March, 1957), p. 59.

[77] A breakdown of the network's rank and status indicates a focus on

in retrospect the party's leadership acknowledged the neglect of the peasantry as a major cause of its previous failures, it made no attempt to remedy the situation during the most favorable conditions afforded the movement at the time of the National Front government.[78]

Apart from these factors, the Soviet attitude toward the nationalist movement should also be considered. Except for general support of the anti-Western aspects of government policies voiced at such international levels as the UN Security Council and through other diplomatic media, the Soviet attitude toward the National Front government was marked by considerable restraint and correctness.[79]

In early 1953, when Moscow demanded an extension of the Caspian Fishery Concession which had just elapsed, it appeared for a while that a severe crisis analogous to that of the 1945–1946 oil dispute would develop. A quick reversal of Soviet policy, however, avoided this, and the issue of new arrangements to replace the expired concession was solved without adversely affecting relations between the two countries.

Similarly, the change of leadership in the Soviet Union following the death of Stalin in March, 1953, failed to introduce any novel element. Although some initiative was taken for a rapprochement between the two countries at the end of Dr. Mossadegh's government, virtually the same restraint on the diplomatic level and the absence of communication on the ideological plane continued to characterize the Soviet stand toward Iran's nationalist upsurge.[80] In view of its past total subordina-

---

the middle class elements of the intelligentsia, which had its counterpart in the civilian leadership of the party.

[78] *Seyre Komonism*, pp. 324–325.

[79] On the whole, Soviet authors treat Dr. Mossadegh's premiership and eventual overthrow with reticence and caution. It would appear that the Soviet government was doubtful of the exact significance of his movement and preferred not to commit itself toward it. See *CAR*, Vol. IV, No. 4 (1956), 382–432.

[80] On August 8, 1953, Premier Georgi Malenkov spoke about mutual interests in solving outstanding problems between his country and Iran, and two days later the start of talks between the two was announced in

tion to the Soviet Union, the Tudeh leadership may well have been discouraged by these evidences of Soviet coolness, to the point that it was unable to act resolutely when political conditions in the country seemed opportune.

Finally, there was the difficulty of maintaining close contact between the front organizations and the clandestine party, and thus the impossibility of well-coordinated moves at the crucial juncture. An almost total breakdown of communication left the party unable to cope with the sudden turn of events and the subsequent shift to the left by a considerable sector of the National Front leadership. Thus, although there was a hasty demand for abolition of the monarchy and a governmental request for arms to resist the counterrevolution, the Communists made no actual steps to resort to arms, even though they had long prepared for it and had carefully infiltrated the military for that very purpose.

Indeed, it could be argued that the Tudeh leadership helped the cause of the royalist conservative opposition by default, for it was primarily in reaction to the Communist anti-American agitation that Mossadegh ordered larger units of the army into action, thereby putting them into a position for their subsequent participation in the counterrevolution against the government.

The Tudeh party's preliminary analysis of the developments of these years showed a strict adherence to classic Communist doctrines. Quoting from Stalin's formula about the three-stage revolution in colonial and semicolonial countries, the Central Committee contended that "despite more than ten years of experience, the revolutionary movement in Iran was still in its first stage — namely, that of a national anti-imperialist phase, which had to pass through a second stage of bourgeois-democratic revolution before it could embark on the final proletarian socialist stage." [81]

Teheran; these were interrupted because of the sweeping events that followed. See Klaus Mehnert, "Iran and UdSSR 42–53," *Osteuropa*, Yearbook, Vol. 3, No. 5 (October, 1953), 381–82.

[81] Central Committee of the Tudeh Party, *Darbarehe Bistohashte Mordad*

By so characterizing the nationalist movement, the party, in effect, blamed its failure to exploit or alter the course of its evolution on the objective conditions of Iranian society, which were allegedly beyond its control. Given these conditions, the party believed it had done all it could in securing some of the Communist movement's immediate goals, among which the following were the most fundamental: convincing the anti-imperialist masses of the necessity of extending their struggle against the United States as well as Great Britain; enlightening the anti-imperialist masses about the role of the Soviet Union; convincing many of the National Front followers of the futility of compromise with reaction and imperialism; campaigning for the slogan of the anticolonial united front; and, above all, intensifying the antimonarchist struggle.[82]

These optimistic evaluations of the party's performance were not held valid for long, however. For reasons to be examined later, the party's leadership had to initiate a thorough reappraisal of these views following the overthrow of the National Front government and subsequent to the fundamental post-Stalin revision of the doctrine of national liberation movements.

[About August 19, the Date of the National Front Government's Overthrow] (Teheran, 1954), p. 11.

[82] *Ibid.*, pp. 21–25.

6

COMMUNISM IN THE
POST-MOSSADEGH EPOCH

The violent overthrow of Dr. Mossadegh's government and the established regime's subsequent consolidation of power signified more than a mere restoration of the status quo ante for the Communist movement. For although the post-Mossadegh era embodies many characteristics analogous to those of the period following the ban on Communist organizations in 1949, there are also important differences. Some of these are related to doctrinal changes made by international communism's supreme leadership after the death of Stalin. Others are due to a corollary shift in Soviet diplomatic posture, not only toward Iran but toward all underdeveloped areas. Still others are the result of the policies and attitudes of the reinstated Iranian regime and the reaction they produced among various domestic political forces after 1953.

The Government's Reorientation

The most fundamental change in the government's general orientation had to do with the regime's internal security. To ensure its security, a systematic and often ruthless policy of repression of all political opposition was instituted, in order to eradicate the very conditions from which the Communist movement had previously benefited. Not only were all cover and affiliate Tudeh organizations suppressed and many of their leaders and militant cadres imprisoned or executed, but nationalist parties and groups that had remained loyal to the Front were also severely prosecuted.[1] Active prosecution of the Communists was further intensified with the discovery of the movement's military network in the summer of 1954, at the same time that restrictive measures against the nationalist elements were gradually relaxed as effective opposition to the regime from this quarter abated. By early 1955, with the prosecution of Tudeh military and civilian leaders and the flight of others, the authorities could justly claim that their policy of repression had succeeded and that the Tudeh party as an organized force within Iran was almost completely crushed.[2]

Government prosecution was aided by large-scale defection from the party, on a pattern almost identical to the one that followed the Azarbayjan crisis of 1947. However, because the prosecution of the party was in this instance more systematic and determined than it had been before, it is impossible to say how genuine the avowed motives for defection were. In 1947, disillusioned party members still had relatively unhindered freedom of expression; in 1953 and after, this was definitely not the case. It is therefore difficult to know whether defection was, as

---

[1] Although there are no reliable statistical data on the extent of the effectiveness of these measures, some reports indicate that as a result of mass arrests of some 3,000 active members and the exile of some to Kharkh Island in the Persian Gulf, Tudeh party membership dropped to somewhere between 3,000 and 4,000 by January, 1954. Government authorities later reported that only 580 of these were still in prison. See *New York Times*, Jan. 15, 1954. To reinforce the legal foundation of the anti-Communist policy, a new Subversive Activities Control Act was adopted on November 2, 1954, to replace the old 1931 Act. *Interparliamentary Union, Constitutional and Parliamentary Information*, III, No. 21, 8–9.

[2] Of a total of 548 members of the Tudeh military network, 28 officers constituting its top leadership were executed and the others received prison sentences ranging from life to six-month suspended terms. Military Governorship of Teheran, *Ketabe Siyah* [The Black Book], (Teheran, 1955) pp. 345–372.

many said, prompted by disillusionment with the party and its
ideology or simply by fear of government prosecution.[3]

Undoubtedly, the issue of what policy was to prevail toward
the National Front was one of the major causes of the defection
of many party members and sympathizers. Related to this was
a feeling of abandonment — even betrayal — shared by members
who had never accepted Soviet hegemony of all Communist
movements — a hegemony which in its extreme form demanded
the subordination of the interests of Communist parties everywhere to the Soviet raison d'état.[4] It has been reported that some
of these elements, especially certain young intellectuals who favored complete cooperation with the National Front in opposition to the Central Committee's indecisive attitude, were active
in Marxist circles claiming to be the real Tudeh party.[5] It is
evident from the course of events, however, that these elements
failed to make any serious challenge to the former leaders, even
though the latter were for the most part in exile. Gradually, the
former leaders retrieved their control of the party, through circumstances to be examined more fully below.

Another major change in the government's orientation was
in its international outlook, which in almost every respect was
wholeheartedly pro-Western. The restored regime resumed relations with Great Britain; it worked out a new arrangement with
an international consortium for marketing oil from the nationalized industry; it secured further U.S. military and economic
aid; and finally, in the fall of 1955, it pledged Iran as a member

---

[3] With the active encouragement of the authorities, some attempts were
made at political rehabilitation of party members, even including some of
its prominent leaders. Most of these attempts took the form of new journals which specialized in anti-Communist articles and revealing accounts
of activities written by former leading figures of the organization. Invariably
these contained professions of repentance and protestations of loyalty to
the regime. *Seyre Komonism*, esp. chap. 23.

[4] Gianroberto Scarcia, "Aspetti giurdici e politici della recente polemica
fra Persia e Unione Sovietica," *Oriente Moderno*, Vol. XXXIV, No. 7
(1959), 499–513.

[5] Leonard Binder, *Iran; Political Development in a Changing Society*
(Berkeley and Los Angeles, 1962), p. 204.

of the Baghdad defense alliance with Iraq, Pakistan, Turkey, and Great Britain, thereby bringing full circle the process of reorientation of her foreign policy.

As for relations with the Soviet Union, not long after the consolidation of the new government in power a rapprochement was effected on some outstanding border and monetary questions — clear proof of the Soviet Union's eagerness to stabilize relations with its neighbors as a prelude to the post-Stalin liberalization of policies.[6] This improvement in relations was soon offset by Iran's signing of the Baghdad Pact (renamed CENTO in 1959), to which the Soviet Union seriously objected, but even in this matter Soviet reaction was tempered by the prevailing search for a détente with the West which characterized the era of the Bulganin–Khrushchev collective leadership. Instead of breaking with Iran or intensifying its propaganda warfare against the regime, Moscow attempted more subtle persuasion once the Majlis had ratified the Pact.

This policy of cordial relations culminated in an official visit by the Shah and Queen Soraya to the Soviet Union in late June and early July, 1956. It afforded a splendid occasion for wooing Iran at the formal level. In a speech welcoming the Shah, Soviet Prime Minister Marshal Bulganin mentioned his government's objection to the Baghdad Pact, "which like all military groups created by Western powers, harms the cause of peace and is a new disguised form of the old colonial policy which has damaged the vital interests of the people of the Near and Middle East."[7] The Shah's reassurance that his country had never entered an anti-Soviet military alliance did nothing to remove Soviet objections, and soon after his departure from Moscow, Soviet propaganda resumed its hostile tone. This state of affairs continued almost unabated for two and a half years.

Early in 1959, apparently in an effort to force the United

---

[6] For texts of these documents see J. C. Hurewitz, *Diplomacy in the Near and Middle East, A Documentary Record: 1914–1956* (New York, 1956), II, 305–308.

[7] *Pravda*, July 11, 1956; cited in *CAR*, Vol. IV, No. 4 (1956), 397.

States into a more explicit commitment for the defense of the regime, the Shah initiated talks for an accommodation with Moscow. The Soviets responded favorably, glad of this opportunity to oppose Iran's further identification with U.S. policy in the Middle East.[8] At the beginning of February, 1959, a Soviet mission headed by a vice-deputy minister of foreign affairs arrived in Teheran to conduct high-level talks with the Shah and his government on a treaty of nonaggression and peaceful cooperation. Specifically, the Soviets seemed to be aiming at securing Iran's withdrawal from the Baghdad Pact, thwarting the conclusion of the impending U.S.–Iran bilateral agreement, and preventing the establishment of foreign bases in Iran.

With the negotiations in progress, the West made it clear that it considered the prospect of any accommodation between the two countries detrimental to the Baghdad Defense Alliance. The United States, in particular, reacted bluntly, warning the regime against dire consequences of the contemplated change in Iran's international posture.[9] These pressures, combined with an understanding that the United States, although it would not join the Baghdad Pact outright, would sign bilateral defense agreements with the pact's signatories, brought an abrupt end to the Shah's negotiations with the Soviet delegation. Moscow was deeply offended by this move, which, with the signing of the U.S.–Iran agreement on March 4, 1959, made it all too evident that Iran's overtures had been a calculated bid to exploit the Soviet readiness for diplomatic accommodation as a lever of pressure for securing firmer American commitments.[10]

This visible affront brought relations between Iran and the Soviet Union to their lowest ebb since the failure of Moscow's oil offensive in 1947. Both traditional and revolutionary elements of Soviet diplomacy were joined in a violent propaganda assault on the regime, and the Tudeh party, which had undergone several years of ideological crises and organizational dis-

---

[8] See George Lenczowski, *The Middle East in World Affairs* (Ithaca, N.Y., 1962), p. 222.
[9] Binder, *op. cit.*, p. 181.
[10] Lenczowski, *op. cit.*, p. 222.

integration, was restored as the chief instrument for inciting the Iranian people to revolutionary actions.

These features rather consistently characterized the Soviet attitude toward Iran until the fall of 1962. In July of that year, following Dr. Ali Amini's resignation as prime minister, the Shah once again took more direct control of the government, and immediately resumed negotiations with the Soviets. These ultimately resulted in an exchange of letters pledging Iran's refusal to grant military bases to any foreign power — in effect, the minimum goal Moscow had failed to achieve in the 1959 negotiations.[11] The significance of this exchange was almost immediately brought out during the Cuban crisis of October, 1962, which dramatically highlighted the role of foreign bases in the delicate balance of international relations. It was then revealed that the Iranian–Soviet understanding was due as much to U.S. acquiescence as to Soviet abandonment of its previous insistence on Iran's withdrawal from CENTO as a prerequisite to friendly relations between the two countries.[12]

New Ideological Development

On the ideological level, there occurred in this period important changes which affected the entire world Communist movement. The milestones in the post-Stalin doctrinal development were the Twentieth Congress of the Communist Party of the Soviet Union in 1956, the Consultative Conference of Communist Parties in 1957, and, above all, the Advisory Conference of eighty-one Fraternal Communist Parties at the end of 1960. The Advisory Conference was particularly significant because it provided the first comprehensive ideological pronouncements since the 1928 Sixth Comintern Congress, at which decisions were made on fundamental issues concerning the upsurge of national liberation movements in the vast underdeveloped parts of the world.

Most importantly, the Sixth Congress had taken up the ques-

---

[11] Text in *Keyhan International*, Oct. 11, 1962.
[12] *New York Times*, Oct. 24, 1962.

tion of the attitude of Communist parties toward bourgeois nationalism and its organizational expressions, the nationalist movements for economic and political liberation. It was an issue that was of concern from 1928 on, but particular attention was given to it in the few years before the CPSU's Twentieth Congress. Early in 1955, new Soviet publications devoted to the East began to appear. The most prominent of these, *Sovetskoye Vostokovedeniye*, initially reflected the standard Communist views concerning the leading position of working class parties in the bourgeoisie's struggle for national liberation. Accordingly, the journal, citing Mao Tse-tung, spoke of a dual role for bourgeois nationalism, which, "on the one hand came into conflict with imperialism and the leading feudalists, in which fight it has a revolutionary character, and on the other hand because of its economic and political weaknesses and the existence of the unbroken economic bonds connecting it with feudalism and imperialism, fails to wage the struggle against them to the end." [13]

In the Middle East, where bourgeois nationalism was relatively weak and developing slowly under conditions of foreign capital domination, a leading Soviet author argued, only the proletariat seemed capable of leading the national liberation movements, "because it alone was the consistently revolutionary class, which, supported by the broad masses of the peasantry, occupied the front ranks in the struggle for peace, freedom, and national independence." [14] Thus, any contribution of bourgeois nationalism to liberation movements was regarded with utmost suspicion. Any Communist alliance with political organizations representing it must be temporary and tactical, and unquestionably under Communist party leadership.

The Tudeh party, which had remained largely faithful to these concepts during the nationalist movement in the early 1950's, hesitated to alter its attitude toward the bourgeois na-

---

[13] Mao Tse-tung, *Selected Works*, I, (London, 1954), 162.

[14] L. N. Vatolina, "The Growth of National Consciousness Among the Arab Peoples, 1945–46," *Sovetskoye Vostokovedeniye*, No. 5 (1955); cited in *CAR*, Vol. III, No. 3 (1955), 251.

tionalists without the sanction of the recognized leadership of international communism. In early 1956 and immediately after the Twentieth Congress the authority sanctioning a drastic revision of these orthodox views became available. The former suspicion about the bourgeoisie's potential betrayal of national liberation was rejected as sectarian. *Sovetskoye Vostokovedeniye*, which a year earlier had echoed these views on the authority of Mao, now asserted: "The national bourgeoisie is not always prone to betray the cause of national independence; on the contrary, it is the natural and almost irreconcilable enemy of imperialism."[15]

Perhaps a more radical change of attitude concerned the role of the working class parties. The orthodox view was based on the well-known proposition of Marxism–Leninism which foresaw that, "In the epoch of the general crisis of capitalism the proletariat of dependent and colonial countries where capitalism is comparatively developed may become the leader of national liberation and anti-feudal revolutions."[16] Hence, the Communist parties, which consider themselves the true representative of the proletariat, had consistently endeavored to assume leadership of these revolutions irrespective of their weakness and their slim chances for success.

This attitude was now denounced as an incorrect deduction from the above-cited proposition, which "not only had failed in its purpose but had also prevented the objective appreciation of the victory in such a struggle in a number of Eastern countries like India, Burma, Indonesia, and Egypt where the proletariat, the avant-garde of the patriotic forces, had not been able to take the lead."[17] The truth was now said to be that these victories had become possible because at certain moments in the anti-imperialist struggle, the interests of the bourgeoisie

---

15 *Sovetskoye Vostokovedeniye*, No. 1 (1956); cited in Walter Z. Laqueur, ed., *The Middle East in Transition* (New York, 1958), p. 391.

16 "The 20th Congress of the CPSU and the Tasks Set for the Study of the Contemporary East," *Sovetskoye Vostokovedeniye*, No. 1 (1956); cited in CAR, Vol. IV, No. 4 (1956), 344.

17 *Ibid.*

and those of the majority of people basically coincided and forced the withdrawal of imperialism.

Similarly, the former tendency to ignore the multiple nature of the national liberation struggles of the East was now criticized. A high authority of international communism commented:

> Liberation from the colonial yoke may be attained in different ways in different countries. In some cases the people first fight and win their complete political and economic independence and then undertake the task of bringing about not only a democratic but a socialist transformation. This is true of North Korea and China where the working class plays the leading role and directs the struggle for socialism. But emancipation is a long process and presently many other forces participate in it. Because the peasantry and the proletariat are weak, they are obliged to ally themselves with the national bourgeoisie.[18]

The new concept also entailed a more profound appreciation of the notion of independence in the East. Soviet theorists under Stalin had always emphasized the strict Marxist–Leninist teaching that social liberation was the inevitable precondition of national liberation and that a prerequisite for independence was freedom from foreign capital.[19] Now, though admitting that political independence was not complete independence, Communist theorists saw at least two advantages in achieving sovereignty in the East without immediately attaining economic independence. In the first place, by achieving political independence, the sovereign state would be free to initiate policies to redress its economic backwardness; such measures as the nationalization of foreign assets and the introduction of a planned economy, though far from socialistic, were nevertheless regarded as conducive to ultimate complete independence. In the second place, political independence would permit a different course in international relations: "Because they are no longer isolated by the powerful capitalist system and in view of the existence of

---

[18] M. E. Zhukov, "The Break-up of the Imperialist Colonial System," *Party Life* (August, 1956); cited in Laqueur, ed., *The Middle East in Transition*, p. 392.
[19] *Ibid.*

the Socialist revolution and consolidation, they would be able to rely on the anti-imperialist camp whose very existence has made the struggle against colonialism easier." [20]

These were sharp departures from the former Stalinist doctrine which measured the value of anti-imperialist movements primarily in terms of their relation to Soviet policies. It was in no small measure owing to this oversimplified criterion that the Communists had failed to exploit fully such nationalist outbursts as the movement for oil nationalization in Iran. In theory, at least, the Communist parties were now armed with modern ideological weapons designed to overcome difficulties all too frequently encountered in the past. It is not clear, however, whether their acceptance as the key concept of Soviet policy toward the East from 1956 on was motivated by a realistic recognition of the extreme weakness of the Eastern proletariat or by an attempt to offset that weakness by entrusting the bourgeoisie with the burden of leading these countries to socialism.

As Alexandre Bennigsen has pointed out, these new concepts have necessitated fundamental changes in tactics and policies of non-Western Communist movements: the Number One enemy of the working class is now foreign rule rather than the national bourgeoisie; non-Soviet Communist parties no longer seek a vanguard position in the anti-imperialist front but simply wish to participate in it; unlike the Leninist–Stalinist concept, the new doctrine envisages a permanent alliance between the proletariat and the bourgeoisie resting on a genuine community of interests; and, finally, civil war is no longer regarded as indispensable because in this area the capitalist structure lacks a solid foundation.[21]

To effect these revised concepts the Communist parties of the East incorporated important changes in their program after 1956, including the goal of a popular front — an alliance among workers, peasants, the lower and middle classes, and the demo-

---

[20] Mme Carrere d'Encausse, "The Evolution of Soviet Policy Since the 20th Congress," in *ibid.*, p. 393.

[21] Alexandre Bennigsen, "The National Front in Communist Strategy in the Middle East," in *ibid.*, pp. 363–364.

cratic intelligentsia. In some cases, the plans for alliance are even broader, with the entire industrial bourgeoisie also included because the interests of local factory owners are believed to be opposed to those of the foreign imperialists.[22]

As Walter Laqueur has noted, tactically, the patriotic anti-imperialist fronts are not radically different from the various united and popular fronts of the 1930's. But the aim is entirely different. The purpose of the Popular Front was to combat fascism without hoping to bring about final salvation. The national anti-imperialist front, on the other hand, may well serve as a step toward establishing a regime like that of the National Front under Dr. Mossadegh. A further difference relates to composition. Whereas the Popular Front of the 1930's joined socialist and democratic parties with the Communists in an alliance against fascism, which permitted no democratic parties, the anti-imperialist front in the Middle East implies cooperation with groups whose attitude toward democracy is hardly more positive than that of the Communists themselves: "The decisive criterion is not the party's class character, its social and economic program or its general stand on domestic issues, but its international outlook and foreign policy orientation."[23]

The Tudeh Party's Attempt at Revival

Along with other Middle Eastern Communist parties, the Tudeh party quickly made an effort to translate these new concepts into definite policies. It particularly welcomed the new theoretical sanctions for evaluating national liberation movements, seeing in them the possibility of somehow recovering from the recent setbacks caused by government repression and the intraparty and ideological crisis.

The revision of orthodox Communist views might help the party in several areas, the leaders reasoned. First, the reevalua-

---

[22] Walter Z. Laqueur, *Communism and Nationalism in the Middle East* (New York, 1956), p. 296.
[23] *Ibid.*

tion of the role of the national movement gave the party some good arguments to explain its past errors: it could now say that responsibility for blunders in the conduct of individual Communist parties transcended the confines of their native leadership. In other words, the party hoped the de-Stalinization process would extend its shield to those Communist parties which, like itself, considered their solidarity with the Soviet Union as the supreme test of ideological excellence. The Tudeh leadership expected this process to strengthen its authority over the remaining party cadres, who, despite great despair and an almost complete breakdown of the party apparatus, had not abandoned their basic ideological affinity for Soviet communism. For this group of diehard members the process of de-Stalinization led to a reassertion of the Soviet hegemony of international communism, thereby benefiting the Tudeh and other pro-Soviet parties.

Second, by conceding a more dominant role to the bourgeois nationalists in the struggle for national liberation, the party counted on retrieving many members who had left the movement mainly because they disapproved of the party's stand on this issue.[24] To critics who believed that the party had in the past continually oscillated between outright hostility or indecision and conditional support for the nationalist movement, the party could now offer a more consistent attitude which would surely result in genuine cooperation with the nationalist forces.

Finally, the party was optimistic that these revised concepts would appeal to the broad spectrum of members who had opposed joining a united anti-imperialist front primarily because they held the orthodox Communist views about its goal and composition.

The task of appraising the Mossadegh era had always been, of course, a formidable challenge for the party. In its first reaction to the reversal of political developments in favor of the conservative ruling class at the time of the 1953 counterrevolu-

---

[24] Mme Carrere d'Encausse, "Le Toudeh Iranien," *Revue Militaire d'information* (February–March, 1957).

tion, the exiled Central Committee had blamed the National Front government for having failed to accept its offer of cooperation "to defeat the forces of imperialism."[25] But this argument had brought strong criticism from the party's rank and file as well as from many of those in actual charge of the party in Iran during this critical period. Outright condemnation of the National Front hardly satisfied their fundamental misgivings about the party's failure to make a sound evaluation of the Front's role and its delay in adopting concrete policies once such an evaluation had been made. Mindful of these pressures and fearful of another massive defection, the Central Committee had acknowledged some "tactical" errors. But it had remained faithful to the orthodox Communist doctrine on the role of nationalist movements — which, after all, did not undergo thorough revision until the mid-1950's.[26]

The fourth plenum of the Tudeh Central Committee, which met in East Germany on July 17, 1957, was a landmark in the process of revitalization of the Tudeh party. Not only was it the first enlarged session of the committee since the summer of 1948, but it was also the Tudeh leadership's first opportunity for a full review of past developments and an analysis of future policies in the light of the revised doctrinal interpretations.[27]

The plenum agreed that "the counterrevolution of 1953 had been a tragedy for our country which temporarily reversed the course of its history by nullifying the gains of our people and strengthening the domination of reaction and imperialism." And the reason for the reversal? It was chiefly the lack of close cooperation between the party and the nationalist forces, for which both were to blame: "The natural distrust with which the bourgeois nationalists regarded the working class was aggravated by

---

[25] Central Committee of the Tudeh Party, *Darbarehe Bistohashte Mordad* [About August 19].

[26] *Les Activités Communistes au Moyen-Orient* (a compilation of documents and commentaries based on Persian material, edited by le Centre de documentation et de synthèse, Paris, 1954; mimeo.).

[27] Davoud Nowrouzi, "Hezbe Tudehe Iran, Yek Zorourate tarikhi baraye Keshvare ma" [The Tudeh Party of Iran, A Historical Necessity for Our Country], *Donya*, Vol. II, No. 1 (1958), 29.

the party's failure to understand the nature of bourgeois nationalism and its anti-imperialist potential, and this led to the adoption of the wrong tactics in relation to the Mossadegh government." [28]

For the first time, the party was admitting serious doctrinal errors in the period of the National Front government. Once the admission had been made, the party set in motion its vast machinery of propaganda to present to its following, especially among the intelligentsia, a new image.[29] In successive meetings the Central Committee's plenum sought to portray the Tudeh as a realistic and nonsectarian party, ready to accept its share of blame for past errors and eager to learn from them in determining its future program.

The fifth plenum, held in February, 1958, went a step further in formulating concrete demands and specific goals. In a resolution dealing with prevailing political conditions in Iran, it advocated the transition to a regime of "national democracy, because we believe that the people's basic wishes are unattainable without a radical change in the present regime's composition through the unity of all national and democratic forces." [30] In a general way, of course, these resolutions conformed to the revised concept of the role of the nationalist movement, but the new goals were still vague.

At last, in its seventh enlarged plenum, held August 19–29, 1960, the Central Committee put the finishing touches on its ultimate political program. The language was clear and to the point:

---

[28] Abdolsamad Kambakhsh, "Iran at the Crossroads," *World Marxist Review*, Vol. II, No. 9 (1961), 38.

[29] In early 1958 the party's leadership intensified its propaganda campaign through a more regular publication of its clandestine organs and other literature in East Germany, addressed to several thousand Iranian students in Europe. A year later the leadership was supplied with a short-wave transmitter called Peyke Iran and beamed to Iran on 19.37–25.37 mtrs from East Berlin. (Based on regular monitoring service conducted by the British Department of Information.)

[30] Central Committee of the Tudeh Party, "Resolution of the Vth Plenum, March, 1958," *Masaele Hezbi* [Party Problems], No. 5 (April, 1958), 44.

The reactionary regime of Iran, composed of big landlords and capitalists dependent on imperialism and led by the Shah, is the genuine and positive manifestation of the domination of imperialism and feudalism in our country. Therefore, the main task of the revolution in the present stage must be the transference of political power from these big landlords and capitalists to a regime of national democracy representing the united independence-seeking, patriotic, and freedom-loving forces, i.e., workers, peasants, the petty bourgeoisie (tradesmen, shopkeepers), intellectuals, civil servants, and the nationalist capitalists whether merchants or owners of industries.[31]

Specifically, such a regime had to be composed of a coalition of all "progressive" classes and dependent on the broad strata of the people. It had to be capable of eliminating the influence of imperialism and the remnants of feudalism, of transforming the peasants into landowners, of securing democratic freedoms for all, of withdrawing from military pacts, and of effecting fundamental economic and cultural development programs. Any government that succeeded in realizing these essential goals would enjoy the party's support, even without its active participation in the machinery of government.[32]

By accepting a broader basis for alliance with other "democratic" political forces and a pledge of cooperation without sharing in political power, the leadership hoped to avoid past errors in these important areas. Simultaneously, it attempted to give an impression of the utmost harmony in its own rank and file by unifying the Tudeh party and the other underground organizations of the Communist movement, notably the segment of the Azarbayjan Democratic party leadership that had fled to

---

[31] "Tarhe Barnameh va Assassnamehe Mossavebe Plenome Haftom va Konferance Vahdat" [Draft Party Program and Statute Adopted by 7th Plenum and Unity Conference], *Nashriyeh Hezbi*, September–October, 1960.

[32] "Dowlate Demokrassiye Melli" [Government of National Democracy], *Donya*, Vol. II, No. 4 (March, 1961), 73. For a more detailed analysis of this concept consult Klaus Westen, *Der Staat der nationalen Demokratie* (Cologne, 1964).

Russia after the failure of the insurrection and continued its propaganda campaign against the Iranian regime.[33]

Throughout the Mossadegh era when the Tudeh party was actively employing front-organization tactics along with an expanded clandestine network, the Democratic party maintained its separate identity, although it gave general support to Communist efforts to exploit the turbulent political developments. Its refusal to join the Tudeh leadership in exile was due in part to confusion of doctrinal concepts regarding cooperation with nationalist forces and in part to the traditional rivalry between the two parties. Under the pressures for unity and after the solution of some of the most crucial ideological issues, leaders of the two organizations were ready by 1960 to agree on unification. A joint conference was held concurrent with the seventh plenum, and a resolution was issued to hail the unification as "the realization of a fifteen-year-old desire of party members and all friends of progress and freedom."[34]

The revival of the "united party of the working class" was accompanied by the final agreement on its revolutionary nature. The 1952 draft program of the Tudeh party, a document which incorporated many of the revolutionary aims of the Democratic party, was formally adopted by the joint meeting of the seventh plenum and the unity conference. This development also indicated a clear reinstatement of the pro-Soviet element of the leadership; there was no question that the Democratic party's leadership, composed mostly of the remnants of the Caucasian immigrants involved in the Azarbayjan revolt, was intended to represent the pro-Soviet wing of the movement's leading bodies.[35] Furthermore, by incorporating the Democratic party's goals in its program, the Tudeh party had finally nationalized

---

[33] Since 1946 a radio transmitter calling itself the Free Voice of Iran and aimed mainly at the Azarbayjani members of the armed forces has been the chief indication of the continued existence of the remnants of the Azarbayjan Democratic party in Soviet Caucasia.

[34] Nowrouzi, *op. cit.*, p. 39.

[35] Carrere d'Encausse, "Le Toudeh Iranien."

the sectional revolutionary demands of that wing of the leadership whose long-standing radicalism had now become accepted
policy. In the words of the new program: "The masses of the
Iranian people are confronted with the task of overthrowing
the imperialist regime and its agents, securing political economic
independence, and eradicating the feudal landlord-serf relations
through the overthrow of the present reactionary government,
and by the concentration of all power in the hands of the people
and the consolidation of popular sovereignty in the form of a
people's democratic republic." [36]

In a political resolution the party identified the tactical means
of achieving this goal:

> The common interest of the Iranian people from workers and
> peasants to the middle classes, the intellectuals, the national bour-
> geoisie, and all patriotic and freedom-seeking elements in the over-
> throw of the oppressive and antinational regime of the Shah consti-
> tutes the rallying cause for an alliance of these forces. Hence the
> practical step for the creation of a broad united front to encompass
> them is an historical necessity stemming from our society's objective
> condition. It is for this reason that our party considers the creation
> of a broad united front of all independence and freedom-seeking
> forces as its most fundamental task in the present era.[37]

The struggle for a regime of "national democracy" was evidently only the immediate goal of the now unified organizational expression of the Communist movement. Likewise, it
was abundantly clear that the formation of a united national
front by no means implied the party's total assimilation in the
alliance or its loss of identity as the embodiment of a distinctive
social and political ideology. The proposed front represented its
participants' common goals and interests in the current phase of
struggle.[38] The party's long-term goal, jointly confirmed by the
seventh plenum and unity conference, was still the establishment
of a people's democracy.

---

[36] "Tarhe Barnameh."
[37] Nowrouzi, *op. cit.*, p. 42.
[38] *Ibid.*

Concurrent with these developments there occurred certain changes in the evolution of Iranian domestic politics. In the spring of 1960 a limited freedom of activity was afforded all political forces in connection with the general election for the 20th Majlis, scheduled to begin in midsummer. Once again, the comparative easing of governmental control of political activity proved most beneficial to the opponents of the regime, which was at this point attempting to introduce the concept of a two-party system into Iranian politics.

On the Shah's initiative, measures had been taken a year before the election to organize the supporters of the regime into two political formations, one representing the government in power and its majority in the Majlis and the other purporting to function as a loyal opposition with which the former could alternate in the control of the cabinet. Accordingly, members of the Majlis, top government officials, businessmen, and other social and political groups enjoying the trust of the regime were regrouped into a Melliyoun (Nationalist) and a Mardom (People's) party. A bitter struggle to win the majority of parliamentary membership, which the Shah had promised would determine the choice of the ministry, ensued. Despite the obvious artificiality of the new arrangement, the competition for the right to form the new cabinet through the process of election introduced a measure of freedom and liveliness that had been nonexistent in Iranian politics since the reinstatement of the regime in 1953.[39]

The Tudeh party, strengthened by its recent organizational unification and doctrinal consolidation, moved to exploit the new opportunity in pursuance of its immediate goal, a government of national democracy. Rather than boycotting the elections, as it had done since 1953, it decided to participate in them by an active struggle for an alliance of all antigovernment political forces in accordance with the revised concept of united front strategy. In a symbolic gesture, the party urged all supporters to vote for Mossadegh as an at-large write-in candidate, even

---

[39] Binder, *Iran*, pp. 222 ff.

though he was neither legally eligible to run nor permitted to do so by the authorities.[40]

Taking heart from the bitter feud between the competing pro-regime "parties," the Tudeh appealed to the people to restore the nationalist movement to power: "The dissatisfaction and the disgust of the workers, peasants, artisans, intellectuals, and bourgeois nationalists with the existing regime grows daily. . . . Even those segments of society which constitute the social base of the regime are voicing their discontent with its policy. . . . An analysis of the situation in Iran shows that the decline of the national liberation in our country is coming to an end and a new upsurge is approaching — the signs of which are already apparent."[41]

It was hoped that even a small electoral gain by a patriotic popular front could pave the way for achieving some, at least, of the main Communist goals, such as a shift in Iran's foreign policy toward nonalignment, withdrawal from CENTO, and termination of the U.S.–Iran bilateral pact. This optimism was evidently due to the National Front's record both in and out of government, when, by utilizing legitimate channels, it had succeeded in bringing about important policy changes favorable to the attainment of these minimum goals.[42]

The outcome of the elections hardly showed much real success for the proposed united front of antigovernment forces; the government received a majority, thus retaining its effective ban on the Tudeh and nationalist parties. Undaunted, these joined the "loyal opposition" of the Mardom party in loudly clamoring for the invalidation of the elections because of gross fraud. When the demand was finally granted, it was generally interpreted as

---

[40] Under the electoral laws in force since the grant of the constitution in 1905, persons over seventy cannot be candidates for the Majlis. Mossadegh had attained this age limit in the late 1950's; furthermore, he had been under house detention since his release from prison in 1956 after serving three years in solitary confinement.

[41] Kambakhsh, *op. cit.*, p. 40.

[42] Bozorg Alavi, "Der Iran in den Fanger des Neokolonialismus," *Deutsche Aussenpolitik* (East Berlin), No. 1 (January, 1961), 77.

a victory for the opposition's claims that the regime's attempt at party election was a self-defeating device.

The Conference of Fraternal Parties

Meanwhile, the world Communist movement initiated another attempt at setting straight its ideological and tactical course. For the second time in the post-Stalin epoch, fundamental ideological issues facing Communist parties throughout the world were discussed in a conference held in Moscow in November, 1960. The Iranian party was particularly interested in the deliberations of the eighty-one "fraternal parties" attending this advisory conference, for one of the major issues raised was that of the ramifications of nationalist and revolutionary upheavals in the developing countries and the tasks of their Communist parties.

Three years earlier, following the Twentieth Congress of the Soviet Communist Party, another advisory conference had dealt with some aspects of this issue, such as a reevaluation of the nationalist movements and the tactical changes in the united front composition designed to bring to power a regime of "national democracy."[43] Many of these revisions, however, had been only tentatively formulated and experimentally put into practice, as in the isolated case of Iran's Tudeh party. Now, the Moscow conference brought to conclusion the process of reinterpretation of a number of major fundamental concepts. As an avowed Communist party, loyal to Soviet leadership and proud of its pioneer application of some of these concepts, the Tudeh party actively participated in the conference and faithfully attempted to enforce its many resolutions.

A few days after the publication of the conference's declaration on December 6, the Iranian delegation, consisting of the party secretary and four other high-ranking members of the Central Committee, convened a special session of the committee's executive board to report on the declaration and their par-

---

[43] *Donya*, Vol. II, No. 4, 73.

ticipation in the proceedings. After voicing general support for the declaration, the session examined its relevance to Iran and the task of the party in carrying it out. It resolved that the party's goal could be inferred from the way in which the conference had summed up the contemporary era: "A period whose main content is the passage of capitalism to socialism, a transformation which began with the October Revolution and continues to be characterized by the conflict of the two contradictory social systems. An era of socialist and national liberation revolutions, of collapse of imperialism and colonial systems in which every day new masses of people set out on the path of socialism. . . . In short, an era of socialist victory on a universal scale." [44]

As for current Iranian political developments, the executive board resolved, on the authority of the declaration, that these developments reflected the general social contradiction and called for an all-out effort to establish a regime of national democracy. The criterion for identification of such a regime was the pursuance of a specific policy tending to undermine the dominance of the West and to assure local Communists freedom of action: "The national-democratic state should defend its political and economic independence, fight against imperialism and its military blocs, against the existence of military bases on its territory, new forms of colonialism and the penetration of the country by imperialist capitalists, and give its population the chance to fight for the enforcement of agrarian and other reforms designed to achieve social and democratic goals." [45] In addition to the general support given all Communist movements, a state that met this standard would also be entitled to the Soviet bloc's political and economic support.

Commenting on this concept, the Tudeh journal *Donya* identified Cuba, Indonesia, and India as prototypes of the regime

---

[44] "Report of the Executive Board to the C.C., Meeting on Dec. 9–10," *Masaele Hezbi*, No. 16 (October, 1961), p. 3.

[45] Walter Z. Laqueur, "Towards National Democracy: Soviet Doctrine and the New Countries," *Survey*, No. 37 (July–September, 1961), 3–11. For the full text see Dan N. Jacobs, ed., *The New Communist Manifesto and Related Documents* (Evanston, Ill., 1961).

of national democracy "in which various strata of bourgeoisie and progressive elements participate, and though the nationalist and anti-imperialist bourgeoisie retain its leadership the peasants and the working class play a significant role in its political and social organization." [46]

As we have seen, this question had preoccupied the Tudeh leadership long before the Moscow conference. In fact, the party's seventh plenum and conference of unity had pioneered the advocacy of such a regime. Now that the Communist movement's international leadership sanctioned the tactic, the party could advocate its program with firmer conviction. The resolution on the tasks of the "fraternal" Communist parties was therefore readily accepted and maximum efforts for its fulfillment were pledged. [47] Along with other Communist parties, the Tudeh party undertook to fight for the completion of a democratic, anti-imperialist, antifeudalist revolution; to struggle for the creation of a democratic regime; to support any nationalist regime that would consolidate the gains achieved in this struggle; to oppose antidemocratic measures of the ruling class; and to discredit the reactionary wing of the bourgeoisie. [48]

The party took pains to stress that a regime of national democracy was merely its immediate goal and that it remained faithful to the ultimate program of building a socialist society in Iran. "Our efforts to fulfill this immediate goal," it said, "were due to the conviction that a regime of national democracy can attract the broad masses of people to political action, and through far-reaching social reforms will be able to pave the way for a more progressive society." For the same reason the party accepted the conference's resolution regarding work among the masses, proclaiming that "next to organizational unity, the task of infiltration of the masses and mobilization of various classes and strata of the society was the most important condition for the spread of the revolutionary movement of the working class." [49]

[46] *Donya*, Vol. II, No. 1, 35.
[47] *Masaele Hezbi*, No. 16 (October, 1961).
[48] *Donya*, Vol. II, No. 1, 74.

To overcome the obvious difficulty in achieving this aim, given the current situation in Iran, the party recommended a combination of clandestine and public techniques of political struggle: all organizations, leagues, and trade unions (no matter how reactionary) could be infiltrated. And when left wing Communists objected to such a scheme on theoretical grounds, the party dismissed their objections as dogmatic sectarianism. Lenin himself, the Central Committee said, sanctioned total infiltration of the working classes: "Our goal of working among the masses must be focused on organization of open trade unions. Our party members should actively participate in the existing mass legal organizations even though the leadership of these may be in the hands of reactionary elements." [50]

Call for a United Patriotic Front

Political developments within Iran, in the meantime, were assuming a course that made it possible for the party to test almost at once revised Communist tactics for cooperating with nationalist groups.

In the winter of 1960–1961 a second election was held for the 20th Majlis. In making plans, the Tudeh party once more sought the cooperation of the National Front as the sole political organization of the nationalist movement. But whereas, in the election of the previous summer, the party had campaigned for Mossadegh as a write-in candidate throughout the country, this time it announced its support for all candidates opposed to the regime, regardless of their social and political backgrounds. In other words, the sole criterion for Communist support was the degree of opposition of the regime to the candidate – a thing which, under the prevailing political conditions, was not difficult to ascertain.

The Tudeh Central Committee in an open letter to the Front made a desperate appeal for an alliance of progressive forces,

---

[49] *Ibid.*, p. 75.
[50] *Ibid.*

reminding the Front of how, in the past, only defeat had followed their refusal to cooperate with the party, and predicting that "if we strengthen the alliance between the party and the Front, if we create a united front of all patriotic and freedom-loving forces from every sector of the population, our success is assured and our country will be saved from the treacherous policy of the present regime." [51]

The Executive Board of the Central Committee enumerated the specific tasks facing party members and "all other patriotic forces" with whom they sought cooperation. Of chief importance were the following: The creation of joint active nuclei in the vicinity of factories, institutions of learning, and offices for securing freedom in elections; the establishment of committees of free elections in every electoral district with the participation of all elements ready to resist government interference in the electoral process; the support of nationalist candidates in all electoral districts; press and radio campaigns for maximum publication of the aims of this struggle as well as an international propaganda campaign to mobilize world opinion against the regime's antidemocratic measures; the establishment of contact with those opposed to the Shah. [52]

Primarily because of the objection of the center leadership of the Front, no formal electoral alliance came about in consequence of the Tudeh invitation. Only the two major proregime parties submitted candidates, although an independent wing was also permitted to participate and in fact held the balance of power between the two progovernment parties. [53] Thus, since the forces of genuine opposition had no part in the final results of the elections, the question of any tacit Communist–Nationalist cooperation in this area is more or less academic. [54]

---

[51] "Open Letter to the National Front," dated Feb. 9, 1961, cited in Kambakhsh, *op. cit.*, p. 43. See also Radmanesh's interview in *L'Humanité*, Feb. 28, 1961, cited in *Oriente Moderno*, Vol. XLI, No. 6 (1961), 444–445.

[52] *Masaele Hezbi*, No. 16, 25.

[53] The distribution of seats in the new Majlis represented a configuration of about 45 percent for the government party and 35 percent for the "loyal opposition," with the rest belonging to the independents.

[54] Only one candidate of the National Front, in a remote constituency,

As the party saw it, there were two basic obstacles to the establishment of a workable united popular front: first, the active opposition of the regime, which, "haunted by the spectre of unity of action of all democratic forces, knew well that such a development would alter quantitatively and qualitatively the course of the mass struggle"; [55] second, the opposition of former Tudeh members and of other ultranationalist groups, who were consistently against close cooperation with the Communists.[56] Nonetheless, the Communists declared themselves satisfied with the results of the election. It even maintained that, although organizationally there had been no united front in these elections, in reality the common struggle during the campaign created such an alliance.[57] This claim was based on the favorable response given by certain left wing elements of the National Front to the party's open letter. The Youth Branch of the liberal Iran party, in a declaration on the eve of the second election, had supported the slogan, "A Struggle for Freedoms Guaranteed in the Constitution," as the minimum goal of all parties and groups with different or even contradictory views on the program for social and economic revolution in Iran.[58] The declaration said in part:

The question of securing social and political rights is the paramount issue in the struggle for political parties; the economic and social doctrines are of secondary importance. That is why political groups and parties with different and even opposing philosophic and economic views are fighting together against the enemy that has

---

was elected, by a solid bloc of sectional support which gave no clue to a possible electoral alliance with the Communists. Lenczowski, *The Middle East in World Affairs*, p. 224.

[55] *Masaele Hezbi*, No. 16, 26.

[56] The party has singled out Maleki's Third Force and Baghai's followers as the chief standard-bearers of anticommunism. See Ardeshir Ovanessian, "Anti-Communism, the Enemy of Mankind: Behind the Smokescreen of Positive Nationalism" [résumé of a seminar held in Leipzig by the Institute of World History], *World Marxist Review*, Vol. V, No. 9 (1962), 74–79.

[57] "Communique of the Central Committee of the Tudeh party," *Mardom*, Vol. V, No. 14 (April, 1961), 1–4.

[58] *Djavanane Iran* (clandestine organ of the Iran party's youth branch), in Kambakhsh, *op. cit.*, p. 40.

abolished these freedoms. They know that if there is no possibility of free expression of their opinions, there can be no talk about ideological views.[59]

Seemingly ignoring the insignificance of these token indications of a willingness to cooperate, the party continued to talk of a united front. The constant theme of its propaganda at this stage was the absolute necessity of coordinating the Communist–Nationalist struggle against the regime:

> Our endeavors will be fruitful only when all other national forces, particularly that of the Tudeh party, join it. The belief that the Front alone and without the cooperation of the party will be capable of performing the difficult task ahead will in practice produce dissension among progressive forces, divide their ranks, and finally weaken them. The unity of action of these forces is both feasible and necessary for the simple reason that their program in this phase of the struggle is fully agreeable to all, or at least possessed of many common aspects.[60]

Since there was no chance of public agitation against the regime, the Tudeh party concentrated its efforts on Iranians residing in Europe and even in the United States, where, in addition to the usual political expatriates, there were many students at various universities. The attempt to reach these Iranians abroad increased in scope and intensity in the spring of 1961, as it became more and more evident that they were impatient with the regime's failure to solve the fundamental malaise of Iranian politics.[61]

The cabinet crisis of early May, 1961, was the latest manifestation of this impotence. The 20th Majlis, which had finally convened after two elections, had been in session but a few months when student-teacher demonstrations forced the resignation of the caretaker ministry of Sharif Emami and its replacement by

---

[59] *Ibid.*

[60] Gholamhossein Forutan, editorial in *Donya*, Vol. II, No. 4 (1961), 1–2.

[61] For an analysis of some of the problems facing the regime, see Caylor T. Young, "Iran in Continuing Crisis," *Foreign Affairs*, Vol. XL, No. 2 (January, 1962), 275–292.

that of Dr. Ali Amini. Although the crisis owed its immediate cause to the teachers' strike and alleged police brutality in coping with it, there was little doubt that it reflected the deep discontent of the politically articulate over the regime's continued denial of political participation to its genuine opponents.[62]

The choice of the new prime minister and the policies he initiated implied that the regime had at last realized the necessity of some accommodation with the opposition. Ali Amini had long questioned the validity of the two elections for the 20th Majlis, and on his request both houses of parliament were dissolved. Also, a reform program was adopted, an understanding for a temporary restoration to the cabinet of its pre-1953 powers was reached with the Shah, and some measure of freedom for political activity was granted the National Front opposition.[63]

Though not directly affected, the Tudeh party was heartened by these developments. Not only could it claim credit for having itself advocated the dissolution of parliament, but it could also look forward to conditions favorable to its own open activity, as in the years before the Mossadegh era. Speculations about the political orientation of the new cabinet and a possible shift in Iran's foreign policy had also aroused hopes of being able to satisfy at least some of the prerequisites for a national democracy.[64]

In short, the party's first reaction to the new cabinet and to the regime's token accommodation of the genuine opposition was not unlike the enthusiasm it had shown for Mossadegh's return to power after the uprising of July, 1952. Rather than

---

[62] *Ibid.*

[63] At its first authorized public meeting, the Front had an impressive attendance of about 80,000; it demanded immediate elections in accordance with the constitutional provisions governing the dissolution of parliament by the sovereign. *Ibid.*

[64] The inclusion in the cabinet of a former Communist, Noureddin Alamouti, as minister of justice, and a former leader of the Iran party, Gholamali Farivar, as minister of mines and industry, were viewed in this light. The fact that Farivar was chairman of the Iranian Society of Afro–Asian Solidarity was interpreted as showing at least a partial inclination of the new cabinet toward neutralism, one of the avowed Communist goals at this time. Kambakhsh, *op. cit.*, p. 42.

offering its cooperation to the new government, however, the party joined the nationalist parties in a vigorous campaign to force a new election and further isolate Dr. Amini's ministry from the traditional sources of the regime's power.

In a report on the political events leading to the formation of the new cabinet, the Tudeh executive board contended that the coincidence of two simultaneous retreats on the domestic and international scenes was responsible for Iran's latest political crisis. Although, as they saw it, the Amini government was composed of representatives of the landlord and capitalist class "dependent on imperialism," its policy and action seemed to indicate that the prime minister himself considered some concession necessary in order to prevent the growth of the popular movement. This was one retreat. The other was said to have occurred in American policy toward Iran, which now "aimed at preventing the massive unity of all nationalist forces, isolating the Tudeh party, and diverting Iranian nationalism to the path of compromise with imperialism and reaction through superficial reforms."[65]

These alleged concessions stemmed from the regime's fundamental contradictions, which, in the opinion of the party, reflected the larger conflict of the two world social systems as enumerated by the recent Conference of Fraternal Communist Parties. Specifically, these contradictions were: the necessity to win the confidence of the masses or at least of the middle class to prevent a violent upheaval against the regime; the imperativeness of a relaxation of the authoritarian features of the government attitude toward the opposition to meet this necessity; and the fear of a free general election as the most simple and democratic means of satisfying the public, lest its outcome precipitate the regime's downfall.[66] The party was confident that these contradictions would result either in continued government oscillation between seemingly harmless alternative con-

---

[65] *Masaele Hezbi,* No. 16, 21.
[66] *Ibid.,* p. 28.

cessions or in a return to the more conventional policies pursued by successive governments in the preceding eight years.

By the summer of 1961 the latter course seemed to be prevailing. Most of the concessions granted the opposition were withdrawn, and the cabinet gradually came to be subordinate to the Shah in much the same manner as before, throughout the post-Mossadegh era. Obviously, there was no longer any reason to expect any substantial shift in the government's over-all political orientation. Prime Minister Amini had failed to perform the catalyst function for the Communists that Mossadegh's government had carried out in at least the latter part of his rule in 1953.

Thus, when the ninth plenum of the party's unified leadership met in September, 1961, it had to face the same old problems, though in slightly different perspective. Thirty-two full and advisory members of the Central Committee met from Sept. 10 to Sept. 16 (presumably in East Berlin). They unanimously approved the report of Dr. Radmanesh, the party's first secretary, on the conference of the eighty-one fraternal parties,[67] and they listened to organizational and political reports submitted by Eskandari on behalf of the party's executive board. But the major part of the plenum's deliberation was devoted to a study of the work of the Moscow conference and of the task of giving maximum publicity to the conference's declarations on such issues as the regime of "national democracy," neocolonialism, and the progress of revolutionary movements in Iran. As for the domestic situation, the plenum made a resolution:

Despite some blows inflicted on the regime, the national movement of the people has not as yet achieved that degree of power and consolidation necessary to overthrow the regime. Hence, the destruction of the despotic and antinational regime of the Shah, the establishment of a national government, and the restoration of democratic freedoms continue to constitute the principal goals of the independence and freedom-loving movement of our people in the current phase of the struggle.[68]

---

[67] "Communique of the 9th Plenum of the Central Committee of the Tudeh Party," *ibid.*, pp. 1–2.
[68] *Ibid.*

The struggle to secure democratic freedoms was declared to be the most pressing demand, and the leading party organs were instructed to increase their efforts in its behalf. More concretely, the plenum defined the major tasks of the party as the restoration of the parliamentary system by means of an immediate free election; reinstatement of the fundamental political freedoms guaranteed in the constitution and the Declaration of Human Rights; and the struggle against CENTO and the U.S.–Iran bilateral agreement. Mindful of the past experience of the Tudeh party and other "fraternal" parties, the plenum also emphasized the necessity of a systematic struggle against local nationalism and expansionist chauvinism. These were cited as major sources of ideological deviation to be combated by indoctrinating party members with the "true spirit of proletarian internationalism." [69]

It was evident from the election of a new three-man secretariat, chosen from the eleven-man executive board, that the trend in party leadership was to be pro-Soviet. Radmanesh, a compromise candidate representing several different factions, retained his post as first secretary, but Eskandari and Kambakhsh, both of the pro-Soviet faction, replaced Ehsan Tabari and Dr. Keshavarz as second and third secretaries. [70]

A month later the new secretariat and several other party leaders, including Reza Rusta, secretary of the United Council, attended the Twenty-second Congress of the CPSU in Moscow. They were as one in expressing their party's unconditional acceptance of the Soviet leadership in all major international and national domains. Radmanesh's address to the congress embodied the usual characteristics that have distinguished pronounce-

---

[69] *Ibid.*

[70] Tabari, who first took office as second political secretary in 1948, is well known for his long-standing rivalry with the old guard, now reestablished in power. Keshavarz, according to Iranian sources, has left the party altogether; he is said to be presently residing in Switzerland on an Iraqi passport. Of the original members of the Central Committee elected by the Second Congress in 1948, two (Dr. Bahrami and Dr. Yazdi) were arrested in Iran in 1953 and received life terms, another (Ollovi) was executed, and three others were expelled from the party for cooperating with the authorities after their arrest.

ments of Soviet-dominated foreign Communist parties in the post-Stalin era. Echoing the party's admiration for the CPSU's new program in adulating terms, he said in part:

It opens up a new and bright chapter in Marxist–Leninist learning and knowledge, in the life of the CPSU, and in the history of the world Communist and workers' parties. The toilers of our country, like all the toilers of the world, rejoice in the victories and achievements of the Soviet Union and sincerely congratulate the CPSU and its Leninist Central Committee led by comrade Khrushchev, the most outstanding fighter for peace and defender of the people's freedom from slavery and colonialism.

He also endorsed, on behalf of his party, Moscow's condemnation of its ideological opponents of both Left and Right: "The new program with its great material and intellectual value is a powerful psychological and political weapon against the bourgeois and reformist factions and against revisionism and dogmatism within the Communist and workers movement."

To remove any doubts about where his party stood in the emerging Sino–Soviet ideological dispute, reflected in Moscow's denunciation of the Albanian Communist party, Radmanesh declared: "We regard the unity of the Socialist camps as dear to us as the apple of our eye. For this reason we approve the criticism against the Albanian workers' party for the breach of the pronouncements of the Communists and workers' parties approved in 1957 and 1960 and the resulting weakening of international bonds."

The parts of the address relating to Iran's domestic politics and foreign relations were simply a restatement of the party's evaluation of the post-Mossadegh trends. But Radmanesh made an effort to inject a note of optimism into an otherwise pessimistic account of the party's travails under the current regime:

The struggle of our masses in the last two years shows that we are now at the beginning of a great national liberation movement. Our party, making use of past experience, is gaining strength and is striving to unite all democratic and national forces in a united front of the masses against imperialism and feudalism, for the overthrow of the regime and the achievement of democratic freedoms, the withdrawal from aggressive blocs, and the formation of a national government. In this struggle the victories and achievements of the Soviet Union and other countries of the Socialist camp give us inspiration and strength.[71]

There has been no substantial changes in the party's pronouncements on its domestic and international policy since this address by Radmanesh in October, 1961. Since then, although prospects for fulfilling party goals have not radically improved, it is evident that the party continues to work in this direction. In early November, 1961, for example, government authorities announced the smashing of a major Communist cell in Isfahan and the arrest of some ninety party activists allegedly directed by exiled leaders in eastern Europe.[72] Confiscated Tudeh literature also allegedly indicated nationalist–Communist cooperation, and the regime has used this as its strongest argument in favor of continued suppression of opposition from these sources.

Rapprochement with the Soviet Union

The more recent developments likely to be of even greater significance to the future course of communism in Iran have to do with the latest Soviet diplomatic posture toward the regime's social and economic reforms and the Sino–Soviet ideological schism.

Since 1962, when Iran pledged its refusal to allow foreign military bases on her soil, relations between Iran and the Soviet Union have slowly, but unmistakably, improved. Inevitably, this has had an impact on the Tudeh party's line of propaganda and action.

---

[71] Radmanesh, "Address to CPSU's 20th Congress on Oct. 28, 1961," as reported in *Communist Propaganda and Developments in the Middle East*, No. 97 (November, 1961); compiled by the British Information Dept. For a review of this congress consult Charlotte Saikowski and Leo Gruliow, eds., *Current Soviet Policies. IV: The Documentary Records of the 22nd Congress of the C.P.S.U.* (New York, 1962).

[72] Dr. Kiyanouri, then residing in Graz, Austria, was identified as the head of this particular cell. *Oriente Moderno*, XLI, 881.

At the core of Soviet relations with Iran is the U.S.S.R.'s revised assessment of the regime's capability to undertake radical — even revolutionary — social and political reforms through conventional, nonrevolutionary means. A move in this direction aimed at large-scale land reforms and an anticorruption campaign was initiated under Dr. Amini's government in May, 1961, with the Shah's apparent, but perhaps half-hearted, support.[73] The move lost most of its momentum, however, in the latter part of Amini's term of office and did not resume its initial intensity until the change of cabinet in July, and the Shah's subsequent resumption of more direct control of government affairs.

The coincidence of this development with the exchange of letters about foreign bases resulted in an extension of the new accommodating Soviet attitude to the regime's domestic policies. With the favorable Soviet reaction to the Shah's referendum on the six major reform measures several months later, the Tudeh party once again faced the difficult task of compromising its ideological and political hostility toward the regime with a new Soviet diplomatic posture.[74] Indeed, the Iranian–Soviet détente in recent years, culminating in a number of symbolic gestures to the further discredit of the party, has raised the question of whether the Soviets have not written off the Tudeh permanently.[75] The adverse effects of this development on the party should not be overstated, however. In the first place, the predominantly pro-Soviet leadership could take refuge in the tactical necessity of the new shift. As in the past, its silent acquiescence to this shift may again be justified in the context of "proletarian internationalism," which provides all pro-Soviet Communist

---

[73] The text of the Royal Firman authorizing the reform measures and an analysis of the circumstances prompting their initiation through extraparliamentary devices can be found in *the Middle East Journal*, Vol. XVI, No. 1 (1962), 86–92.

[74] The government-controlled Iranian press gave prominent coverage to favorable accounts in *Pravda* and *Izvestia* of the Shah's "revolution from above," put to referendum on January 26, 1963. *Ettelaat* (air ed.), Feb. 21–24, 1963.

[75] These symbolic gestures included the surrender to the Iranian police of a number of convicted Tudeh fugitives, one of whom, a former police officer, was executed in July, 1964.

parties with the rationale for accepting changes dictated by Soviet raison d'état.

Secondly, the party could present the regime's somewhat less anti-Soviet attitude and its proposed social and economic reforms in the contexts both of the revised concepts of national liberation movements and of the orthodox Leninist views on the relevance of objective conditions to the revolutionary potentials of backward societies. Thus, Iran's refusal to grant military bases to the Western powers and the social and economic reforms for consolidation of her economic emancipation could be regarded as in part satisfying the prerequisites for a regime of "national democracy."

Similarly, the party could rely on favorable long-range changes which the reform measures are likely to bring about.[76] Just as the modernizing policies of Reza Shah proved conducive to the revival of communism after 1941, the present Shah's "white revolution" could radically alter the country's traditional power bases to the ultimate benefit of the party.[77] In sum, this development alone is unlikely to dishearten the party's leadership, particularly as long as the Soviet Union and its European allies continue to serve as the main sanctuary for the majority of Tudeh fugitives. As in the past, however, the lower echelons of the party and the membership at large will probably not remain impervious to the growing Soviet accommodation with the Iranian regime.

The Challenge of Polycentrism

As to the Sino–Soviet dispute, which in recent years has strained the relations of most foreign Communist parties with Moscow,

---

[76] One commentator has attributed to some of the leaders of the Iranian regime in recent years a fallacious contention that no significant change in power relationships will result from revolutionary or conventional alteration of the pattern of economic and production relations. See Binder, *Iran*, p. 309.

[77] For a critical appraisal of these measures see Hossein Mahdavy, "The Coming Crisis in Iran," *Foreign Affairs*, XLIV, No. 1 (October, 1965), 134–146.

there is little doubt that the Iranian party has also been affected.[78] If the Tudeh party had been able to operate outside the sphere of Soviet influence, the impact of polycentrism on the Iranian movement might be more accurately discerned. Until recently, however, not only have party followers remained under strict surveillance inside the country but also the Tudeh leadership has given every appearance of a unified pro-Soviet stance on all international and ideological issues. On various occasions since the CPSU's 22nd Congress in October, 1961, the Tudeh Central Committee has upheld the Moscow position unequivocally. It has only recently become known that on these occasions the leadership was not always unanimous.

Even as early as the 1961 meeting of the ninth plenum, when the question of the Tudeh attitude toward the Albanian Workers' Party was raised, a small faction of the Central Committee refused to go along with the CPSU's condemnation of the Albanian party which even then portended the forthcoming Sino–Soviet rift. The façade of unanimity and solidarity with the CPSU was nevertheless preserved until the summer of 1965, when the party's old guard faced another crisis reminiscent of the intraparty upheavals of 1947 and 1953.

Two interrelated developments in the summer of 1965 helped to bring into the open the brewing crisis in the party's leadership. One was the continuing improvement of Soviet–Iranian relations, climaxed by a second visit of the Shah to Moscow and the reported acquiescence of the Central Committee to the combined pressure of the two governments for the repatriation of other convicted Tudeh fugitives.[79] The other was a turn for

---

[78] For an analysis of the Asian Communist stand in this respect see Robert A. Scalapino, "Moscow, Peking, and the Communist Parties of Asia," *ibid.*, Vol. XLI, No. 2, (January, 1963), 323–343. For a review of the impact of polycentrism on the Middle Eastern parties, see W. A. C. Adie, "The Middle East: Sino–Soviet Discords," in Walter Laqueur and Leopold Labedz, eds., *Polycentrism* (New York, 1962).

[79] This visit paved the way for several financial agreements, including a long-term Soviet credit of 286 million dollars to build an industrial complex consisting of a steel mill, a machine tool plant, and other factories. *The Economist* (London), April 2, 1966.

the worse in Sino–Soviet relations after a brief interlude of mutual restraint following the change of Soviet leadership in the fall of 1964.

In July and August, 1965, three prominent members of the Tudeh Central Committee issued a series of sharp statements dissenting from the committee's strongly pro-Soviet line.[80] In one statement they reasserted their dedication to a "violent revolution as the only way to the liberation of the Iranian masses." In another, they appealed to the rank and file of the party to join them in the struggle "to revive and reorganize the revolutionary activity of the Iranian working class."

In response, the eleventh plenum of the Central Committee meeting at the end of the summer branded the three an antiparty faction and voted to expel two from the Central Committee and to suspend the third. The plenum also appointed a three-man bureau in an attempt to streamline the committee and to fill the gap caused by the expulsion of the three. The defectors wrote to the newly elected bureau on October 7, 1965, to denounce all the decisions of the eleventh plenum and to declare their intention of organizing a separate party under the same name but dedicated to "reviving the revolutionary tradition of the Tudeh Party of Iran." By then the three, along with an undetermined number of supporters, had left their East European countries of residence and had proceeded to Peking via Albania, thus making a formal split in the party leadership and a clear establishment of a pro-Peking faction.

In a lengthy communique issued in January, 1966, the Central Committee, acknowledging the split, put the blame on the leadership of the Chinese Communist party, which had publicly urged Marxist–Leninist parties to draw a clear line of distinction in political and organizational respects between themselves and

---

[80] These were Ahmad Ghassemi and Dr. Gholamhossein Forutan, full members, and Abbas Shaghai, a consultant member. Ironically, both Forutan and Ghassemi, particularly, were among the most vigorous champions of party unity and the leadership authority in the major party crisis of 1947–1948.

"the revisionists who serve American imperialism."[81] Once the split became a fait accompli, the pro-Soviet Central Committee formally joined the ranks of other parties following the Soviet lead. Thus, for example, the party organ *Mardom* condemned the "evil effects" of the CCP's policy in a sweeping indictment which ranged from charges of flouting the genuine Marxist–Leninist tenets to neglecting the "anti-imperialist struggle of the heroic people of Vietnam" by divisive tactics.[82] Similarly, at the CPSU's 23rd Congress held in Moscow in April, 1966, the Tudeh delegation reaffirmed its Soviet affiliation in unequivocal terms.

Outside the Tudeh party, other leftist elements, especially among the intellectuals, have also been vulnerable both to the shift in Soviet policy toward Iran and to the disintegration of the monolithic world Communist movement. Quite apart from the effect of a determined Chinese offensive to vie for the allegiance of the Middle Eastern Communists, there are other factors that might eventually give Chinese communism a lead in the Middle East. Particularly, there is the indigenous nature of the Communist movement in China, and the similarity of some of the social and economic features of China to those of Middle Eastern societies. Also of importance is China's non-involvement in the area, which spares Peking from probable conflict with the inherent nationalist sentiment of the Middle Eastern people. And, not least important, there is the radicalism of Maoism, which is likely to attract some of the younger generation of Marxists in the Middle East.[83]

---

[81] The communique, broadcast over the clandestine Radio Peyke Iran on January 3, 1966, made especial mention of an editorial in *People's Daily* and *Red Flag* on November 12, 1965, entitled "The Unity of Action of the New Leadership of the Soviet Communist Party." This was, the broadcast said, the green light for the Tudeh and other Communist defectors to Peking.

[82] From an editorial broadcast on Radio Peyke Iran on January 8, 1966.

[83] Iranian students abroad, particularly in Western Europe, have been most susceptible to Maoist propaganda. A trial arising out of an attempt on the Shah's life in April, 1965, implicated scores of British-educated intel-

Some of these factors are evidently an integral part of the appeal of the more universal Communist ideology, which even now is still identified with the Soviet Union and to which further reference will be made in the concluding pages.

---

lectuals whose activity has allegedly exceeded a purely academic concern for Maoism. In another trial in April, 1966, a military tribunal sentenced to death two young Iranians on a charge of conducting pro-Peking subversion. *New York Times*, April 20, 1966.

CONCLUSION

The main body of this work has inquired into the dynamics of the Communist movement in Iran since its inception in early 1920 — the evolution of its principal doctrines, the changes and continuity in Soviet diplomacy, and various efforts to apply new doctrinal interpretations to traditional objectives.

What follows is an attempt, first of all, to identify the main source of the ideological appeal of communism, next, to examine the interaction of communism with competing traditional or modern social forces, and, finally, to determine the social characteristics of those strata of Iranian society that have been most susceptible to communism.

The role of communism as the most radical challenge to the established political order, especially in the interwar period when the Communist movement assumed a more indigenous nature, has been the main source of its appeal in Iran.[1] Throughout its evolution the movement had served as a vehicle of a nega-

---

[1] A recent study of Iranian politics has distinguished between two types of negative and positive forms of challenging the established political order, determined by the degree of alienation and the goals of the challengers. In its most extreme form a negative challenge is believed to be manifested by participation in a subversive party conspiracy to overthrow the regime by force. Communism is one of the major ideologies seeking to satisfy this mode of challenge. Others have been identified as extreme nationalism, militaristic dictatorship, and the Islamic fundamentalism. Binder, *Iran*, pp. 286–287.

tive, and, on occasion, a positive process for challenging the system. And as in other protest movements, the fulfillment of this function has corresponded to the degree to which the politically articulate elements are alienated from the regime.

Our inquiry has amply confirmed the strong attraction of this function of Communist ideology for those politically articulate Iranians who have been more or less estranged from the regime. For them, the movement provided a channel for at least a negative challenge to the social and political system. By joining a party dedicated to overthrowing the regime in power, the participants satisfied the most extreme form of this type of challenge. They could also use its less extreme forms of passive resistance, refusal to vote, and so on — modes of protest in which, according to Leonard Binder, alienation from the system is not overtly displayed for fear of deprivation.

One offshoot of this negative protest in Iran has been the attitude toward major foreign powers, which is directly connected with their support of or opposition to the established Iranian regime. The closer the identification of the regime with a foreign power, the more intense the hostility has been toward that power; the more pronounced the hostility of a foreign power to the regime, the more frequent, however vague, the support for it.[2] The pro-Soviet orientation of the Tudeh movement, despite its obvious conflict with nationalistic sentiments, can be at least partly understood in this context.

This has been particularly true of three phases of the movement: (1) the long period since 1947, when the Soviet Union has not been directly involved in the struggle for influence over the Iranian system, except for the brief crisis over fishery agreements in the winter of 1952–1953; (2) when government repression closed other channels of the system-challenging process, as in the post-Mossadegh era; and (3) when competing ideologies like nationalism did not effectively challenge communism, as in the periods after the Azarbayjan episode and the Mossadegh regime.

---

[2] *Ibid.*, p. 328.

In Iran, as elsewhere, the varieties of alienation have produced different types of susceptibility, depending on the particular needs and interests of the participants. Besides the general political alienation from the system, the role of social alienation, caused by racial, ethnic, and cultural discrimination, is important. In Iran, with its substantial minority groups, this has been a significant factor, which the party has actively exploited through its advocacy of autonomy and self-determination as well as cultural and religious toleration for minorities. The Communist movement in Iran has included members of all minorities, not only those officially recognized by the regime — Armenians, Jews, Zoroastrians — but also those, like the Azarbayjanis and the Kurds, who have not been so acknowledged. Indeed, the linguistic isolation of the latter was frequently exploited in the immediate postwar phase. Advancement for the minority groups in the party's higher echelons has been fairly easy, as indicated by their rather heavy representation in the leadership organs as compared with their small total numerical strength. In the case of certain ethnic minorities, including the Armenians, Kurds, and Assyrians, whose problems and grievances transcend the boundaries of Iran, the attraction of communism is largely to be explained in tactical and practical rather than deep-rooted ideological terms. Few of these, except the Armenians, have been especially represented in the higher echelons of the party.[3]

The movement in Iran has operated under conditions typical of underdeveloped societies, except that it has had, in addition to the estrangement of class and status, alienations of race and of ethnic and cultural discrimination. It is precisely this type of environment, according to Gabriel Almond, that "has enabled the movement to draw the destructive energies and the desperate impatience from all these varieties of protest and resentment

---

[3] The Armenian case presents a special exception, probably because of the large-scale Soviet offensive to bring them into the Soviet Armenian Republic as well as the existence of a considerable number of non-Iranian Armenians among the well-trained cadres of the Communist leadership. For a description of some of the particularly volatile minorities in Iran, see Laqueur, ed., *The Middle East in Transition*, pp. 225–228.

and harness them in the service of a controlled and comprehensive destructiveness." [4] In its general characteristics, the Tudeh party closely resembles the type of national and anti-Western organizations that flourish in poor and backward countries:

Such a party is comprised necessarily of professional people, formally trained or self-taught, with some large element of Western education or influence. It is so comprised because the intelligentsia is the conductor through which Western influences penetrate non-Western cultures and because this party, to win and hold power, must provide a ruling class capable of governing in the conditions of that rapid industrialization and cultural metamorphosis which we call Westernization. Such a party is a national party because its basic aim is national power through the development of modern industry.[5]

As our inquiry has shown, the Tudeh party has consistently attempted to exploit all varieties of alienation. Its concentration on the urban population, for example, rather than on the peasantry was in part due to a recognition that the peasants were still to a large extent integrated in their traditional unit, whereas the semiskilled or unskilled laborers were uprooted from their usual system of social relationships and in an unfamiliar setting. In fact, the Iranian experience shows that, although the Communist movement had an essentially middle class and intellectual social basis, the semiskilled and unskilled laborers proved most susceptible to Communist proselytizing, in contrast to the skilled workers, who frequently defected when the government-sponsored trade unions offered more attractive concessions. Unskilled labor has seemed little interested in any shift from a positive to a negative process of system-challenging which in practice amounts to collective bargaining designed to

---

[4] Gabriel A. Almond, *The Appeals of Communism* (Princeton, N.J., 1954), p. 381. See also Morris Watnick, "The Appeal of Communism to the Underdeveloped Peoples," *Economic Development and Cultural Change*, Vol. I, No. 1 (1952), 22–36.

[5] R. V. Burks, *The Dynamics of Communism in Eastern Europe* (Princeton, N.J., 1961), p. 186.

secure the maximum economic concessions from the regime
with the minimum degree of political concessions by the unions.
The question of rival ideologies, such as nationalism and
Islam, and their attraction for the politically articulate has been
emphasized in recent sociopolitical studies of Middle Eastern
countries.[6] Our inquiry into the Iranian experience, though
largely substantiating the ineffectiveness of these ideologies as a
serious challenge to the Tudeh party, does not rule out their
relevance to the complex problem of resistance to communism.
This is particularly true of nationalism whenever a conflict
between Russian and Iranian interest exists, as during the oil
crisis of 1945–1947.

In Iran, as in other countries of similar cultures, nationalism
has been the object of different interpretations. For the alienated
population, it embodies social reform, free elections, industrialization, land distribution, and a tendency toward neutralism.
For the present regime it has a different connotation.[7] According to the regime, "positive nationalism," as it has been defined,
in contradistinction to the "negative nationalism" of Mossadegh's era, is a nationalism that equates the aggrandizement of
state power with that of the nation.[8] And for the Communist
movement for most of its existence, there was its own special
brand of leftist nationalism. This particular nationalism was
intended for the general public, which, until 1955, was rarely
exposed to the movement's Marxist–Leninist orientation.[9]

---

[6] *The Middle East in Transition*, ed. Laqueur, contains pertinent articles on this subject. For a more general review of the impact of modern
ideologies on changing societies, consult John Kautsky, ed., *Political Change
in Underdeveloped Countries: Nationalism and Communism* (New York,
1962).

[7] See L. P. Elwell-Sutton, "Nationalism and Neutralism in Iran," *Middle East Journal*, Vol. XII, No. 1 (1958).

[8] See the Shah's detailed analysis of "positive nationalism" in his memoirs, *Mission for My Country* (New York, 1961). For a more comprehensive
study of Iranian nationalism, consult Richard Cottam, *Nationalism in
Iran* (Pittsburgh, 1964).

[9] Ehsan Tabari's essay, "Esteghlal Chist?" [What Is Independence?], is
a typical statement of the Tudeh party's conception of independence during
its period of legal existence. See *Mardom*, Vol. II, No. 10 (June, 1948), 1–3.

The Tudeh party's leftist nationalism strongly emphasized national independence, democracy, social equality, and similar objectives, which were particularly attractive to recruits who knew little, if anything, about the real nature of the party program and ideology. Since 1955, however, when the party abandoned all pretense of noncommunism, party leaders have had to cope not only with so-called negative nationalism but also with its most extreme forms of chauvinism and xenophobia. In response to charges of pro-Sovietism and antinationalism frequently expressed by such extreme nationalists, the party has consistently sought protection under the cover of proletarian internationalism. In a recent pronouncement, the party's pro-Sovietism was attributed to "the analysis of the Soviet state and the international front of peace and freedom, i.e., proletarian internationalism which only the ignorant and the antagonists can confuse with antinationalism." [10]

Although the party's higher echelons have accepted these concepts, as our study has shown, serious misgivings persist on this issue, particularly among the intellectuals and the middle class. Similarly, the party's support of "negative nationalism" — negative, that is, in relation to the imperialists and positive from the point of national interests — has not markedly improved the chances of solving this perplexing problem.[11]

As for Islam as a force to weaken the Communist appeal, the Iranian case substantiates the accepted notion that religious beliefs cannot in themselves significantly offset the attraction of radical ideologies. By and large, the segments of society that have been the target of the most intensive Communist proselytizing and indoctrination either have been nonreligious or have justified their response to the party within the context of their religious beliefs. The latter was particularly true during the period of front-organization strategy, when a large number of presumably religious lower middle class groups in urban regions responded favorably to Communist agitation for such seem-

---

[10] Nowrouzi, "Hezbe Tudehe Iran."
[11] See Ovanessiyan, "Anti-Communism."

ingly innocent goals as universal peace and anti-imperialism. Party propaganda directed toward this group often sought to identify its social objectives with the "true" teachings of Islam.

The ineffectiveness of religion in general as a serious competitor of communism in the struggle for the allegiance of the politically articulate in the Middle East has been attributed to several factors, some of which apply to Iran.[12] As Bernard Lewis has pointed out, certain of the accidental elements of Islam, which are part of the recent historical situation, such as the anti-Western motif or the identification of the West with imperialism, have been instrumental in attracting predominantly religious elements of the small-trade bourgeoisie to various Communist front organizations, particularly during the Mossadegh era.[13]

Although the Tudeh party has never made any concentrated effort to attract the religious hierarchy, it has shown a fair measure of success when tactical reasons have required it, as the participation of certain religious figures in the peace offensive of the early 1950's would indicate. The Shia hierarchy, likewise for tactical reasons, has not been averse to accepting Communist support in the face of a common enemy.[14] No doubt the Moslem religion will remain of little influence on the Communist movement as long as the Communists, despite their loud protestations of mass basis of appeal, cater primarily to the educated elite. Party records show that except for occasional attempts to glorify Shia martyrdom or to exploit the alleged religious tolerance in the Soviet Union, it has not been much interested in the religious aspect.

A survey of Tudeh literature, however, indicates that in the

---

[12] Laqueur, ed., *The Middle East in Transition*, p. 6.

[13] Bernard Lewis, "Communism and Islam," *International Affairs*, Vol. XXX (January, 1954), pp. 17–19.

[14] The most extreme example of participation in the Communist movement by a religious figure was that of Ayatollah Borghei, the so-called Red Mullah, whose membership in the Iranian Society of Peace Partisans brought him, among other benefits, several East European trips in 1952–1953 to represent his affiliates in Peace Festivals. See Binder, *Iran*.

process of recruiting for its subversive organization, the party had to resort to antireligious indoctrination when religious reservations were found to be troubling the minds of potential recruits.[15] In these cases, the transition from religious belief to communism was not difficult because other signs of susceptibility to its appeal could be successfully exploited. Some specialists in Islamic religion attribute the ease with which this transition is often made to such fundamental features of Islam as obedience to effective authority and collective obligation. Others have mentioned the supernatural character of the universal systems advocated by both ideologies.[16]

Quite apart from whatever fundamental conflicts and similarities may exist in Islam and communism, the experience of Communist movements in predominantly Moslem societies shows that Islam is certainly no more anti-Communist than Christianity is. On the other hand, it is not improbable that, once Moslem countries recognize the atheistic nature of communism, Islam will prove formidably resistant. Certainly this will be true in the higher echelons of the Shia clergy and the predominantly religious peasantry, neither of whom have so far been systematically courted by the Iranian Communists.

The extent of the party's success in utilizing different elements of its ideological appeal in recruiting has, of course, varied greatly during the history of the movement. In this, the Iranian experience has been little different from that of other Communist movements whose fluctuations in membership are known.[17] In Iran, the heaviest recruiting occurred in three kinds of situations:

---

[15] This was a significant factor in the recruiting of army officers. In cases where potential recruits had been found to satisfy other requirements on an elaborate personality questionnaire, religious belief was frequently discovered to be the last obstacle to surmount. *Ketabe Siyah*, p. 114.

[16] See Lewis, *op. cit.*, and Nabih Amin Faris, "The Islamic Community and Communism," in Laqueur, ed., *The Middle East in Transition*, pp. 357–358.

[17] Almond, *The Appeals of Communism*, pp. 297–332.

1. In situations where the party appeared to have good prospects for success, as during the Azarbayjan crisis, particularly in the spring of 1946.

2. At the time of the accommodation of the movement in the fabric of Iranian politics, as in the early part of the Second World War, or at the time of a serious social breakdown when the radicalism of the party became more attractive, as was at least partly true just before 1953.

3. At times when the party was "protectively colored," such as in the latter part of the wartime occupation and in the Mossadegh era when it was associated with broad moderate and patriotic aims.

These inflationary phases in the evolution of the movement were invariably followed by periods of decline:

1. The disillusionment of participants as a result of the abrupt elimination of the party's prospects for success, demonstrated in the post-Azarbayjan crisis at the end of 1946 and early 1947, and to some extent in the post-Mossadegh era.

2. The reversal of the government's accommodating policies combined with a severe repression of the party which occurred after the movement was outlawed in 1949 and more systematically after the overthrow of the National Front government in 1953.

3. The situation that ultimately follows the era of popular alliance in which the movement suffers from disillusionment, as was the case in the second part of the Mossadegh era and indeed continues to be so even today when a numerically much smaller party shows signs of inability to solve the crisis of alliance with the nationalist forces.

Each of these situations has been highlighted by a party crisis, ostensibly as a result of changes in party line. However, dissatisfaction with and defection from the movement cannot be primarily attributed to these tactical changes. As it has been shown in other similar cases, these changes are like "the opening of the

flood gates, permitting the already disenchanted and the dissatis-
fied to move out in the comparative safety and anonymity of
party crisis." [18] The major Tudeh party crises at the beginning
of 1947 and after 1953 fully fit into this pattern of crisis defection. As we have seen, the largest group of party defectors in 1947
publicly acknowledged that their dissatisfaction could be traced
to the dissension that developed during the First Party Congress
in 1944.

Just as the susceptibility to Communist appeal is multifaceted,
so is the process of defection attributable to many factors. Party
policies that affect the interests of a specific party stratum, such
as an unpopular strike or acccommodation with the government,
are likely to lead to defection among workers and intellectuals.
Similarly, any action that has the effect of placing the participants at a distance from the control of the Communist organization and communication can lead to defection — military
enlistment, for example, transfer from urban to rural areas, and,
among student groups, travel abroad for higher education.

A corollary of the defection process is the postdefection attitude, which is greatly affected by the absence or presence of other
alternatives for defectors. The Iranian experience indicates the
importance of the lack of satisfactory alternatives to the Communist movement. As our inquiry into the party's evolution has
shown, several attempts to absorb the non-Communist Left into
new organizations such as the Toilers party and the Third Force,
active during the National Front era, failed to hold Tudeh defectors for any length of time.[19] As a result the Tudeh party
could by and large retain its professed monopoly of leftist radicalism. If anything, this claim has been reinforced since 1953,
when the party began to advocate publicly its Communist ideals.

---

[18] *Ibid.*, p. 327.

[19] The suggested hypothesis about the availability of satisfactory alternatives or the sanction and disability imposed on defectors, based on
Western and notably the Italian and French experiences, is confirmed in
the Iranian case where a large percentage of these defectors have either
remained totally indifferent or have joined one or the other of non-
Communist parties for brief periods of time. *Ibid.*

The severe repression of the party since then has contributed to its revolutionary image and provided it with many martyrs.

The past experience indicates that a successful challenge to the Tudeh party's monopoly of leftist radicalism cannot emanate from non-Communist sources, even though at times some of the more extreme nationalist groups have outdone the party in support of revolutionary methods to gain political objectives. An effective challenge to this function of the party from within the party, however, should not be ruled out. The recent defection of the pro-Peking Tudeh leaders and the evidence of the susceptibility of Iranian intellectuals to the more revolutionary Maoism may well prove the most serious threat to the established Tudeh leadership. It may be conjectured that, given the opportunity to express their preference, a substantial sector of the leftist elements, including disillusioned former Tudeh followers, would opt for the splinter Tudeh faction that has identified itself with Peking.

As for the social characteristics of the participants in the Communist movement, an analysis of the composition of the Tudeh party's chief governing bodies yields a number of observations.[20] First of all, it bears out the notion that susceptibility to communism is not the simple consequence of poverty. The largest proportion of the party's elite belonging to the urban and industrial groups fell in the middle income category; only a small percentage of the leadership's lower echelon belonged to the poorer groups. To the extent that it could be ascertained,

---

[20] Three segments of the Tudeh elite were analyzed: (1) members of the Central Committee and the larger plenum consisting of former members and nonvoting alternate members as well as the parliamentary group; (2) the entire membership of the party's military network; (3) the 50 or so principal defectors of the Maleki faction, who constituted the bulk of the party's intelligentsia before 1947. The chief sources of data on former Tudeh members are *Seyre Komonism* and *Ketabe Siyah*, *Activités Communistes au Moyen-Orient*, Steiner's "Der Iranische Kommunismus," "Biographical Sketch of Tudeh Leaders," and "Report on the Second Congress," and the party journal *Mardom*, especially Vol. I, Nos. 3–6 (1946–1947), and Vol. II, Nos. 1–4 (1948).

this situation also characterized the membership and sympa-thizers. Since the party never took the sympathizers seriously, it may be concluded that the Tudeh leadership was aware of the temporary nature of their susceptibility. Therefore an analysis of the social background of party sympathizers is unlikely to produce concrete evidence of a correlation of social character-istics and attraction to communism. The same is not true of the party elite, which, judged by longer membership, awareness of party goals, and the degree of commitment to the party's action program, has shown a more lasting and genuine response.

This analysis substantiates many conclusions and generaliza-tions made in the preceding chapters. Thus, for example, the contention that despite claims to the contrary, the movement has been led by middle class, better-educated groups through its existence is borne out by the predominance of these social strata among party cadres and leaders. In terms of occupation, white collar and professional categories predominated, including students, particularly at the later stages of secondary and the lower stages of higher education.

The Tudeh's successful recruitment of a large number of the military indicates that, where other elements of susceptibility are present, the profession itself, even when it involves formal commitment to the security of the regime, is no particular bar-rier to be overcome. An analysis of the rank and status of military members of the Tudeh party confirms the relevance of the variety of alienations to the attractions of Communist radicalism. Since, until recently, the military profession offered the only oppor-tunity for free education and career advancement, it is not sur-prising that most of the military party recruits were found to come from the lower middle class, which has been traditionally deprived of these opportunities.

As for higher education and types of institutions, it is interest-ing to note that our analysis shows a predominance of medical and physical sciences over the humanities among the fields of the higher-echelon members. Another finding, based on statements of defectors, indicates the apparent incompatibility of advanced studies in the humanities at French-oriented institutions with rigid party discipline.[21]

The continued presence of many of the sociopolitical characteristics reviewed here as conducive to the furtherance of the Communist cause in the past tends to project an optimistic picture for its future prospects.

Viewed in the domestic context, the past experience suggests that although many of the objective conditions for successful communization of Iran are still lacking, the persistence of various elements of susceptibility to the Communist appeal could make it easier for determined and militant cadres to try to operate once again. Recent doctrinal revisions have given theoretical sanction for the successful use of such subjective factors. Cadres may now be composed of any stratum of Iranian society: student groups, intelligentsia leading a peasant movement, nomadic tribes in revolt against the central government — in short, all those who may benefit from a radical change in the status quo. Similarly, the abandonment of the principle of proletarian exclusiveness has made it possible for the Communists to rally all forces of opposition around a concrete program for recasting Iran's social structure and realigning her international stand in favor of the Soviet Union. The overthrow of the present regime, with the subsequent breakdown of state power through the disintegrating action of minorities, may be speculated to be the most likely eventuality of bringing this about in the foreseeable future.

Since the impact of such an eventuality in Iran, and indeed elsewhere in the Middle East, is apt to extend beyond the domestic context, the Communist prospects have to be evaluated also in the international context. In the latter context, the revival of communism either as an indigenous force or as instrument of Soviet diplomacy becomes less likely. The indispensibility to

---

[21] Over nine-tenths of the defectors who complained about the authoritarian nature of the party had received advanced educations, and nearly two-thirds of those with European degrees had been trained in the humanities at French, Belgian, and Swiss universities.

Western strategic and political interests of Iran's independence and the increased identification of the security of Iran with that of the present regime not only has ruled out Soviet intervention as the surest method of communizing Iran but also has committed the West to oppose any radical change in Iran's prevailing power relations. The present international balance of power, in other words, has placed Iran's political situation in the broader perspective of the Cold War conflict, thereby preventing the treatment of any future Communist offensive as a purely indigenous phenomenon.

Although the prospects for a renewed Communist assault on the Iranian system may be remote, Communist radicalism remains a source of ideological attraction despite the fact that the over-all record of the movement has been a mixed one. As we have seen, its numerous attempts to seize power have failed in the face of combined domestic and external forces. But can the movement's record as a genuine opposition force in contemporary Iranian history be dismissed as a total failure? The evidence as reviewed in these pages will not allow for such an outright dismissal. Our account of the evolution of the movement shows that with minimum freedom of political activity the movement could reassert itself as the most effective channel for threatening the foundations of the Iranian sociopolitical order. The ability to do so obviously depends on the continued susceptibility of politically articulate Iranians to the radicalism of the movement. It further depends on the existence of rival political forces on the Left and Right. While in the past, competition from the Left has been quite inconsequential, there is no assurance that it will remain so. The process of modernization and changing patterns of economic relations could produce favorable conditions for the emergence of a non-Communist Left. When and if it does, the politics of the Left, very much as in the developed countries, will become deradicalized. Communism, or at least its Soviet version, will then cease to perform its traditional function of presenting radical alternatives to Iran's social and political problems.

Bibliography

General: Books, Articles and Documents
This section contains sources on: Communist ideology in general;
Communist doctrines related to the East; communism in the Middle
East; Soviet diplomacy in the Middle East; Modern history of Iran;
international relations of Iran and other sources with a general bear-
ing on the focus of this study.

Adie, W. A. C. "The Middle East: Sino-Soviet Discords," in *Polycentrism,* ed. Walter Z. Laqueur and Leopold Labedz (New York:
Frederick A. Praeger, 1962).

Agabekov, George. *O.G.P.U., The Russian Secret Terror.* New York:
Brentano, 1931.

Almond, Gabriel A. *The Appeals of Communism.* Princeton: Princeton University Press, 1954.

Arnold, G. L. "Communism and the Intelligentsia in Backward
Areas: Some Recent Literature," *Problems of Communism,* Vol.
IV, No. 5 (September–October, 1953).

Bahar, Mohammad Taghi (Malekolshoara). *Tarikhe Mokhtassare
Ahzabe Siyasiye Iran: Engheraze Qajariyeh* [A Short History of
Iranian Political Parties: The Fall of the Qajars]. Two vols. Te-
heran, 1944.

Banani, Amin. *The Modernization of Iran, 1921–1941.* Stanford:
Stanford University Press, 1961.

Bennigsen, Alexandre. "The National Front in Communist Strategy
in the Middle East," in *The Middle East in Transition,* ed. Walter
Z. Laqueur (New York, 1958).

———. "Sultan Galiev: The U.S.S.R. and the Colonial Revolution," in *The Middle East in Transition*, ed. Walter Z. Laqueur (New York, 1958).

Binder, Leonard. "The Cabinet of Iran: A Case Study in Institutional Adaptation," *Middle East Journal*, Vol. XVI, No. 1 (1962).

——. *Iran; Political Development in a Changing Society.* Berkeley and Los Angeles: University of California Press, 1962.

Borkenau, Franz. *World Communism.* Ann Arbor: University of Michigan Press, 1962.

Browne, Edward G. *The Persian Revolution of 1905–1909.* Cambridge, England: The University Press, 1911.

Burks, R. V. *The Dynamics of Communism in Eastern Europe,* Princeton: Princeton University Press, 1961.

Carr, Edward H. *The Bolshevik Revolution: 1917–1923.* 3 vols. New York: Macmillan, 1953.

Carrere d'Encausse, Mme H. "The Evolution of Soviet Policy Since the 20th Congress," in *The Middle East in Transition*, ed. Walter Z. Laqueur (New York, 1958).

Centre de documentation et de synthèse. *Les Activités Communistes au Moyen-Orient.* Paris, 1954–1955.

Communist Party of Great Britain. *The 3rd Congress of the Communist International.* London, 1921.

——. *The Fifth Congress of the Communist International.* London, 1924.

——. *The Communist International Between the Fifth and Sixth World Congresses.* London, 1928.

Communist Party of the Soviet Union. "The Twentieth Congress and the Tasks Set for the Study of the Contemporary East," *Central Asian Review.* Vol. IV, No. 4 (1956).

Cottam, Richard. *Nationalism in Iran.* Pittsburgh: University of Pittsburgh Press, 1964.

Davis, Helen Miller. *Constitutions, Electoral Laws, Treaties of States in the Near and Middle East.* 2d ed.; Durham, N.C.: Duke University Press, 1953.

Degras, Jane. *The Communist International*, Vol. I. London: Oxford University Press, 1950.

Dimitroff, G. *The United Front.* New York: International Publishers, 1938.

Elwell-Sutton, L. P. *Persian Oil; A Study in Power Politics.* London: Lawrence and Wishart, 1955.

Eudin, Xenia J., and Robert C. North. *Soviet Russia and the East,*

1920–1927: A Documentary Survey. Stanford: Stanford University Press, 1957.

Faris, Nabih Amin. "The Islamic Community and Communism," in *The Middle East in Transition*, ed. Walter Z. Laqueur (New York, 1958).

Fateh, Mostafa. *Panjah Sal Nafte Iran* [Fifty Years of Persian Oil]. Teheran, 1956.

Fatemi, Nassrollah, S. *Diplomatic History of Iran*. New York: R. F. Moore, 1951.

Fischer, Louis. *The Soviets in World Affairs*. 2 vols. 2d ed.; Princeton: Princeton University Press, 1951.

Florinsky, Michael T. *World Revolution and the U.S.S.R.* New York: Macmillan, 1933.

Ford, Alan W. *The Anglo-Iranian Oil Dispute of 1951–1952; A Study of the Role of Law in the Relations of States*. Berkeley and Los Angeles: University of California Press, 1954.

Glazer, Sidney, ed. *Communism in the Middle East*, Supplement to *Strategy and Tactics of World Communism*. Washington, D.C., 1949.

Grigoryan, M. "Persia After the War," *Mirovye khozyaystvo i Mirovaya politika*, Nos. 4–5, 1946. English summary in *CAR*, Vol. IV, No. 4 (1956).

Gurko-Kryazhin. *Kratkaya istoriya Persii*. Moscow, 1925.

Hamzavi, Abdolhossein. *Persia and the Powers: An Account of Diplomatic Relations, 1941–1946*, London: Hutchinson & Co., Ltd., 1947.

Hurewitz, J. C. *Diplomacy in the Near and Middle East, A Documentary Record: 1914–1956*. 2 vols. Princeton: Van Nostrand, 1956.

Imperial Government of Iran. "Mozakerate Majlis" [Parliamentary Debates], *Rooznamehe Rasmi* [Official Gazette]. Teheran, 1943–1946.

———. "Subversive Activities Control Act," *Interparliamentary Union, Constitutional and Parliamentary Informations*, No. 21. Geneva, 1955.

International Press Correspondence. *The Sixth Congress of the Communist International, 1928*. Vienna, 1928.

Ivanov, M. S. "Istorii ogrableniya Anglo-Iranskoy neftyanoy kompaniyey," *Voprosy istorii*, No. 5 (Moscow, 1952).

———. *Ocherk istorii Irana*. Moscow, 1952.

Jacobs, Dan N., ed. "Declaration of Representatives of the Eighty-one Communist Parties, Meeting in Moscow Nov.–Dec. 1960, " *The New Communist Manifesto and Related Documents.* Evanston, Ill.: Row, Peterson & Co., 1961.

Kautsky, John H. *Political Change in Underdeveloped Countries: Nationalism and Communism.* New York: John Wiley & Sons, 1962.

Kohn, Hans. *Geschichte der nationalen Bewegung im Orient.* Berlin: K. Vowirckel, 1928.

———. *Nationalism and Imperialism in the Hither East.* London: G. Routledge, 1932.

Die Kommunistische Internationale, No. 14. Hamburg, 1923.

Laqueur, Walter Z. *Communism and Nationalism in the Middle East.* New York: Frederick A. Praeger, 1956.

———, ed. *The Middle East in Transition.* New York: Frederick A. Praeger, 1958.

———. *The Soviet Union and the Middle East.* New York: Frederick A. Praeger, 1959.

———. "Towards National Democracy: Soviet Doctrine and the New Countries," *Survey,* No. 37 (1961).

Lenczowski, George. *The Middle East in World Affairs.* 3rd ed.; Ithaca: Cornell University Press, 1962.

———. *Russia and the West in Iran, 1918–1948: A Study in Big Power Rivalry.* Ithaca: Cornell University Press, 1949.

Lenin, V. I. *Sochineniia,* Vol. XXIV. English translation, *Selected Works,* 12 vols. New York, n.d.

———. "Preliminary Draft of Theses on the National and Colonial Questions," *Selected Works,* Vol. X.

Lerner, Daniel. *The Passing of Traditional Society: Modernizing the Middle East.* Glencoe, Ill.: Free Press, 1958.

Lesueur, Emile. *Les Anglais en Perse.* Paris, 1922.

Lewis, Bernard. "Communism and Islam," *International Affairs,* Vol. XXX (January, 1954).

Mahdavy, Hossein, "The Coming Crisis in Iran," *Foreign Affairs,* Vol. XLIV, No. 1 (October, 1965).

Mao Tse-tung. *Selected Works.* 5 vols. London: Lawrence and Wishart, 1954–1961.

Milov, P. *Iran vo Vremya i Posie vtoroy Mirovoy voyny.* Moscow, 1949.

Monterisi, Mario. "Iran," *Manuali di Politica Internazionale,* No. 32 Milan, 1941.

Mossadegh, Dr. Mohammad. "Matne Defa," *Mohakeme Tarikhi* [Defense Statement, Historic Trial]. Teheran, 1954.

Pahlavi, Mohammad Reza Shah. *Mission for My Country*. New York: McGraw-Hill, 1961.

Palmieri, E. *La Politica Asiatica du Bolscevichi*, Vol. I (Cina–Giappone–India–Persia). Bologna, 1924.

Pavlovich, M., and S. Irankii. *Persiia v Bor'be za Nezavisimost*. Moscow, 1925.

Popov, M. V. *Amerikanski y imperializm v Irane v gody vtoroy Mirovoy voyny*. Moscow, 1956.

Protokoll des Zweiten Weltkongresses der Kommunistischen Internationale. Hamburg, 1920.

———. *Des III Kongress der Kommunistischen Internationale*. Hamburg, 1921.

———. *Des Vierten Kongresses der Kommunistischen Internationale*. Hamburg, 1923.

Radek, Karl. *Vneshniaia politika Sovetskoi Rossii*. Moscow, 1923.

Ravandi, Morteza. *Tafsire Qanune Assassiye Iran* [Interpretation of Iran's Constitution]. Teheran, 1944.

Reisner, I. M., and B. K. Rubstova, eds. *Novaia istoriia stran zarubezhnogo vostoka*. 2 vols. Moscow, 1952.

Saikowski, Charlotte, and Leo Gruliow, eds. *Current Soviet Policies. IV: The Documentary Record of the 22nd Congress of the C.P.S.U.* New York: Columbia University Press, 1962.

Salnamehe Majlis [Yearbook of the Iranian Parliament]. Teheran, 1945.

Scalapino, Robert A. "Moscow, Peking, and the Communist Parties of Asia," *Foreign Affairs*, XLI, No. 2 (January, 1963).

Setvati, Nicole. *L'Iran, bastion de nationalisme oriental face à la Russie*. Geneva, 1960.

Sovremennyy Iran: Spravochnik. Moscow: Academy of Sciences of the U.S.S.R., Institute of Oriental Studies, 1957.

Spector, Ivor. *The Soviet Union and the Moslem World, 1917–1958*. Seattle: University of Washington Press, 1959.

Spuler, Bertold. "Moskaus Kirchen-Politische Offenssiv im vorderen Orient," *Ost-Probleme*, June 2, 1951.

Steppat, Fritz. *Iran zwischen den Grossmachten, 1941–48*. Oberursel: Verlag, Europa-Archive, 1948.

Tully, Andrew. *C.I.A.: The Inside Story*. New York: Simon and Schuster, 1962.

Upton, Joseph M. *The History of Modern Iran: An Interpretation.* Cambridge: Harvard University Press, 1960.

U.S. Congress, House, Foreign Affairs Committee. *Strategy and Tactics of World Communism.* 81st Cong., 1st Sess. 1949, House Doc. 158, Supp. 3.

———. House, Committee on Foreign Affairs (Subcommittee No. 5). *Communism in the Near East.* 80th Cong., 1st Sess. 1948.

Vatolina, L. N. "The Growth of National Consciousness Among the Arab Peoples, 1945–1946," *Sovetskoye Vostokovedeniye,* No. 5, 1955. English version in *CAR,* Vol. III, No. 3 (1955).

Warne, William E. *Mission for Peace: Point 4 in Iran.* Indianapolis: Bobbs-Merrill, 1956.

Watnick, Morris. "The Appeal of Communism to the Underdeveloped Peoples," *Economic Development and Cultural Change,* Vol. I, No. 1 (March, 1952).

Westen, Klaus. *Der Staat der nationalen Demokratie.* Cologne: Verlag Wissenschaft und Politik, 1964.

Young, Caylor T. "Iran in Continuing Crisis," *Foreign Affairs,* Vol. XL, No. 2 (January, 1962).

Zhukov, M. E. "The Break-up of the Imperialist Colonial Systems," *Party Life* (Moscow, August, 1956). Summary in *The Middle East in Transition,* ed. Laqueur.

Specific: Books, Articles, Pamphlets and Documents
This section contains sources exclusively related to the Communist movement in Iran and to Soviet–Iranian relations since 1917.

Alatur [pseud.]. *Hezbe Tudehe Iran* [The Tudeh Party of Iran]. Teheran, n.d.

Alavi, Bozorg. "Der Iran in den Fangen des Neokolonialismus," *Deutsche Aussenpolitik* (East Berlin), No. 1 (January, 1961).

———. *Kämpfendes Iran.* Berlin, 1955.

———. *Panjaho-se Nafar* [The Fifty-three]. Teheran, n.d.

Anonymous. *Hezbe Tudeh Bar Sare Do Rahi* [The Tudeh Party at The Crossroads]. Teheran, January, 1947.

Ardakani, A. "Pages from History: A National Hero," *World Marxist Review,* Vol. V, No. 10 (1962).

Atyeo, Henry C. "Political Development in Iran, 1951–1954," *Middle East Affairs,* Vol. V, Nos. 8–9 (1954).

Bashkirov, A. K. *Ekspansiya Angliiskikh i Amerikanskikh Imperialistov v Irane, 1941–1953.* Moscow, 1954.
———. *Rabocheye i Profsoyuznoye Drisheniye v Irane.* Moscow, 1949.
Bassir, E. "Barkhi Moshakhassate Sabke Erani dar Tarvije Afkare Marxisti dar Iran" [Some of the Characteristics of Erani's Style of Dissemination of Marxist Thoughts in Iran], *Donya,* Vol. II, No. 1 (Clandestine) (1958).
Carrere d'Encausse, Mme H. "Le Parti Toudeh" Mimeographed lecture notes published by the Centre des Hautes Etudes d'Administration Musulmane, Paris, 1956.
———. "Le Toudeh Iranien," *Revue Militaire d'information,* February–March, 1957.
Ducroq, Georges. "La Politique du gouvernement des Soviets en Perse," *Revue du Monde Musulman,* Vol. LII (1922).
"Dowlate Demokrasiye Melli" [The Government of National Democracy], *Donya,* Vol. II, No. 4 (Clandestine) (March, 1961).
Dunsterville, Major-General L.C. "Military Mission to North-West Persia, 1918," *Journal of Royal Central Asian Society,* Vol. VIII, No. 2 (1921).
Efimenco, N. Marburg. "An Experience with Civilian Dictatorship in Iran: The Case of Dr. Mossadegh," *Journal of Politics,* Vol. XVII, No. 3 (August, 1955).
Elwell-Sutton, L. P. "Nationalism and Neutralism in Iran," *Middle East Journal,* Vol. XII, No. 1 (1958).
———. "Political Parties in Iran, 1941–1948," *Middle East Journal,* Vol. III, No. 1 (1949).
Eprim, Dr. A. *Che Bayad Kard?* [What Is to Be Done?]. Teheran, 1946.
Erani, Taghi. *Bashar az nazare Maddi* [Man from a Materialistic Viewpoint]. 4th ed.; Teheran, 1945.
———. *Erfan va Osule Maddi* [Mysticism and Principles of Materialism]. Teheran, n.d.
———. *Matne Defa* [Defense Statement]. Teheran, 1945.
———. *Teorihaye Elm* [Theories of Science]. Teheran, 1943.
Eskandari, Iraj. "Conditions of the Working People in Iran," *World Trade Union Movement,* No. 2 (January, 1951).
———. "Federasione Jahani Sandikaha va Nehzate Kargari Iran" [World Federation of Syndicates and Iranian Labor Movement], *Razm,* Vol. II, No. 6 (December, 1948).

————. "For Bread, Peace, and National Independence," *World Trade Union Movement*, No. 9 (May, 1951) .

————. "Histoire de Parti Toudeh," *Moyen-Orient*, Nos. 5–12 (1949–1950).

————. "What Do We Mean by the National Bourgeoisie?" *World Marxist Review*, Vol. II, No. 8 (September, 1959).

Farboud, Parviz H. "L'Evolution politique de l'Iran pendant la Second Guerre Mondiale." Doctoral dissertation, University of Lausanne, 1957.

Fischer, Von Alfred Joachim. "Hat der Kommunismus Chancen in Persien?" *Die Zukunft* (Wien), No. 3 (March, 1954).

Forutan, Gholamhossein. "Sarmaghaleh" [Editorial], *Donya*, Vol. II, No. 4 (March, 1961).

G.V.O., von. "Der Persische Tudeh," *Freie Rundschau* (Munchen), Nos. 2–3 (March–June, 1959).

Ghassemi, Ahmad. "Dar Sarashibe Ensheab" [On the Brink of Split], *Mardom*, Vol. II, No. 5 (February, 1948) .

————. *Hezbe Tudeh Che Miguyad va Che Mikhahad?* [What Does the Tudeh Say and Want?]. Teheran, 1944.

————. "Marahele Enghelabe Mashruteh" [Phases of the Constitutional Revolution], *Razm*, Vol. II, No. 7 (January, 1949).

————. *Qanoun chist va cheguneh bevojud amadeh?* [What Is Law and How Has It Been Created?]. Teheran, 1944.

————. "Tarbiyate Kadrha" [Training Cadres], *Mardom*, Vol. II, No. 10 (June, 1948).

Geyer, Dietrich. *Die Sowjetunion und Iran: Eine Untersuchung zur Aussenpolitik der U.D.S.S.R. in Nahen Osten, 1917–1954.* Tübingen, 1955.

Harries, E. P. "W.F.T.U. Delegation to Iran," *Trade Union Congress* (mimeographed confidential monthly report of British delegation prepared for the Labor Party). London, May 29, 1947.

Hezbe Tudeh. *Assassnamehe Movaghat* [The Provisional Statute]. Teheran, 1942.

————. *Assassnamehe Mossavebe Kongerehe Avval* [Statute Adopted by First Party Congress]. Teheran, 1944.

————. *Assassnamehe . . .* [2nd Congress, 1948].

————. *Barnamehe Hezbe Tudeh Baraye Marhalehe Konuni az Takamole Ejtemaiye Keshvare Ma* [Draft Program of Tudeh Party for the Contemporary Stage of Our Country's Social Evolution]. Teheran, 1952.

———. *Mamlekate bi-Naghshe va bi-Hadaf* [The Planless and Goal-less Country]. Teheran, 1952.

———. *Manifesto.* December 24, 1946.

———. *Nashriyeh Hezbi* [Party Publication], No. 5.

———. *Nashriyehe Hayate Ejraiyehe Movaghat* [Communique of the Provisional Executive Board]. Teheran, December, 1946.

———. "Sharhe Hal Rahbarane Hezb" [Biographical Sketch of Party's Leaders], *Mardom*, Vol. II, Nos. 3–6 (1946–1947).

———. "Tarhe Barnameh va Assassnamehe Mossavebe Plenome Haf-tom va Konferance Vahdat" [Draft Party Program and Statute Adopted by 7th Plenum and Unity Conference], *Nashriyeh Hezbi*, September–October, 1960.

Hezbe Tudeh, Central Committee. *Darbarehe Bistohashte Mordad* [About August 19, the Date of the National Front Government's Overthrow]. Teheran, 1954.

———. "Elammiyeh bemonasebate Eftetahe Majlese Bistom," [Com-munique on the Opening of the 20th Majlis], *Mardom*, Vol. V, No. 14 (April, 1961).

———. "Elammiyeh plenome Nohom" [Communique of the 9th Plenum], *Masaele Hezbi* [Party Problems], No. 16 (October, 1961).

———. *Hezbe Ma va Jonbeshe Enghelaby Salhaye Akhir* [Our Party and the Revolutionary Movement of Recent Years]. Teheran, Sep-tember, 1955.

———. "Namehe Sargoshadeh be Jabheye Melli" [Open Letter to the National Front]. English summary in *World Marxist Review*, Vol. XIV, No. 9.

———. "Qatenamehe Plenome Haftom" [The Resolution of the 7th Plenum], *Masaele Hezbi* [Party Problems], No. 5 (April, 1958).

———. "Qatenamehe Siyassiye Plenome Haftom" [The 7th Plenum's Political Revolution], *Donya*, Vol. II, No. 1 (1958).

Hezbe, Tudeh, Executive Board of Central Committee. "Gozaresh be Komitehe Markazi" [Report to the Central Committee], *Masaele Hezbi*, No. 16 (October, 1961).

International Labor Office. *Labor Conditions in the Oil Industry in Iran.* Geneva, 1950.

———. *Record of Proceedings of 27th Session International Labor Conference.* Paris, 1945.

Irandust. "Aspects of the Gilan Revolution," *Istorik-Marksist*, No. 5, 1927. English summary in *CAR*, Vol. IV, No. 3 (1956).

Iransky. "Russko-Persitskiye otnoshenia za piat let," *Novyi Vostok*, Vol. IV, Nos. 3–4 (1923).

Ivanova, M. N. "The National Liberation Movement in Gilan Province of Persia in 1920–21," *Sovetskoye Vostokovedeniye*, No. 3, 1955. English summary in *CAR*, Vol. IV, No. 3 (1956).

Kambakhsh, Abdolsamad. "Iran at the Crossroads," *World Marxist Review*, Vol. II, No. 9 (1961).

Kapeluik Amnon. "Mifleget Tudeh be Iran," *Hamizrach Hachadash* (Tel Aviv), No. 4 (Summer, 1954).

Keshavarz, Freydoun. "Jebheye Matbouate Zede Diktatori" [Antidictatorship Press Front], *Mardom*, Aug. 22, 1948.

Kiyanouri, Mohammad Hossein. *Mobarezate Tabaghati* [Class Struggles]. Teheran, 1948.

———. "The National Bourgeoisie, Their Nature and Policy," *World Marxist Review*, II, No. 8 (August, 1959). Summary of a seminar on bourgeois nationalism and the liberation movements in Asia, Africa, and Latin America held by the Leipzig Institute of World History, May, 1959.

———. "Siyasate Shoravi va Siyasate Ampriyalizm dar Iran" [The Soviet and the Imperialist Policies in Iran], *Razm*, Vol. II, No. 5 (November, 1948).

———. *Tafsiri az Ozaye Siyasi va Ejtemai Iran* [A Commentary on the Sociopolitical Conditions of Iran]. Teheran, n.d.

Kusha, M. R. *Diplomasiye Shoravi, diplomasiye Amperialisti* [Soviet Diplomacy, Imperialist Diplomacy]. Teheran, 1951.

Lacoste, Raymond. *La Russie Sovietique et la question d'Orient*. Paris, 1946.

Lambton, Ann K. "Some of the Problems Facing Persia," *International Affairs*, Vol. XXII, No. 2 (1946).

Lavrentyev, A. K. *Imperialisticheskaya politika SSHA i Anglii v Irane*. Moscow, 1960.

Lenczowski, George. "The Communist Movement in Iran," *Middle East Journal*, Vol. I, No. 1 (1947).

Maleki, Khalil. *Do Ravesh baraye Yek Hadaf* [Two Approaches Toward the Same Goal]. Teheran, 1946.

———. Editorials in *Elm va Zendegi* [Science and Life], Vol. I, Nos. 1–3 (1953).

———. *Nirouye Sevvom Piruz Mishavad* [The Third Force Will Be Victorious]. Teheran, 1951.

————. *Nirouye Sevvom va Tudeyha darbareh Solh* [The Third Force and the Tudehites on Peace]. Teheran, n.d.

Manshur, Mohammud Ali. *Siyasate Dowlate Shoravi dar Iran az 1296 ta 1306* [The Soviet Policy in Iran, 1917–1927]. Teheran, 1948.

Margold, Stella. "The Streets of Teheran," *The Reporter*, Nov. 10, 1953.

Massudi, Ghassem. *Mossaferat be Mosko* [Mission to Moscow]. Teheran, 1946.

Mazyar, L. "Struggle for Persian Oil and the Task of the Communist Party in Iran," *Inprecor*, Vol. XV (1932).

Mehnert, Klaus. "Iran and UdSSR 42–53," *Osteuropa*, October 1953.

Military Governorship of Teheran. *Ketabe Siyah* [The Black Book]. Teheran, 1955.

————. *Seyre Komonism dar Iran az Sharivar 1320 ta Farvardin 1336* [The Evolution of Communism in Iran, September, 1941–March, 1958]. Teheran, 1958.

Mobarez, P. Sh. *Aya Hezbe Tudeh Shekast khorde ast?* [Has the Tudeh Party Been Defeated?] Teheran, n.d.

Modjtehedi, M. "La Question d'Azerbaidjan: Le Mouvement des Democrates et les efforts de l'O.N.U." Doctoral Dissertation, University of Paris, 1952.

Mohammad-Zadeh. "Report on the Trade Union Movement in Iran," *World Trade Union Movement*, December, 1949.

Naderi. "The United Front in the Middle East," *Inprecor*, Vol. XV, No. 39 (1932).

Nowrouzi, Davoud. "Hezbe Tudehe Iran, Yek Zorourate tarikhi baraye Keshvare ma" [The Tudeh Party of Iran, a Historical Necessity for Our Country], *Donya*, Vol. II, No. 1 (1958).

Ossietroff, V. "Les Partis politiques de la Perse," *Revue du Monde Musulman*, Vol. LII (1922).

Ovanessian, Ardeshir. "Anti-Communism, the Enemy of Mankind: Behind the Smokescreen of Positive Nationalism," *World Marxist Review*, Vol. V, No. 9 (1962).

————. *Tashkilate Hezbi* [Party Organizations]. Teheran, 1943.

Pesyan, Najafgholi. *Marg Bud Bazkasht Ham Bud* [There Were Both Death and Retreat]. Teheran, 1947.

"Proletarian Party," *The Times* (London), Oct. 6, 1945.

Radmanesh, Reza. "Gozaresh be Kongerehe Bisto-dovvom Hezbe Komoniste Shoravi" [Report to the CPSU's 22nd Congress]. English version in *Communist Propaganda and Developments in the Middle East* (London), No. 97 (October, 1961).

————. "Hezbe Tudehe Iran, Hezbe Taraze Novine Tabaghehe Kargar" [The Tudeh Party of Iran, the Modern Type Working Class Party], *Donya*, Vol. II, No. 2 (Summer, 1961).

Rambout, L. *Les Kurdes et le Droit*. Paris, 1947.

Rondot, Pierre. "L'Union Sovietique et les confins Irano–Kurdes du Moyen-Orient," *Politique Etrangère* (publication of the Centre d'ètudes de politiques etrangères, Paris). Vol. X, No. 3 (1945).

Roosevelt, Archie. "Kurdish Republic of Mahabad," *Middle East Journal*, Vol. I, No. 3 (July, 1947).

Rostow, Robert. "The Battle of Azarbayjan, 1946," *Middle East Journal*, Vol. IX (Winter, 1956).

Saillant, Louis. "Letter to the Prime Minister of Iran," *World Trade Union Movement*, Supp. No. 6 (March, 1950).

Scarcia, Gianroberto. "Aspetti guiridici e politici della recente polemica fra Persia e Unione Sovietica," *Oriente Moderno*, Vol. XXXIX, No. 7 (1959).

Sergeyev. "The Struggle of Democracy Against Reaction in Persia," *Bolshevik*, Nos. 11–12 (1946). English summary in *CAR*, Vol. IV, No. 3 (1956).

Shahed (Organ of the Toilers party of Iran). *Hezbe Tudeh che migoft va che mikard?* [What Was the Tudeh party Saying and Doing?] Teheran, 1951.

Shareghi, A. "Report of the 9th Session of the Sixth Congress of Comintern," *Inprecor*, Vol. VIII, No. 48 (1928).

Shoraye Mottahede. *Tarikhehehe Mokhtasare Nehzate Kargari dar Iran* [Brief History of Workers' Movement in Iran] Teheran, n.d.

Shteynberg, Ye. L. *Sovestsko-Iranskiye otnosheniya i proiski Anglo-Amerikanskogo imperializma v Irane*. Moscow, 1947.

Steiner, C. "Der Iranische Kommunismus," *Ost-Probleme*, Sept. 30, 1955.

Sultan Zadeh, A. [spelled Sultan-sade in German sources] "Der erste Kongress der persischen Kommunisten der Partei Adalat," *Die Kommunistische Internationale*, No. 14. Hamburg, 1923.

————. "Persia an Outpost of British Imperialism, War Preparations on the Near Eastern Frontiers of the Soviet Union," *Inprecor*, Vol. II, No. 25 (1931).

————. *Sovremennaya Persiya*. Moscow, 1922.

————. "Der Zweiter . . ." *Die Kommunistische Internationale*, No. 51. Berlin, 1927.

Tabari, Ehsan. "Barresiye Sharayete Zohur va Marahele Roshd va Mobareze va Khasaese Tarikhiye Hezbe Tudehe Iran" [Survey of Condition of Emergence, Stages of Development and Struggle, and the Historical Peculiarities of the Tudeh Party of Iran], *Mardom*, Vol. I, No. 8 (May–June, 1947).

————. "Esteghlal Chist?" [What Is Independence?], *Mardom*, Vol. II, No. 10 (June, 1948).

————. "Haft Sal Mobarezeh" [Seven Years of Struggle], *Razm*, Vol. II, No. 4 (September–October, 1948).

————. "Hezb Chist?" [What Is Party?], *Mardom*, Vol. I, No. 9 (May, 1947).

————. "Konferance Baraye Faaline Hezbi" [Address to Party Activists], *Mardom*, Vol. II, No. 11 (August, 1948).

————. "Kongerehe Dovom" [Second Congress], *Mardom*, Vol. II, No. 9 (May, 1948).

Tamimi-Taleghani, Ahmed. *Jangal Iran Che Budeh?* [What Was the Jangal of Persia?] Teheran, 1945.

Tehrani-Afshari, Hasan. *Mirza Kuchek Khan*. Teheran, 1941.

"Der Umsturz in Teheran," *Osteuropa*, Yearbook, Vol. III, No. 6 (December, 1953).

World Federation of Trade Unions. "Central Council of Unified Trade Unions in Iran," in *Report of Activity to Second World Trade Union Congress*. Paris, 1949.

————. "Report on Violation of Trade Union Rights," in *World Trade Union Movement*, Special Appendix, No. 26.

Periodicals and Newspapers

The following list includes publications in Persian, Azari-Turkish, French, and English which have been produced by Iranian sources and frequently used in this work.

Azarbayjan (in Azari-Turkish; Tabriz; Official organ of the Democratic party, 1945–1946)

Azhir (Teheran; daily and irregular, 1943–1945)

Besouye Ayandeh (Teheran; daily, 1951–1953)

Beyraghe Adalat (Resht; irregular, 1918–1920)

Damavand (Teheran; weekly, 1943–1945)

Donya (Teheran; monthly, 1935–1937; clandestine, quarterly and irregular, 1959–1965)

Elm va Zendegi (Teheran; monthly and irregular, 1950–1953)

Enghelabe Sorkh (Resht; irregular, 1920)

Ettelaat (Teheran; daily since 1925)

Golshan (Resht; weekly, 1920–1925)

Haqiqat (Resht and Teheran; daily and irregular, 1920–1925)

Iran (Teheran; daily and irregular, 1920–1953)

Jangal (Resht; daily and irregular, 1919–1921)

Javanane Iran (clandestine; irregular, 1960–1962)

Journal de Teheran (Teheran; daily since 1939)

Keyhan International (Teheran; daily since 1960)

Komonist (Resht; irregular, 1920–1921)

Majelehe Forough (Resht; monthly and irregular, 1925–1930)

Mardom (Teheran and clandestine; daily, monthly, and irregular since 1942)

Maslehat (Teheran; weekly and monthly, 1951–1953)

Parvaresh (Resht; irregular and daily, 1922–1930)

Rahbar (Teheran; daily, 1942–1946)

Razm (Teheran; daily and monthly, 1943–1949)

Rooznamehe Rasmi (Teheran; daily and irregular, 1944–1950)

Setarehe-Iran (Teheran; irregular, 1922–1930)

Shahbaz (Teheran; daily, 1951–1953)

Shahed (Teheran; daily, 1949–1955)

Zafar (Teheran and clandestine; daily and irregular, 1943–1947)

Index